SIR HALLEY STEWART TRUST: PUBLICATIONS

Volume 1

THE HEART OF THE BIBLE

THE HEART OF THE BIBLE

Volume One: The Literature of the Hebrew People

JEANNIE B. THOMSON DAVIES

Routledge
Taylor & Francis Group
LONDON AND NEW YORK

First published in 1933 by George Allen & Unwin Ltd

This edition first published in 2025
by Routledge
4 Park Square, Milton Park, Abingdon, Oxon OX14 4RN

and by Routledge
605 Third Avenue, New York, NY 10158

Routledge is an imprint of the Taylor & Francis Group, an informa business

© 1933 Sir Halley Stewart Trust

All rights reserved. No part of this book may be reprinted or reproduced or utilised in any form or by any electronic, mechanical, or other means, now known or hereafter invented, including photocopying and recording, or in any information storage or retrieval system, without permission in writing from the publishers.

Trademark notice: Product or corporate names may be trademarks or registered trademarks, and are used only for identification and explanation without intent to infringe.

British Library Cataloguing in Publication Data
A catalogue record for this book is available from the British Library

ISBN: 978-1-032-88962-7 (Set)
ISBN: 978-1-032-88718-0 (Volume 1) (hbk)
ISBN: 978-1-032-88720-3 (Volume 1) (pbk)
ISBN: 978-1-003-53936-0 (Volume 1) (ebk)

DOI: 10.4324/9781003539360

Publisher's Note
The publisher has gone to great lengths to ensure the quality of this reprint but points out that some imperfections in the original copies may be apparent.

Disclaimer
The publisher has made every effort to trace copyright holders and would welcome correspondence from those they have been unable to trace.

This book is a re-issue originally published in 1933. The language used and views portrayed are a reflection of its era and no offence is meant by the Publishers to any reader by this re-publication.

THE HEART OF THE BIBLE

CONTENTS OF VOLUME TWO

I. A PERIOD OF REFORMATION
II. THE PRIESTLY CODE AND THE DAWN OF HISTORY
III. LITERATURE OF PROTEST
IV. THE PROBLEM OF SUFFERING
V. THE HYMNAL OF THE JEWISH CHURCH
VI. WRITINGS OF THE WISE MEN
VII. LATER POST-EXILIC PROPHETS
VIII. THE FORMATION OF THE CANON
IX. THE CHRONICLER
X. THE STORY OF QUEEN ESTHER
XI. THE WISDOM OF JESUS SON OF SIRACH
XII. THE BOOK OF DANIEL
XIII. THE STORY OF JUDITH
XIV. A HISTORY OF PERSECUTION AND THE MACCABEAN REVOLT
XV. TWO GREEK ADDITIONS TO OLD TESTAMENT LITERATURE
XVI. THE LAST CENTURY BEFORE CHRIST

CONTENTS OF VOLUME THREE

I. THE FIRST CENTURY OF THE CHRISTIAN ERA
II. THE BEGINNINGS OF NEW TESTAMENT LITERATURE
III. MORE LETTERS OF THE NEW TESTAMENT
IV. A NEW DEVELOPMENT IN LITERATURE: THE FIRST GOSPEL
V. LATER LITERATURE OF THE PERSECUTIONS
VI. THE LATEST LITERATURE OF THE NEW TESTAMENT

THE HEART
OF THE BIBLE

by

JEANNIE B. THOMSON DAVIES, M.A.

IN THREE VOLUMES

VOLUME ONE
THE LITERATURE OF
THE HEBREW PEOPLE

LONDON
GEORGE ALLEN & UNWIN LTD
MUSEUM STREET

FIRST PUBLISHED IN 1933

All rights reserved
PRINTED IN GREAT BRITAIN BY
UNWIN BROTHERS LTD., WOKING

PREFACE

It was my privilege to be born into a home where the presence of God could not be evaded and where acceptance of fresh truth was never less than whole-hearted. This has been my fundamental preparation for a bold venture into the ranks of those who struggle to restore to modern readers the knowledge and love of the Bible.

The aim of this particular venture is to present the writings now collected in the volume called the Bible in an order approaching that in which they came into being. Mrs. Allen Warner first drew my attention to this possibility. The hope is that a considerable amount of both the Old and New Testaments may be read in a fresh setting, so that questions about the inconsistencies in the Bible, or about its varying levels of morality, or about its uneven value for religious education can no longer be fired as poisoned darts to attack its life and influence. Many readers, fortunate in knowing the generally approved results of modern Biblical scholarship, find in the new approach to the Bible not only the conservation of all its old values, but also a wonderful and fresh revelation of God. But for ordinary readers and for immature minds such knowledge has been somewhat hard to acquire and assimilate, its presentation being too far removed from the reading of the Bible itself. This is an attempt to combine reading the Bible with learning to understand it.

Many were the difficulties in the way of this venture. Where selection is so much a matter of taste, the choice of a single individual cannot be acceptable to all: nor can all approve the use of the Authorized Version. Teaching experience, familiarity with the minds of young people, knowledge of the difficulties of teachers and ministers are assets of a kind. But the work had to be done by one who is no scholar in the technical sense of that term. My husband, who has a first-hand acquaintance with the problems of Biblical scholarship, safeguarded me against the worst blunders. Dr. A. J. Grieve, Principal of the Lancashire Independent College, has, in the course of the last few years, read the whole of the manuscript, answering questions, suggesting sources and marking definite errors. This great kindness has given the work the support of a scholar whose mind is at home in the most recent developments of Biblical study. He too it was who suggested the title, "The Heart of the Bible".

A serious difficulty has been the high cost of setting up the type for so much Biblical material arranged in a fresh form, as contrasted with the low cost of printing off great numbers of Bibles from the same sets of type. To ensure publication at the present price it was necessary to cover all non-recurring expenditure by an endowment of considerable size. The greater part of this endowment has been raised by personal friends, but open thanks must here be given to the Halley Stewart Trust for a generous contribution made in order to reduce the published price to the lowest figure possible. Another friend has undertaken the laborious task of correcting the proofs, while others have assisted in the compilation of the index.

I wish in particular to express my gratitude to my publishers for encouragement and guidance first given several years ago, and steadily continued until all difficulties in the way of publication have been overcome.

J. B. T. D.

May 1933

CONTENTS

		PAGE
I.	**THE FIRST LITERATURE**	11
	1. INTRODUCTION	11
	2. THE EARLIEST POETRY	12
	Fragments	12
	Song of Deborah	13
	Fable of Jotham	15
	Song of the Bow	16
	3. THE EARLIEST NARRATIVES	20
	The Court History of King David	21
	Other Narratives of the Early Monarchy	27
	4. FOUR GREAT PROPHETS	29
	Amos to Luxurious Oppressors of the Poor	30
	Hosea and the Love of God	33
	Isaiah, the Prophet-Statesman	36
	Micah, the Prophet of the People	44
	5. EARLY LAWS	46
	The Book of the Covenant	47
	The Ten Commandments	53
II.	**DEUTERONOMY—A REMARKABLE LAW-BOOK**	56
	1. INTRODUCTION AS FROM MOSES	59
	2. LAWS OF SOCIAL RIGHTEOUSNESS	60
	3. LAWS CONCERNING RELIGION	62
	4. CONCLUSION AS FROM MOSES	65
III.	**JEREMIAH—A PERSECUTED PROPHET OF JUDAH**	67
IV.	**OTHER PROPHETS—ZEPHANIAH, NAHUM, HABAKKUK**	82
V.	**THE BOOK OF KINGS—A HISTORY FROM DAVID'S DEATH TO THE EXILE**	89
	1. INTRODUCTION	89
	2. A WISE KING AND A DIVIDED KINGDOM	93
	3. THE LAST TWO CENTURIES OF THE NORTHERN KINGDOM	112
	Elijah, an Opponent of Baal	115
	Elisha, the Prophet-Friend	124
	The Fall of Samaria	134
	4. JERUSALEM ATTACKED BY THE ASSYRIANS	136
	5. THE REFORMATION IN JUDAH	142
VI.	**THE CONCLUSION OF THE BOOK OF KINGS**	146

10   THE HEART OF THE BIBLE

		PAGE
VII.	THE TRAGEDY OF PATRIOTISM	151
	1. The Psalm of an Exile	151
	2. The Malicious Spirit of Edom	152
	3. A Song of Sorrow for the Woes of Jerusalem	153
VIII.	THE PROPHET EZEKIEL	155
IX.	AN EXILIC CODE OF LAW	172
X.	A HISTORY OF THE ESTABLISHMENT OF THE KINGDOM	176
	1. Introduction	176
	2. Stories of Judges in Israel	181
	Deborah and Gideon	184
	Jephthah's Daughter	190
	A Tragedy of Strength	192
	Two Primitive Tales	197
	Samuel, the Last of the Judges	202
	3. The Choice of Saul as King: Two Narratives	208
	4. The Decline and Fall of King Saul: Two Narratives	218
	5. David the Outlaw and David the King	227
XI.	THE GREAT UNKNOWN PROPHET OF THE EXILE	240
	1. Comfort for the People	240
	2. To Cyrus the Conqueror	243
	3. The Suffering Servant of Jehovah	244
	4. The Return to Jerusalem	247
XII.	OTHER ANONYMOUS PROPHECIES OF THE EXILE	251
	1. The Fall of Babylon	251
	2. The Return to Jerusalem	252
	3. A Curse on Edom	253
XIII.	THE FIRST POST-EXILIC PROPHETS	255
	1. Introduction	255
	2. Haggai and the New Temple	258
	3. The Visions of Zechariah	260
XIV.	A PERIOD OF DISILLUSION AND MISERY	266
	1. Malachi's Picture of His Times	266
	2. A Psalm of Hope	268
	3. The Hope of an Unknown Prophet	269
	4. A Priestly Code of Law	273
	INDEX	276
	MAP OF THE WORLD OF OLD TESTAMENT HISTORY	At end

THE LITERATURE OF THE HEBREW PEOPLE

I

THE FIRST LITERATURE

1. INTRODUCTION

THE Bible is both one book and a collection of separate books. It is not only one book in the sense of being bound in one volume, but one book also in that its contents, in spite of their manifold variety and evident complexity, give us one great message about God and His ways with humanity. The message is so wonderful and many-sided that only through a complex book could it be revealed. Thus we need to give the Bible more patient study than can easily be achieved in busy days. It is hoped that this selection will help us to follow the thread of the whole so that we may return to our complete long Bible with a clue to its difficulties and complexities.

The Old Testament contains most of what is left to the world of the literature of the Hebrew people, chosen and arranged with a deep religious purpose. This literature, like our own English literature, came into being in different ways. Fathers and mothers told their children stories of what they had seen and heard; the children in turn told their children, and, after many generations of young people had listened in this way to the stories, these were written down in a more permanent form. Again in times of great excitement, poets are born and songs are composed telling of the wonderful events, and these songs and poems are more easily remembered than stories and so are handed down from father to son more accurately. It happened that often different forms of a story, the same in essentials but varying in details, were in circulation among the Hebrews.

There are, for instance, in the Bible two quite different accounts of the choosing of Saul as the first king (see p. 208): while we have just one version of the "Song of Deborah" (see p. 13). It is not likely that any of the early stories or of the first poems were set down in writing until a long time after the events of which they tell.

2. THE EARLIEST POETRY

FRAGMENTS

It is possible to pick out from the books of the Bible a few of these fragments of early verse, although no quotation marks appear to indicate that they belong to an earlier time than the rest of the book. For much of our difficulty in understanding the Bible arises from the fact that the books, as we now have them, are in many cases compilations of earlier literature made for a religious purpose, and quotations from earlier sources are given with seldom a hint as to their source. It has taken much effort on the part of students of the Hebrew language and Biblical scholars to find out the simplest literary forms in the Old Testament.

Of these forms the simplest is the poem: we give a selection from the earliest poetical fragments.

The Warrior Lamech's Cry of Revenge
    Adah and Zillah, hear my voice:
    Ye wives of Lamech, hearken unto my speech:
    I would slay a man in my wound,
    And a young man in my hurt.
    If Cain shall be avenged sevenfold,
    Truly Lamech seventy and sevenfold.
                                             [*Genesis* iv. 23
                                               (*A.V. Margin*)

Miriam's Red Sea Song
    Sing ye to the Lord,
    He hath triumphed gloriously;
    The horse and his rider
    Hath He thrown into the sea.
                                                 Exodus xv. 21

A Song of the Well

> Spring up, O well; sing ye unto it:
> The princes digged the well,
> The nobles of the people digged it,
> By the direction of the law-giver,
> With their staves.
>
> [*Numbers* xxi. 17]

The Song of Deborah

One of the greatest Hebrew war songs goes back to these early days, the "Song of Deborah". After the children of Israel had come out of Egypt and at last reached Canaan, they settled in scattered groups surrounded by heathen foes. Their lives were saved by great warrior leaders who from time to time under God led them to victory. One of these was Deborah. In the Book of Judges a prose account of her work appears side by side with this poem (see p. 186). Both historians and lovers of good literature place the highest value on the "Song of Deborah".

Praise

> Praise ye the Lord for the avenging of Israel,
> When the people willingly offered themselves.
> Hear, O ye kings; give ear, O ye princes;
> I, even I, will sing unto the Lord;
> I will sing praise to the Lord God of Israel.

To Jehovah Who cometh from Sinai to aid His people

> Lord, when Thou wentest out of Seir,
> When Thou marchedst out of the field of Edom,
> The earth trembled, the heavens dropped,
> The clouds also dropped water.
> The mountains melted from before the Lord,
> Even Sinai from before the Lord God of Israel.

Deliverance from Evil Times

> In the days of Shamgar, the son of Anath,
> In the days of Jael, the highways were unoccupied,
> And the travellers walked through byways.
> The inhabitants of the villages ceased, they ceased in Israel.
> Until that I, Deborah, arose,
> That I arose, a mother in Israel.
> My heart is toward the governors of Israel,
> That offered themselves willingly among the people.
> Bless ye the Lord.

Speak, ye that ride on white asses,
Ye that sit in judgment, and walk by the way.
They that are delivered from the noise of archers
In the places of drawing water,
There shall they rehearse the righteous acts of the Lord,
Even the righteous acts toward the inhabitants of His villages in Israel:
Then shall the people of the Lord go down to the gates.

The Victory

Awake, awake, Deborah:
Awake, awake, utter a song:
Arise, Barak, and lead thy captivity captive, thou son of Abinoam.
Zebulun and Naphtali were a people that jeoparded their lives unto the death
In the high places of the field.
The kings came and fought,
Then fought the kings of Canaan
In Taanach by the waters of Megiddo;
They took no gain of money.
They fought from heaven;
The stars in their courses fought against Sisera.
The river of Kishon swept them away,
That ancient river, the river Kishon.
O my soul, thou hast trodden down strength.
Then were the horsehoofs broken
By means of the pransings, the pransings of their mighty ones.

Jael slays the Enemy's Captain

Blessed above women shall Jael be,
The wife of Heber the Kenite.
Blessed shall she be above women in the tent.
He asked water, and she gave him milk;
She brought forth butter in a lordly dish.
She put her hand to the nail,
And her right hand to the workman's hammer;
And with the hammer she smote Sisera, she smote off his head,
When she had pierced and stricken through his temples.
At her feet he bowed, he fell, he lay:
At her feet he bowed, he fell:
Where he bowed, there he fell down dead.

The mother of Sisera looked out at a window,
And cried through the lattice,
"Why is his chariot so long in coming?
Why tarry the wheels of his chariot?"

Her wise ladies answered her,
Yea, she returned answer to herself,
"Have they not sped? Have they not divided the prey?
To every man a damsel or two;
To Sisera, a prey of divers colours,
A prey of divers colours of needlework,
Of divers colours of needlework on both sides, meet for the necks of them that take the spoil?"

So let all thine enemies perish, O Lord:
But let them that love Him be as the sun when he goeth forth in his might.

[*From Judges* v

In poetical form also have come down to us a few very early proverbs and riddles and fables. For instance, we find in 1 Samuel xxiv. 12, in the story of David sparing Saul's life in the cave:—

David said to Saul. . . . "The Lord judge between me and thee: the Lord avenge thee of me: but mine hand shall not be upon thee. As saith the proverb of the ancients,

'Wickedness proceedeth from the wicked:
But mine hand shall not be upon thee.'"

Many of these oldest proverbs and riddles can never have reached a written form, and are lost to us. But we have left the riddle asked by Samson, and the answer given by his guests in riddle form (to which the correct answer is "Love").

Riddle

Out of the eater came forth meat,
Out of the strong came forth sweetness.

Reply

What is sweeter than honey?
What is stronger than a lion?

[*Judges* xiv. 14 and 18

FABLE OF JOTHAM

We have also the remarkable "Fable of Jotham", telling of the trees' choice of a king. It may belong to later times, but many scholars think that it is very old indeed.

The trees went forth on a time
To anoint a king over them;
And they said unto the olive tree,
"Reign thou over us."
But the olive tree said unto them,
"Should I leave my fatness,
Wherewith by me they honour God and man,
And go to be promoted over the trees?"

And the trees said to the fig tree,
"Come thou, and reign over us."
But the fig tree said unto them,
"Should I forsake my sweetness,
And my good fruit,
And go to be promoted over the trees?"

Then said the trees unto the vine,
"Come thou and reign over us."
And the vine said unto them,
"Should I leave my wine,
Which cheereth God and man,
And go to be promoted over the trees?"

Then said all the trees unto the bramble,
"Come thou and reign over us."
And the bramble said unto the trees,
"If in truth ye anoint
Me king over you,
Come, put your trust in my shadow:
And if not, let fire come out of the bramble,
And devour the cedars of Lebanon."

[*Judges* ix. 8–15

Song of the Bow

Most scholars agree that such poetical fragments as have been given above belong to the days before there were any kings in Israel; that is, roughly, to the period before about 1000 B.C. We know a little also about poems which appear to be not later than the early monarchy, that is, not later than the century 1000–900 B.C. There are, for instance, two brief fragments, one celebrating David's first victories, the other giving Solomon's dedicatory prayer after he had completed the building of the Temple:—

Saul hath slain his thousands,
And David his ten thousands.
[1 *Samuel* xviii. 7

The Lord said that He would dwell in the thick darkness.
I have surely built Thee an house to dwell in,
A settled place for Thee to abide in for ever.
[1 *Kings* viii. 12

To this century belong, it is thought, the "Blessing of Jacob" in Genesis xlix, although some parts of this poem may be earlier: the "Oracles of Balaam" in Numbers xxiii and xxiv: also the "Blessing of Moses" in Deuteronomy xxxiii. 6–25 (see p. 66). Here we give two poems which were surely composed by David himself, and which show us at once how great a poet he was. The first is the famous "Song of the Bow", a lament over the death of Saul and Jonathan; the second a brief, unimpassioned but sincere lament over the death of Abner, his former enemy who had secretly made peace with him.

Song of the Bow

The beauty of Israel is slain upon thy high places:
How are the mighty fallen!
Tell it not in Gath,
Publish it not in the streets of Askelon;
Lest the daughters of the Philistines rejoice,
Lest the daughters of the uncircumcised triumph.

Ye mountains of Gilboa,
Let there be no dew, neither rain upon you, nor fields of offerings:
For there the shield of the mighty is vilely cast away,
The shield of Saul, as not anointed with oil.
From the blood of the slain, from the fat of the mighty,
The bow of Jonathan turned not back,
The sword of Saul returned not empty.

Saul and Jonathan were lovely and pleasant in their lives,
And in their death they were not divided:
They were swifter than eagles,
They were stronger than lions.
Ye daughters of Israel, weep over Saul,
Who clothed you in scarlet, with delights,
Who put ornaments of gold upon your apparel.
How are the mighty fallen in the midst of the battle!

O Jonathan, slain in thine high places!
I am distressed for thee, my brother Jonathan:
Very pleasant hast thou been unto me:
Thy love to me was wonderful,
Passing the love of women.

How are the mighty fallen,
And the weapons of war perished.

[2 *Samuel* i. 19–27

Lament over Abner

Died Abner as a fool dieth?
Thy hands were not bound,
Nor thy feet put into fetters:
As a man falleth before wicked men, fellest thou.

[2 *Samuel* iii. 33

Why do we give so few extracts from the poetry of King David? In the answer to that question lies the clue to the solution of many difficulties in understanding the Bible. First, we are assured that so great a poet as David shows himself here, and so deeply religious a man as we know him to have been, composed religious poetry or psalms. But it has baffled students of the Bible to select a certain definite psalm and say, "David actually composed that as it now stands."

A DIFFICULTY ABOUT AUTHORSHIP

The Hebrews had no idea of the literary copyright of modern times. To us, what a man has written belongs to himself and to his publishers; it is wrong in our eyes to attach any other name than the author's to any writing; we regard it as stealing. But the Hebrew idea of right and wrong in literary matters was entirely different. Who would give due honour to songs or stories or laws composed or formulated by some little known local person? The more they remembered and revered the great religious leaders of the past, such as Moses or David or Isaiah, the less likely they would be to acknowledge that any good thing could come out of the present. Even of Jesus they said that he must be Elijah, or John the Baptist, or one of the prophets come again.

But some men with insight knew that God chooses to reveal

Himself through things and people that are despised. To these men the ethically right custom was to publish the writings of unknown or little known men under the name of the best-known leader in that side of literature. All proverbs are "of Solomon", all laws "of Moses", all psalms "of David", while many prophetic messages, even ones as inspiring as those found in the second half of the Book of Isaiah, are attached to the writings of well known earlier prophets. So was God glorified and His work done.

We give illustrations to show how necessary it is to remember this literary custom, if we would decipher aright God's message in the Old Testament. Under the words: "Moses called Israel and said unto them: 'Hear, O Israel, the statutes and judgments which I speak in your ears this day' " (Deut. v. 1), we read, "One from among thy brethren shalt thou set king over thee: thou mayest not set a stranger over thee, which is not thy brother. . . . Neither shall he multiply wives to himself, neither shall he greatly multiply to himself silver and gold" (Deut. xvii. 15). But in the time of Moses there was no thought of any need for a king over Israel. In this passage, however, the kingship is taken for granted; stress is laid on the king being no foreigner and on his moderation in the matter of wives and wealth. It must belong to later days when Solomon's disappointing career showed the value of such moderation, and when the Northern kingdom showed a tendency to permit foreign rulers.

Again in one of the "Psalms of David" (Ps. cxxxvii), we read:—

> By the rivers of Babylon,
> There we sat down;
> Yea, we wept,
> When we remembered Zion.

And Psalm lxxix begins:—

> O God, the heathen have come into Thine inheritance:
> Thy holy temple have they defiled; they have laid Jerusalem on heaps.

In the time of David no temple was in Jerusalem, and it was many years after his death before Judah went into exile by the rivers of Babylon or Jerusalem was laid on heaps.

Many scholars think that parts of at least several psalms in the Book of Psalms were composed by David himself. We feel how near to the known circumstances of David's life comes the Shepherd Psalm (Ps. xxiii); much of Psalm xviii, for instance, is very likely David's. But these religious songs have been sung over and over again, added to and altered from century to century, until it is impossible at the present time to say with any assurance exactly when each part of each psalm took its present form. So it is that we must in this section on the earliest poetry confine our selections from the poems of David within very narrow limits.

3. THE EARLIEST NARRATIVES

To recover the earliest poetry from the Bible as it now stands has required much knowledge of the Hebrew language, and of the whole development of Hebrew religion and literature. We note again that neither these first poems nor the earliest stories were set down in writing until a long time after the events of which they tell.

But sometime during the tenth century B.C., probably in the first half of Solomon's reign, some man deeply impressed by the dramatic appeal of the time felt moved to record permanently the events which he remembered. He was the first Hebrew historian. We know that this man was a member of David's court: so vividly and with such detailed knowledge does he write what is usually called "The Court History of David" that he must have been an eye-witness of the events and personalities which he depicts for us. Probably this historian was Abiathar: we find his work in 2 Samuel ix–xx very much as it must originally have come from his pen. From this earliest narrative we now give selections.

The Court History of King David

David's Great Sin

And it came to pass at the time when kings go forth to battle, that David sent Joab and his servants with him, and all Israel; and they destroyed the children of Ammon, and besieged Rabbah. But David tarried still at Jerusalem. And it came to pass in an evening that David arose from off his bed, and walked upon the roof of the king's house: and from the roof he saw a woman washing herself; and the woman was very beautiful to look upon. And David sent and enquired after the woman. And one said, "Is not this Bath-sheba, the wife of Uriah the Hittite?" And David sent messengers and took her.

And David sent to Joab, saying, "Send me Uriah the Hittite." And Joab sent Uriah to David. And when Uriah was come unto him, David demanded of him how Joab did, and how the people did, and how the war prospered. And David said to Uriah, "Go down to thy house and wash thy feet." And Uriah departed out of the king's house, and there followed him a mess of meat from the king. But Uriah slept at the door of the king's house with all the servants of his lord, and went not down to his house.

And it came to pass in the morning, that David wrote a letter to Joab, and sent it by the hand of Uriah. And he wrote in the letter, saying, "Set ye Uriah in the forefront of the hottest battle, and retire ye from him, that he may be smitten and die." And it came to pass when Joab observed the city, that he assigned Uriah unto a place where he knew that valiant men were. And the men of the city came out, and fought with Joab: and there fell some of the people of the servants of David; and Uriah died also.

Then Joab sent and told David all the things concerning the war: and charged the messenger saying, "When thou hast made an end of telling the matters of the war unto the king, and if so be that the king's wrath arise, and he say unto thee, 'Wherefore approached ye so nigh unto the city when ye did fight? Knew ye not that they would shoot from the wall? Who smote Abimelech the son of Jerubbesheth? Did not a woman cast a piece of a millstone upon him from the wall, that he died in Thebez? Why went ye nigh the wall?' then say thou, 'Thy servant Uriah the Hittite is dead also.'" So the messenger went, and came and shewed David all that Joab had sent him for. Then said David unto the messenger, "Thus shalt thou say unto Joab, 'Let not this thing displease thee, for the sword devoureth one as well as another: make thy battle more strong against the city and overthrow it': and encourage thou him."

And when the wife of Uriah heard that Uriah her husband was dead, she mourned for her husband. And when the mourning was past David sent and fetched her to his house, and she became his wife, and bare him a son. But the thing that David had done displeased the Lord.   [*From 2 Samuel* xi

Nathan sent to Rebuke David: David's Sorrow

And the Lord sent Nathan unto David. And he came unto him, and said unto him, "There were two men in one city; the one rich, and the other poor. The rich man had exceeding many flocks and herds: but the poor man had nothing, save one little ewe lamb, which he had brought and nourished up; and it grew up together with him, and with his children; it did eat of his own meat, and drank of his own cup, and lay in his bosom, and was unto him as a daughter. And there came a traveller unto the rich man, and he spared to take of his own flock and of his own herd, to dress for the wayfaring man that was come unto him; but took the poor man's lamb, and dressed it for the man that was come to him."

And David's anger was greatly kindled against the man; and he said to Nathan, "As the Lord liveth, the man that hath done this thing shall surely die: and he shall restore the lamb fourfold, because he did this thing, and because he had no pity." And Nathan said to David, "Thou art the man. Thus saith the Lord God of Israel, 'I anointed thee king over Israel, and I delivered thee out of the hand of Saul; and I gave thee thy master's house, and thy master's wives, and gave thee the house of Israel and of Judah; and if that had been too little, I would moreover have given unto thee such and such things.' Wherefore hast thou despised the commandment of the Lord, to do evil in His sight? Thou hast killed Uriah the Hittite with the sword, and hast taken his wife to be thy wife, and hast slain him with the sword of the children of Ammon."

And David said unto Nathan, "I have sinned against the Lord." And Nathan said unto David, "The Lord hath put away thy sin; thou shalt not die. Howbeit, because by this deed thou hast given great occasion to the enemies of the Lord to blaspheme, the child also that is born of thee shall surely die." And Nathan departed unto his house.

And the Lord struck the child that Uriah's wife bare unto David, and it was very sick. David therefore besought God for the child; and David fasted, and went in, and lay all night upon the earth. And the elders of his house arose, and went to him, to raise him up from the earth; but he would not, neither did he eat bread with them. And it came to pass on the seventh day, that the child died. And the servants of David feared to tell him that the child was dead: for they said, "Behold, while the child was yet alive, we spake unto him, and he would not hearken unto our voice: how will he then vex himself, if we tell him that the child is dead?"

But when David saw that his servants whispered, David perceived that the child was dead: therefore David said unto his servants, "Is the child dead?" And they said, "He is dead." Then David arose from the earth, and washed, and anointed himself, and changed his apparel, and came into the house of the Lord, and worshipped: then he came to his own house; and when he required, they set bread before him, and he did eat. Then said his servants unto him, "What thing is this that thou hast done? Thou didst fast and weep for the child, while it was alive; but when the child was dead, thou didst rise and eat bread." And he said, "While the child was yet alive, I fasted and wept: for I said, 'Who can tell whether God will be gracious to me, that the child may live?' But now he is dead, wherefore should I fast? Can I bring him back again? I shall go to him, but he shall not return unto me."

And David comforted Bath-sheba his wife: and she bare a son, and he called his name Solomon: and the Lord loved him.

[*From* 2 *Samuel* xii

Sin and Trouble in David's Household

And it came to pass after this, that Absalom the son of David had a fair sister, whose name was Tamar; and Amnon the son of David loved her. And Amnon forced her. Then Amnon hated her exceedingly; so that the hatred wherewith he hated her was greater than the love wherewith he had loved her. And Tamar put ashes on her head, and rent her garment of divers colours that was on her, and laid her hand on her head, and went on crying. Tamar remained desolate in her brother Absalom's house. But when King David heard of all these things, he was very wroth. And Absalom spake unto his brother Amnon neither good nor bad.

And it came to pass after two full years, that Absalom had sheep-shearers in Baal-hazor, which is beside Ephraim; and Absalom invited all the king's sons. And Absalom came to the king, and said, "Behold now, thy servant hath sheepshearers; let the king, I beseech thee, and his servants go with thy servant." And the king said to Absalom, "Nay, my son, let us not all now go, lest we be chargeable unto thee." And he pressed him: howbeit he would not go, but blessed him. Then said Absalom, "If not, I pray thee, let my brother Amnon go with us." And the king said unto him, "Why should he go with thee?" But Absalom pressed him, that he let Amnon and all the king's sons go with him.

Now Absalom had commanded his servants, saying, "Mark ye now when Amnon's heart is merry with wine, and when I say unto you 'Smite Amnon'; then kill him, fear not: have not I commanded you? Be courageous and be valiant." And the servants of Absalom did unto Amnon as Absalom had commanded. Then all the king's sons arose, and every man gat him up upon his mule, and fled.

And it came to pass, while they were in the way, that tidings came to David, saying, "Absalom hath slain all the king's sons, and there is not one of them left." Then the king arose, and tare his garments, and lay on the earth; and all his servants stood by with their clothes rent. And Jonadab, the son of Shimeah, David's brother, answered and said, "Let not my lord suppose that they have slain all the young men the king's sons; for Amnon only is dead: for by the appointment of Absalom this hath been determined from the day that he forced his sister Tamar. Now therefore let not my lord the king take the thing to his heart, to think that all the king's sons are dead: for Amnon only is dead."

But Absalom fled. And the young man that kept the watch lifted up his eyes, and looked, and, behold, there came much people by the way of the hill side behind him. And Jonadab said unto the king, "Behold the king's sons come: as thy servant said, so it is." And it came to pass, as soon as he had made an end of speaking, that, behold, the king's sons came, and lifted up their voice and wept: and the king also and all his servants wept very sore. But Absalom fled, and went to Talmai, the son of Ammihud, king of Geshur. And David mourned for his son every day. So Absalom fled, and went to Geshur, and was there three years. And the soul of King David longed to go forth unto Absalom: for he was comforted concerning Amnon, seeing he was dead.

[*From* 2 *Samuel* xiii

Joab, the captain of David's host, perceived that the king was longing for Absalom. He therefore sent to David a "wise woman", himself putting words in her mouth. The woman's mission was successful.

Absalom's Recall from Exile

So Joab arose and went to Geshur, and brought Absalom to Jerusalem. And the king said, "Let him turn to his own house, and let him not see my face." So Absalom returned to his own house, and saw not the king's face. But in all Israel there was none to be so much praised as Absalom for his beauty: from the sole of his foot even to the crown of his head there was no blemish in him. And when he polled his head, (for it was at every year's end that he polled it: because the hair was heavy on him, therefore he polled it:) he weighed the hair of his head at two hundred shekels after the king's weight. And unto Absalom there were born three sons, and one daughter, whose name was Tamar; she was a woman of a fair countenance.

[2 *Samuel* xiv. 23–27

Absalom steals the Hearts of the People

So Absalom dwelt two full years in Jerusalem, and saw not the king's face. Therefore Absalom sent for Joab, to have sent him to the king; but he would not come to him: and when he sent again the second time, he would not come. Therefore he said unto his servants, "See, Joab's field is near mine, and he hath barley there: go and set it on fire." And Absalom's servants set the field on fire. Then Joab arose, and came to Absalom unto his house, and said unto him, "Wherefore have thy servants set my field on fire?" And Absalom answered

Joab, "Behold, I sent unto thee, saying, 'Come hither, that I may send thee to the king, to say, Wherefore am I come from Geshur? It had been good for me to have been there still': now therefore let me see the king's face; and if there be any iniquity in me, let him kill me." So Joab came to the king, and told him: and when he had called for Absalom, he came to the king, and bowed himself on his face to the ground before the king: and the king kissed Absalom.

And it came to pass after this, that Absalom prepared him chariots and horses, and fifty men to run before him. And Absalom rose up early, and stood beside the way of the gate: and it was so, that when any man that had a controversy came to the king for judgment, then Absalom called unto him, and said, "Of what city art thou?" And he said, "Thy servant is of one of the tribes of Israel." And Absalom said unto him, "See, thy matters are good and right; but there is no man deputed of the king to hear thee." Absalom said moreover, "Oh that I were made judge in the land, that every man which hath any suit or cause might come unto me, and I would do him justice!" And it was so that when any man came nigh to him to do him obeisance, he put forth his hand, and took him, and kissed him. And on this manner did Absalom to all Israel that came to the king for judgment: so Absalom stole the hearts of the men of Israel.

[2 *Samuel* xiv. 28–33, 2 *Samuel* xv. 1–6

The narrative goes on (in 2 Sam. xv, xvi, xvii) to tell how Absalom conspired to have himself at Hebron proclaimed king of Israel; how David with his servants and the people left Jerusalem in great sorrow; how Absalom became king in Jerusalem, while David passed to the other side of the Jordan. But David had friends in Absalom's camp, and friends on the far side of Jordan: victory came in sight.

David defeats Absalom, and Absalom dies

And David numbered the people that were with him, and set captains of thousands and captains of hundreds over them. And David sent forth a third part of the people under the hand of Joab, and a third part under the hand of Abishai the son of Zeruiah, Joab's brother, and a third part under the hand of Ittai the Gittite. And the king said unto the people, "I will surely go forth with you myself also." But the people answered, "Thou shalt not go forth: for if we flee away, they will not care for us; neither if half of us die, will they care for us: but now thou art worth ten thousand of us: therefore now it is better that thou succour us out of the city." And the king said unto them, "What seemeth you best I will do." And the king stood by the gate side, and all the people came out by hundreds and by thousands. And the king commanded Joab and Abishai and Ittai, saying, "Deal gently for my sake with the young man, even with Absalom." And all the people heard when the king gave all the captains charge concerning Absalom.

So the people went out into the field against Israel: and the battle was in the wood of Ephraim; where the people of Israel were slain before the servants of David, and there was there a great slaughter that day of twenty thousand men. For the battle was there scattered over the face of all the country: and the wood devoured more people that day than the sword devoured.

And Absalom met the servants of David. And Absalom rode upon a mule, and the mule went under the thick boughs of a great oak, and his head caught hold of the oak, and he was taken up between the heaven and the earth; and the mule that was under him went away. And a certain man saw it, and told Joab, and said, "Behold, I saw Absalom hanged in an oak." And Joab said unto the man that told him, "And, behold, thou sawest him, and why didst thou not smite him there to the ground? And I would have given thee ten shekels of silver, and a girdle." And the man said unto Joab, "Though I should receive a thousand shekels of silver in mine hand, yet would I not put forth mine hand against the king's son: for in our hearing the king charged thee and Abishai and Ittai saying, 'Beware that none touch the young man Absalom.' Otherwise I should have wrought falsehood against mine own life: for there is no matter hid from the king, and thou thyself wouldest have set thyself against me." Then said Joab, "I may not tarry thus with thee." And he took three darts in his hand, and thrust them through the heart of Absalom, while he was yet alive in the midst of the oak. And ten young men that bare Joab's armour compassed about and smote Absalom, and slew him. And Joab blew the trumpet, and the people returned from pursuing after Israel: for Joab held back the people. And they took Absalom, and cast him into a great pit in the wood, and laid a very great heap of stones upon him: and all Israel fled every one to his tent.

Then said Ahimaaz the son of Zadok, "Let me now run, and bear the king tidings, how that the Lord hath avenged him of his enemies." And Joab said unto him, "Thou shalt not bear tidings this day, but thou shalt bear tidings another day: but this day thou shalt bear no tidings, because the king's son is dead." Then said Joab to Cushi, "Go tell the king what thou hast seen." And Cushi bowed himself unto Joab, and ran. Then said Ahimaaz the son of Zadok yet again to Joab, "But howsoever, let me, I pray thee, also run after Cushi." And Joab said, "Wherefore wilt thou run, my son, seeing that thou hast no tidings ready?" "But howsoever", said he, "let me run." And he said unto him, "Run." Then Ahimaaz ran by the way of the plain, and overran Cushi.

And David sat between the two gates: and the watchman went up to the roof over the gate unto the wall, and lifted up his eyes, and looked, and behold a man running alone. And the watchman cried, and told the king. And the king said, "If he be alone there is tidings in his mouth." And he came apace, and drew near. And the watchman saw another man running: and the watchman called unto the porter, and said, "Behold another man running alone." And the king said, "He also bringeth tidings." And the watchman said, "Me thinketh the running of the foremost is like the running of Ahimaaz the son of Zadok." And the king said, "He is a good man, and cometh with good tidings." And Ahimaaz called, and said unto the king, "All is well." And he fell down to the earth upon his face before the king, and said, "Blessed be the Lord thy God, which hath delivered up the men that lifted up their hand against my lord the king." And the king said, "Is the young man Absalom safe?" And Ahimaaz answered, "When Joab sent the king's servant, and me thy servant, I saw a great tumult, but I knew not what it was." And the king said unto him, "Turn aside, and stand here." And he turned aside, and stood still.

And, behold, Cushi came: and Cushi said, "Tidings, my lord the king: for the Lord hath avenged thee this day of all them that rose up against thee." And the king said unto Cushi, "Is the young man Absalom safe?" And Cushi answered, "The enemies of my lord the king, and all that rise against thee to do thee hurt, be as that young man is." And the king was much moved, and went up to the chamber over the gate, and wept: and as he went, thus he said: "O my son Absalom, my son, my son Absalom! Would God I had died for thee, O Absalom, my son, my son!"

[2 *Samuel* xviii

In the last two chapters of this Court History of King David (xix and xx), we may read of David's restoration to Jerusalem, noting the lack of good feeling between the men of Judah (the South) and the men of Israel (the North); also of a later rebellion in the North which was crushed by Joab. Even under David, the union of North and South was more nominal than real.

OTHER NARRATIVES OF THE EARLY MONARCHY

It is thought that the same brilliant writer, having so vividly depicted the Court History of David, began to write other interesting stories of a time just a little more remote from him. First, probably, he wrote down the Story of the Founding of the Kingdom, beginning with the Philistines' grip on the land, the leadership of Samuel, the search for Saul, and continuing with the varying relationship between Saul and David. This occupies a great part of 1 Samuel, along with the beginning of 2 Samuel; but it is so much interwoven with other narratives of the same period that it cannot easily now be disentangled. So we postpone dealing with the complex book of 1 Samuel until we are in a position to understand better the other strands of its story (see p. 177).

In the Story of the Founding of the Kingdom, the historian of David's court very likely still trusted largely to his own recollections or those of older friends. Soon, however, he or another gathered the old Hero Stories which we have in the Book of Judges, such as the stories of Gideon and Samson, and a little later, very old stories which went back to the beginning of things, such as the stories of Abraham and Joseph. But these stories also have been so much mixed with other material in the Books of Genesis, Exodus, Numbers, Joshua, and Judges, that their study too we must postpone to a much later period, when we can understand more of the very varied elements which went to the composition of these books as we now have them (see p. 181).

The inner discord between the North and the South which existed even under King David led to complete separation under Rehoboam, David's grandson. In the reign of this weak and foolish king, the one strong kingdom of David and Solomon became two kingdoms, the North and the South, the Kingdom of Israel and the Kingdom of Judah. See p. 107 for information about the extent of these two, and about the peculiar characteristics of each. Meantime all we need note is the actual division of the people into two separate parts, under different kings and with different histories. Soon vice, oppression, and disloyalty to Jehovah began to eat away the vitality of both South and North. The North was the first to become thoroughly corrupt, but the South followed all too quickly.

Not all in either kingdom went astray. In two different parts of the country (many think in the North and in the South), and probably at different times, two different narratives were compiled giving an account of how God had chosen the Hebrew nation to be His special people, and of the way by which they had developed from a band of wandering nomads into a strong nation. These narratives made use of earlier written stories, such as those mentioned above, and of varied oral tradition. For more details about these two different narratives, called the J and E Documents, see pp. 178, 179.

To sum up, let us remember that the period of the Early Monarchy was the first period rich in the production of written narratives, and that from this time onwards a variety of written sources, such as the "Book of the Acts of Solomon", Royal Annals and Temple Records, was at the disposal of any person anxious to write a true account of events.

4. FOUR GREAT PROPHETS

During the dark years of the decline of both Northern and Southern kingdoms, there arose a succession of prophets, or preachers, as we should call them, who saw far into the lives of their fellow-countrymen and at the same time penetrated deeply into God's plans for their race, who came to be certain that sin and evil could not go unpunished if their nation were ever to be the blessing to the whole world which God intended it to be. It is due to the insight and courage of these prophets that the nation became at last a fit cradle for Jesus of Nazareth. These men at first simply talked or preached to the people, but to preach ill-fortune is a thankless task, and ere long the prophets were forced to *write* what they wished the people to apprehend clearly. The first message in our Bible which was written in this way is one from Amos. Then come messages from Hosea, Isaiah, and Micah.

One difficult problem presents itself in giving selections from the writings of these prophets as expressed in the Authorized Version; it is the problem of how far to arrange the prophetic writings as verse and how far as prose. In certain passages here given, for instance the Dirge with which the message of Amos opens, or Isaiah's Song of the Vineyard, the rhythm is so strongly marked even in the translation of the Authorized Version, and scholars are so unanimous in giving other translations of these passages in poetic form, that we here set out such passages in verse, as we set out the Psalms in verse. But there are other passages where the rhythmic beat is so strong that they also might be set out in verse instead of prose. The reader should read these passages as he reads poetry, stressing to himself the rhythm, and so turning them for himself into free verse. For example, apart from the Dirge, most of the selections from Amos given here, although printed as prose, have so well marked a beat that they can best be read aloud as free verse. Note in contrast the introductory words, "The words of Amos when he was among the herdmen of Tekoa" (i. 1), or much of the last selection which tells of Amos being dismissed from Bethel. No stressing of beats or rhythm will turn these into poetry: they are essentially prose.

Amos to Luxurious Oppressors of the Poor

Amos prophesied in a time when the Northern kingdom under King Jeroboam II felt itself to be almost as mighty as when Israel and Judah flourished together under King David. At this time their old foe Damascus had been reduced, while their coming conqueror, Assyria, still lacked unity and power. Religious feasts were most cheerful occasions, not seasons for worship and repentance. Sacrifices were offered, but, after suitable portions of the slain beasts had been laid on the altar, the worshippers feasted on the remainder with such immense satisfaction that too frequently the festival became an occasion for revelry and greedy tumult.

About the year 760 B.C., at one such gathering, suddenly on the ears of the revellers fell the strange rhythm of the funeral dirge which they were wont to hear only at times of personal sorrow, when loved ones passed away from them.

Rhythm and words alike were startling: so also was the appearance of the stranger Amos, a herdman from Tekoa in the Southern kingdom. Naturally, the king's priest, Amaziah, interfered, and Amos perforce returned to his sheep and sycamores. But there in Tekoa, prevented from preaching the truths which pressed on his heart, he found relief and satisfaction in *writing* God's message to Israel. Thus with Amos begins written prophecy, one reason for his importance.

But Amos is important for another reason. His is the first clear statement of the fact that true religion lies not in ceremonies and forms of public worship, but in righteousness and judgment; not in seeking Bethel, though it be the king's chapel, but in seeking God. So sure was Amos of the moral order of the universe, that in days of the greatest prosperity for Israel, days when no foe loomed on the horizon, he proclaimed a coming doom and captivity, being inwardly convinced that a society based on the luxury of the rich and the oppression of the poor could not be stable. Thus Amos plays a most important part in the development of Hebrew religion: his message also comes near to some features of our modern civilization.

The Author
The words of Amos, who was among the herdmen of Tekoa, which he saw concerning Israel in the days of Uzziah king of Judah, and in the days of Jeroboam king of Israel:

[*Amos* i. 1

A Dirge
Hear ye this word which I take up against you, even a lamentation, O house of Israel.

> The virgin of Israel is fallen,
> She shall no more rise:
> She is forsaken upon her land;
> There is none to raise her up.

[*Amos* v. 1

Hope for those who repent
For thus saith the Lord unto the house of Israel, "Seek ye Me, and ye shall live: but seek not Bethel, for Bethel shall come to naught." Seek the Lord, and ye shall live; lest He break out like fire in the

house of Joseph, and devour it, and there be none to quench it in Bethel, ye who turn judgment to wormwood, and leave off righteousness in the earth. They hate him that rebuketh in the gate, and they abhor him that speaketh uprightly.

Forasmuch therefore as your treading is upon the poor, and ye take from him burdens of wheat: ye have built houses of hewn stone, but ye shall not dwell in them; ye have planted pleasant vineyards, but ye shall not drink wine of them. For I know your manifold transgressions and your mighty sins: they afflict the just, they take a bribe, and they turn aside the poor in the gate from their right. Seek good, and not evil, that ye may live: hate the evil, and love the good, and establish judgment in the gate: it may be that the Lord of hosts will be gracious unto the remnant of Joseph.

[*From Amos* v. 4–15

Worship without Goodness of no Avail

"I hate, I despise your feast days, and I will not smell your solemn assemblies. Though ye offer Me burnt offerings and your meat offerings, I will not accept them, neither will I regard the peace offerings of your fat beasts. Take thou away from Me the noise of thy songs; for I will not hear the melody of thy viols. But let judgment run down as waters, and righteousness as a mighty stream."

[*Amos* v. 21–24

Luxury in Israel

Woe to them that [are in ease in Zion, and] trust in the mountain of Samaria! Ye that put far away the evil day, and cause the seat of violence to come near; that lie upon beds of ivory, and stretch themselves upon their couches, and eat the lambs out of the flock, and the calves out of the midst of the stall; that chant to the sound of the viol, and invent to themselves instruments of music, like David; that drink wine in bowls, and anoint themselves with the chief ointments: but they are not grieved for the affliction of Joseph.

Therefore now shall they go captive with the first that go captive, and the banquet of them that stretched themselves shall be removed. The Lord God hath sworn by Himself, "I abhor the excellency of Jacob, and hate his palaces: therefore will I deliver up the city with all that is therein."

[*Amos* vi. 1–8

Amos dismissed from Bethel

Then Amaziah the priest of Bethel sent to Jeroboam king of Israel, saying, "Amos hath conspired against thee in the midst of the house of Israel: the land is not able to bear all his words. For thus Amos saith, 'Jeroboam shall die by the sword, and Israel shall surely be led away captive out of their own land.' "

Also Amaziah said unto Amos, "O thou seer, go, flee thee away into the land of Judah, and there eat bread, and prophesy there:

but prophesy not again any more in Bethel: for it is the king's chapel, and it is the king's court." Then answered Amos, and said to Amaziah, "I was no prophet, neither was I a prophet's son; but I was a herdman, and a gatherer of sycomore fruit: and the Lord took me as I followed the flock, and the Lord said unto me, 'Go, prophesy unto My people Israel.' Now therefore hear thou the word of the Lord: Thou sayest, 'Prophesy not against Israel, and drop not thy word against the house of Isaac.' Therefore thus saith the Lord: 'Thy sons and thy daughters shall fall by the sword, and thy land shall be divided by line; and thou shalt die in a polluted land: and Israel shall surely go into captivity forth of his land.'"

[*Amos* vii. 10–17

Hosea and the Love of God

About twenty years after the rugged herdman Amos appeared from the South among the revelling worshippers at Bethel, another prophet declared to the North a message from God. He was Hosea, the first to give clear expression to the love of God.

The tenderness of Hosea's message is a wonderful thing to have come out of a time of national chaos and anarchy. For the Northern kingdom by then was fast approaching its fall: no longer was there luxury and prosperity: everywhere was confusion, even to king murdering king. Hosea realized the sin and saw that a God of justice must condemn it; but at the same moment he loved the sinners, and so penetrated into the heart of a God of love. Can we understand why the man should have reached this assurance of the loving-kindness of Jehovah?

The translation of his work in the Authorized Version of the Bible is not very helpful, and the following selections from it are, of necessity, brief. But the earlier chapters of Hosea's work, especially when simplified by better translations, show us how he reached his assurance through his own personal experience of life and love and sin. He was no stranger like Amos, who could come from afar, declare a terrible day of doom, and return to his distant home without sharing in the sufferings. Hosea was a man of the North, intimately concerned in all that the North should suffer. The men and women who sinned were dear to him, and this echo of the love of God in his own heart showed him the heart of God. But it was Hosea's relationship with one particular sinner which taught him most.

In early days he had wedded a simple maid of his country, and loved her dearly and deeply. Three children were born to them, two sons and a daughter, to whom, in the old fashion, Hosea had given names intended to convey meaning to his neighbours. For instance, he had called his third child "Lo-ammi", which meant "Not my people", voicing the lament of God over His people who were now not His people. As time went on, Hosea's wife betrayed his trust, and left her husband and children to go with strange men. Though his heart was nearly broken, his love for his wife held firm. His opportunity came. At last, when she was a desolate woman, he sought her out and took her home. Yet he knew that for the sake of all he could not at once set her up in honour as his wife: sin could not be covered up: only patient repentance could save his beloved sinner. So, for a time, while supporting her in his home, Hosea treated her as a stranger, until, at last, when he was sure that her heart was changed, he joyfully received her again as his honoured wife.

As this man mused on these things, he saw Jehovah as the deserted sorrowing Husband of Israel, yearning after His lost people, compelled in love to chasten, but ready to welcome back the penitent with wonderful loving-kindness and tender mercy. Thus Hosea gave to the Old Testament a version of the parable of the Prodigal Son. Ephraim is the North.

This selection expresses God's grief over the sins of His people, His love for them from the days of old, and His promise of healing and pardon when they again turned to Him.

The Author and his Times

The word of the Lord that came unto Hosea, the son of Beeri, in the days of Jeroboam, the son of Joash, king of Israel.

[*Hosea* i. 1

THE FIRST LITERATURE

God's Sorrow over His People's Sin

O Ephraim, what shall I do unto thee? O Judah, what shall I do unto thee, for your goodness is as a morning cloud, and as the early dew it goeth away? Therefore have I hewed them by the prophets; I have slain them by the words of my mouth. For I desired mercy, and not sacrifice, and the knowledge of God more than burnt offerings. But they like men have transgressed the covenant: there have they dealt treacherously against me. Gilead is a city of them that work iniquity, and is polluted with blood. And as troops of robbers wait for a man, so the company of priests murder in the way by consent.

When I would have healed Israel, then the iniquity of Ephraim was discovered, and the wickedness of Samaria: for they commit falsehood; and the thief cometh in, and the troop of robbers spoileth without. And they consider not in their hearts that I remember all their wickedness. Woe unto them, for they have fled from Me! Destruction unto them, because they have transgressed against Me! Though I have redeemed them, yet have they spoken lies against Me. And they have not cried unto Me with their heart, when they howled upon their beds: they assemble themselves for corn and wine, and they rebel against Me. Though I have bound and strengthened their arms, yet do they imagine mischief against Me. They return, but not to the most High.

[*From Hosea* vi. and vii

God's Love for His People

When Israel was a child, then I loved him, and called My son out of Egypt. I taught Ephraim also to go, taking them by their arms; but they knew not that I healed them. I drew them with cords of a man, with bands of love: and I was to them as they that take off the yoke on their jaws, and I laid meat unto them. My people are bent to backsliding from Me: though they called them to the most High, none at all would exalt Him. How shall I give thee up, Ephraim? how shall I deliver thee, Israel? Mine heart is turned within Me, My repentings are kindled together. I will not execute the fierceness of Mine anger, I will not return to destroy Ephraim: for I am God, and not man; the Holy One in the midst of thee.

[*From Hosea* xi

"Return unto the Lord"

O Israel, return unto the Lord thy God; for thou hast fallen by thine iniquity. Take with you words, and turn to the Lord: say unto Him, "Take away all iniquity, and receive us graciously: so will we render the calves of our lips. Assyria shall not save us; we will not ride upon horses: neither will we say any more to the work of our hands, 'Ye are our gods': for in Thee the fatherless findeth mercy."

[*Hosea* xiv. 1–3

The Forgiveness of God

I will heal their backsliding, I will love them freely: for Mine anger is turned away from him. I will be as the dew unto Israel: he shall grow as the lily, and cast forth his roots as Lebanon. His branches shall spread, and his beauty shall be as the olive tree, and his smell as Lebanon. They that dwell under his shadow shall return; they shall revive as the corn, and grow as the vine: the scent thereof shall be as the wine of Lebanon. Ephraim shall say, "What have I to do any more with idols?" [*Hosea* xiv. 4-8

ISAIAH, THE PROPHET-STATESMAN

Not long after the days of Hosea's prophecy, the Northern kingdom fell for ever, and its people were scattered over the face of the earth. Henceforward the Southern kingdom becomes the centre of our study; we have passed from the history of the Hebrews to the history of the Jews. Judah as well as Israel at this time felt the ocean of danger beating against her rocky mountains, but the waves receded; Jerusalem, her capital and religious centre, was safe for another century. This was of the utmost importance, as it gave the Jews the opportunity of a richer development in knowledge of God.

Thus, when destruction fell on Jerusalem also, the Jewish exiles had among them an element of religious strength: some, at least, of them believed firmly in the power, wisdom, and real effectiveness of the unseen Jehovah. And in time this Remnant returned to Jerusalem from exile in Babylon, and so ensured the continuance of the Jewish people as a race with a unique service to render to all mankind. Through this century of comparative safety followed by a period of great affliction, a section of the Jews grew into a surprising knowledge of Jehovah and His ways.

Samaria fell in 722 B.C.; Jerusalem not until 586 B.C. How did Jerusalem survive the attacks of the Assyrians who swept Israel to destruction? Partly it was that her security was due to her lack of desirable resources and to her better geographical position, but it must be remembered that after the fall of Samaria, the territory of the Assyrians approached to within a day's walk of the Northern walls of Jerusalem. It must be frankly admitted, also, that the moral and religious life of the greater part of the Jews was not one whit better than that of their Northern kinsfolk. Not only did the majority of them fail to rise to nobler ideas of Jehovah, but they worshipped other gods, even, at times, to the extent of offering human sacrifices. Yet a seed of life remained in them, fostered in its first days of weakness by the great prophet-statesman Isaiah, some of whose writings we now give. He it was who cherished this seed of life until it was beyond destruction, able to grow in captivity. This Remnant of godly men in Judah ultimately gave to the world Jesus of Nazareth.

THE MESSAGE OF ISAIAH

This prophet was a man of most varied gifts, all of which he used in the service of his country. Some time about 740 B.C., about twenty years after the appearance of Amos at Bethel, in the last year of the long reign of King Uzziah of Judah, Isaiah felt himself specially called by God to declare His message to Judah. The first selection gives his own account of this deep spiritual experience. The next two picture a state of affairs in Judah very much like that depicted in Israel by Amos and Hosea. We have God's justice, the justice of "The Holy One of Israel", rebuking the same old sins of oppression, luxury, and false worship; we have an expression of the love of God for His people in the parable of the vineyard. But we have in Isaiah something new, a vision of a way of escape. For Isaiah is certain that there is a Remnant in Judah who will continue to seek God, and who will return to Him from their sin: on the existence of this Remnant Isaiah stakes his hopes, and later history reveals how his faith was justified.

The prophet was such a well-known figure in Jerusalem that we find his wife referred to as "the prophetess". Like Hosea, he gave his little boys names which kept the people in remembrance of his message. For instance, he called one of them "Shearjashub", which means "a remnant shall return"; while he called a later baby "Maher-shalal-hash-baz", which means "the spoil speeds, the prey hastens", referring to the rapid approach of the Assyrians.

Isaiah's Call and Commission

The vision of Isaiah, which he saw concerning Judah and Jerusalem in the days of Uzziah, Jotham, Ahaz, and Hezekiah, kings of Judah:
[*Isaiah* i. 1

In the year that King Uzziah died I saw also the Lord sitting upon a throne, high and lifted up, and His train filled the temple. Above it stood the seraphim: each one had six wings; with twain he covered his face, and with twain he covered his feet, and with twain he did fly. And one cried unto another, and said,

"Holy, Holy, Holy is the Lord of hosts:
The whole earth is full of His glory."

And the posts of the door moved at the voice of him that cried, and the house was filled with smoke.

Then said I, "Woe is me! For I am undone; because I am a man of unclean lips, and I dwell in the midst of a people of unclean lips: for mine eyes have seen the King, the Lord of Hosts." Then flew one of the seraphim unto me, having a live coal in his hand, which he had taken with the tongs from off the altar: and he laid it upon my mouth, and said, "Lo, this hath touched thy lips; and thine iniquity is taken away, and thy sin purged."

Also I heard the voice of the Lord, saying, "Whom shall I send, and who will go for us?" Then said I, "Here am I; send me."
[*Isaiah* vi. 1–8

Warning to the Vain Women of Jerusalem

The Lord will enter into judgment with the ancients of His people, and the princes thereof: for ye have eaten up the vineyard; the spoil of the poor is in your houses. "What mean ye that ye beat My people to pieces, and grind the faces of the poor?" saith the Lord of hosts.

Moreover, because the daughters of Zion are haughty, and walk with stretched forth necks and wanton eyes, walking and mincing as they go, and making a tinkling with their feet: therefore the Lord will smite with a scab the crown of the head of the daughters of Zion. In that day the Lord will take away the bravery of their tinkling ornaments about their feet, and their cauls, and their round tires like the moon, the chains, and the bracelets, the bonnets, and the ornaments of the legs, and the headbands, and the earrings, the rings and nose jewels, the changeable suits of apparel, and the mantles, and the wimples, and the crisping pins, the glasses, and the fine linen, and the hoods, and the vails. And it shall come to pass, that instead of sweet smell there shall be a stink; and instead of a girdle a rent; and instead of well set hair baldness; and burning instead of beauty. Thy men shall fall by the sword, and thy mighty in the war. And her gates shall lament and mourn; and she being desolate shall sit upon the ground.

[*Isaiah* iii. 14–26

"Rise up, ye women that are at ease; hear My voice, ye careless daughters; give ear unto My speech. Many days and years shall ye be troubled, ye careless women; for the vintage shall fail, the gathering shall not come. Tremble, ye women that are at ease; be troubled, ye careless ones. They shall lament for the pleasant fields, for the fruitful vine. Upon the land of My people shall come up thorns and briers; yea, upon all the houses of joy in the joyous city; because the palaces shall be forsaken; the multitude of the city shall be left; the forts and towers shall be burdens for ever, a joy of wild asses, a pasture for flocks."

[*Isaiah* xxxii. 9–14

Parable of the Vineyard

Now will I sing to My wellbeloved a song of My beloved touching his vineyard.

> My beloved had a vineyard in a very fruitful hill:
> And he fenced it,
> And gathered out the stones thereof,
> And planted it with the choicest vine,
> And built a tower in the midst of it,
> And also made a winepress therein:
> And he looked that it should bring forth grapes,
> And it brought forth wild grapes.

And now, O inhabitants of Jerusalem, and men of Judah, judge, I pray you, betwixt Me and My vineyard. What could have been done more to My vineyard, that I have not done in it? Wherefore when I looked that it should bring forth grapes, brought it forth wild grapes?

And now go to; I will tell you what I will do to My vineyard:

> I will take away the hedge thereof
> And it shall be eaten up;
> And break down the wall thereof,
> And it shall be trodden down: and I will lay it waste:
> It shall not be pruned, nor digged;
> But there shall come up briers and thorns:
> I will also command the clouds
> That they rain no rain upon it.
>
> For the vineyard of the Lord of hosts is the house of Israel,
> And the men of Judah His pleasant plant:
> And He looked for judgment, but behold oppression;
> For righteousness, but behold a cry.

[*Isaiah* v. 1–7

ISAIAH'S PROTEST—JUDAH AND EGYPT

The next passage requires for its appreciation a greater knowledge of historical detail. Under King Uzziah (or Azariah), who reigned for fifty-two years, Judah was prosperous and successful. But his grandson Ahaz, who succeeded him in 735 B.C., was a weak type. Finally, to save himself from the attacks of Israel and Damascus, despite Isaiah's remonstrances, he placed himself and his kingdom under the protection of Assyria. On this, Isaiah appears to have withdrawn himself from public life, and to have concentrated his energies on the education of the Remnant. Probably at this time he began to *write* his messages.

Ahaz was succeeded by King Hezekiah, who at once began to plan escape from payment of tribute to Assyria, by an alliance with Egypt. The utter folly of this plan brought Isaiah forth again to face the people. He saw that Egypt was a broken reed upon which to lean, that Judah's one chance of peace amid the storms of war was to submit quietly to the Assyrian. In this selection he pours forth in a torrent of rich language his view of the position. Isaiah reckoned the unseen Jehovah as real a factor in the situation as the Assyrian: his faith, as we shall see later, was justified.

Trust in the Shadow of Egypt or Confidence in Jehovah
>Woe to the rebellious children, saith the Lord,
>That take counsel, but not of Me;
>That walk to go down into Egypt,
>And have not asked at My mouth;
>To strengthen themselves in the strength of Pharaoh,
>And to trust in the shadow of Egypt!
>Therefore shall the strength of Pharaoh be your shame,
>And trust in the shadow of Egypt your confusion.
>
>Into the land of trouble and anguish,
>From whence come the young and old lion,
>The viper and fiery flying serpent,
>They will carry their riches upon the shoulders of young asses,
>And their treasures upon the bunches of camels,
>To a people that shall not profit them.
>For the Egyptians shall help in vain, and to no purpose:
>Therefore have I cried concerning this, "Their strength is to sit still."

Now go, write it before them in a table, and note it in a book, that it may be for the time to come for ever and ever: that this is a rebellious people, lying children, children that will not hear the law of the Lord: which say to the seers, "See not"; and to the prophets, "Prophesy not unto us right things, speak unto us smooth things, prophesy deceits: get you out of the way, turn aside out of the path, cause the Holy One of Israel to cease from before us." Wherefore thus saith the Holy One of Israel, "Because ye despise this word, and trust in oppression and perverseness, and stay thereon: therefore this iniquity shall be to you as a breach ready to fall, swelling out in a high wall, whose breaking cometh suddenly at an instant." And He shall break it as the breaking of the potters' vessel that is broken in pieces; He shall not spare: so that there shall not be found in the bursting of it a sherd to take fire from the hearth, or to take water withal out of the pit. For thus saith the Lord God, the Holy One of Israel: "In returning and rest shall ye be saved; in quietness and in confidence shall be your strength": and ye would not. But ye said, "No, for we will flee upon horses"; therefore shall ye flee: and, "We will ride upon the swift"; therefore shall they that pursue you be swift. One thousand shall flee at the rebuke of one; at the rebuke of five shall ye flee: till ye be left as a beacon upon the top of a mountain, and as an ensign on an hill.

> Woe to them that go down to Egypt for help;
> And stay on horses, and trust in chariots,
> Because they are many;
> And in horsemen, because they are very strong;
> But they look not unto the Holy One of Israel,
> Neither seek the Lord!
> Yet He also is wise, and will bring evil,
> And will not call back His words:
> But will arise against the house of the evildoers,
> And against the help of them that work iniquity.
>
> Now the Egyptians are men, and not God;
> And their horses flesh, and not spirit.
> When the Lord shall stretch out His hand, both he that helpeth shall fall,
> And he that is holpen shall fall down, and they shall all fail together.
> For thus hath the Lord spoken unto me,
> Like as the lion and the young lion roaring on his prey,
> When a multitude of shepherds is called forth against him,
> He will not be afraid of their voice,
> Nor abase Himself for the noise of them:
> So shall the Lord of hosts come down
> To fight for mount Zion, and for the hill thereof.

As birds flying,
So will the Lord of hosts defend Jerusalem;
Defending also He will deliver it,
And passing over He will preserve it.

"Then shall the Assyrian fall with the sword, not of a mighty man;
And the sword, not of a mean man, shall devour him:
But he shall flee from the sword,
And his young men shall be discomfited.
And he shall pass over to his stronghold for fear,
And his princes shall be afraid of the ensign,"
Saith the Lord, Whose fire is in Zion,
And His furnace in Jerusalem.

For in that day every man shall cast away his idols of silver, and his idols of gold,
Which your own hands have made unto you for a sin.
[*From Isaiah* xxx, xxxi

DELIVERANCE FROM DESTRUCTION

In spite of this protest, the alliance with Egypt was accomplished. Instead of continuing to pay tribute to Assyria, and so in quietness finding strength, Judah drew the attention of Assyria on herself by this foolish act of revolt. Soon the Assyrians, under Sennacherib, were at the gates of Jerusalem. For the story of how Isaiah saved the city, see p. 138. Out of a sure expectation of destruction, the inhabitants of Jerusalem were gathered into safety by the defence of the Lord of hosts.

Then was great revulsion of spirit. Isaiah preached an important sermon of repentance, which we give next. And his mind became full of high hopes for a great future for Judah, under the rule of some ideal monarch. Here also is his picture of this perfect state, a picture so beautiful that men have thought of it as applying to the Kingdom of God and to Jesus as King.

Sermon on Repentance

Hear, O heavens, and give ear, O earth: for the Lord hath spoken, "I have nourished and brought up children, and they have rebelled against Me. The ox knoweth his owner, and the ass his master's crib: but Israel doth not know, My people doth not consider." Ah sinful nation, a people laden with iniquity, a seed of evildoers, children that are corrupters: they have forsaken the Lord, they have provoked the Holy One of Israel unto anger, they are gone away backward.

Why should ye be stricken any more? Ye will revolt more and more: the whole head is sick, and the whole heart faint. From the sole of the foot even unto the head there is no soundness in it; but wounds, and bruises, and putrifying sores: they have not been closed, neither bound up, neither mollified with ointment. Your country is desolate, your cities are burned with fire: your land, strangers devour it in your presence, and it is desolate, as overthrown by strangers. And the daughter of Zion is left as a cottage in a vineyard, as a lodge in a garden of cucumbers, as a besieged city. Except the Lord of hosts had left unto us a very small remnant, we should have been as Sodom, and we should have been like unto Gomorrah.

Hear the word of the Lord, ye rulers of Sodom; give ear unto the law of our God, ye people of Gomorrah. "To what purpose is the multitude of your sacrifices unto me?" saith the Lord: "I am full of the burnt offerings of rams, and the fat of fed beasts; and I delight not in the blood of bullocks, or of lambs, or of he-goats. When ye come to appear before Me, who hath required this at your hand, to tread My courts? Bring no more vain oblations; incense is an abomination unto Me; the new moons and sabbaths, the calling of assemblies, I cannot away with; it is iniquity, even the solemn meeting. Your new moons and your appointed feasts My soul hateth: they are a trouble unto Me; I am weary to bear them. And when ye spread forth your hands, I will hide Mine eyes from you: yea, when ye make many prayers, I will not hear: your hands are full of blood."

Wash you, make you clean; put away the evil of your doings from before Mine eyes; cease to do evil; learn to do well; seek judgment, relieve the oppressed, judge the fatherless, plead for the widow. "Come now, and let us reason together," saith the Lord; "though your sins be as scarlet, they shall be as white as snow; though they be red like crimson, they shall be as wool."

[*Isaiah* i. 2–18

A Picture of an Ideal Kingdom

And there shall come forth a rod out of the stem of Jesse, and a Branch shall grow out of his roots: and the spirit of the Lord shall rest upon him, the spirit of wisdom and understanding, the spirit of counsel and might, the spirit of knowledge and of the fear of the Lord; and shall make him of quick understanding in the fear of the Lord: and he shall not judge after the sight of his eyes, neither reprove after the hearing of his ears: but with righteousness shall he judge the poor, and reprove with equity for the meek of the earth: and he shall smite the earth with the rod of his mouth, and with the breath of his lips shall he slay the wicked. And righteousness shall be the girdle of his loins, and faithfulness the girdle of his reins.

The wolf also shall dwell with the lamb, and the leopard shall lie down with the kid; and the calf and the young lion and the fatling together; and a little child shall lead them. And the cow and the bear shall feed; their young ones shall lie down together: and the lion shall eat straw like the ox. And the suckling child shall play on the hole of the asp, and the weaned child shall put his hand on the cockatrice' den. They shall not hurt nor destroy in all my holy mountain: for the earth shall be full of the knowledge of the Lord, as the waters cover the sea. [*Isaiah* xi. 1-9]

MICAH, THE PROPHET OF THE PEOPLE

Beside Isaiah, Micah at first sight looks a poor figure. No dweller in Jerusalem is he, no friend of kings. He belonged to a little country town near the border between Judah and the Philistines, and it was the suffering of the common people losing fields and houses to their oppressors which moved his heart to utterance. Like Amos and Hosea, Micah gazed on the sin of the Northern kingdom and awaited the fall of Samaria. Also from afar he feared the danger for Jerusalem. During Hezekiah's reign, he became certain of doom for Jerusalem also, and in terrible words prophesied its destruction.

The Author and his Subject

The word of the Lord that came to Micah the Morasthite in the days of Hezekiah, king of Judah, which he saw concerning Samaria and Jerusalem. [*Micah* i. 1]

The Consequences of Sin

Hear, all ye people; hearken, O earth, and all that therein is: and let the Lord God be witness against you, the Lord from His holy temple. For, behold, the Lord cometh forth out of His place, and will come down, and tread upon the high places of the earth. And the mountains shall be molten under Him, and the valleys shall be cleft, as wax before the fire, and as the waters that are poured down a steep place. For the transgression of Jacob is all this, and for the sins of the house of Israel. What is the transgression of Jacob? Is it not Samaria? And what are the high places of Judah? Are they not Jerusalem? Therefore I will make Samaria as an heap of the field, and as plantings of a vineyard: and I will pour down the stones thereof into the valley, and I will discover the foundations thereof. And all the graven images thereof shall be beaten to pieces, and all the hires thereof shall be burned with the fire, and all the idols thereof will

THE FIRST LITERATURE

I lay desolate: for her wound is incurable; for it is come unto Judah; he is come unto the gate of My people, even to Jerusalem.

Woe to them that devise iniquity, and work evil upon their beds! When the morning is light, they practise it, because it is in the power of their hand. And they covet fields, and take them by violence; and houses, and take them away: so they oppress a man and his house, even a man and his heritage.

But truly I am full of power by the spirit of the Lord, and of judgment, and of might, to declare unto Jacob his transgression, and to Israel his sin. Hear this, I pray you, ye heads of the house of Jacob, and princes of the house of Israel, that abhor judgment, and pervert all equity. They build up Zion with blood, and Jerusalem with iniquity. The heads thereof judge for reward, and the priests thereof teach for hire, and the prophets thereof divine for money: yet will they lean upon the Lord, and say, "Is not the Lord among us? None evil can come upon us." Therefore shall Zion for your sake be plowed as a field, and Jerusalem shall become heaps, and the mountain of the house as the high places of the forest.

[*From Micah* i, ii, and iii

The sixth chapter of the Book of Micah contains one of the greatest utterances of Old Testament prophecy. It evidently came from a man who had lived in the reign of Hezekiah's successor, Manasseh, a king who reverted to such heathenish ways that even the sacrifice of firstborn children was practised. Micah himself may have so lived on beyond the time of Hezekiah, but many scholars think that a message from a prophet who lived just a little after Micah has been added to Micah's own message by a later editor (see note on p. 18). It summarizes the teaching of this group of prophets—Amos, Hosea, Isaiah, Micah.

Jehovah Pleading

    Hear ye now what the Lord saith,
    "Arise, contend thou before the mountains,
    And let the hills hear thy voice."
    Hear ye, O mountains, the Lord's controversy,
    And ye strong foundations of the earth:
    For the Lord hath a controversy with His people,
    And He will plead with Israel.
    "O My people what have I done unto thee?
    And wherein have I wearied thee?
    Testify against Me.

> For I brought thee up out of the land of Egypt,
> And redeemed thee out of the house of servants;
> And I sent before thee Moses, Aaron, and Miriam."
>
> [*Micah* vi. 1-5

True Religion

> Wherewith shall I come before the Lord?
> And bow myself before the high God?
> Shall I come before Him with burnt offerings,
> With calves of a year old?
> Will the Lord be pleased with thousands of rams,
> Or with ten thousands of rivers of oil?
> Shall I give my firstborn for my transgression,
> The fruit of my body for the sin of my soul?
>
> He hath shewed thee, O man, what is good;
> And what doth the Lord require of thee,
> But to do justly, and to love mercy,
> And to walk humbly with thy God?
>
> [*Micah* vi. 6-8

5. EARLY LAWS

ANOTHER FORM OF HEBREW LITERATURE

We have seen how some forms of Hebrew literature, like some forms of our own English literature, arose through the handing down from father to son of story told and verse sung. We have noted how the dramatic and eventful nature of some periods urged men irresistibly to write annals of their times, and this before men thought of collecting the oral tranditions in writing. And we have seen how some prophets, unable to find sufficient listeners, began to write their messages.

The early literature of the Hebrews took yet another form. Wherever life is social and not solitary, be it life of animals or of men, if there is to be peace and efficiency, order and not chaos must be the keynote of the life; some form of law and of obedience to law is essential. Kipling's *Jungle Book* illustrates this in a delightful way for animals, the law of the pack being clear and consistently enforced on each new generation. In human families the laws of health and cleanliness have to be taught afresh to each new member, if the family life is to be a wholesome thing. "If one member suffer, all the members suffer with it" is true of every social community from a pack of gregarious animals to a highly complex empire like our own; and the more highly developed the community, the more definite and comprehensive must be its laws. We need remember only our own lawyers, law-courts, police and judges.

The young Hebrew nation felt this need for law early in its career. Probably the first leader wise enough to diagnose these deep necessities and define laws to meet them was Moses. But even Moses must have based his rulings on the common use and wont of the people. Variety of custom is usual in a society, but a wise man sees far into the relative values of these customs, and, guided by God, unhesitatingly selects the best custom and gives it the enhanced status of a law. To the Hebrew then the Law had always the sanction of Jehovah behind it: "Thus saith the Lord." And so great was the debt to Moses that the main part of all the laws the nation ever had throughout its varied career was called "the Law of Moses" (see note on p. 19).

THE BOOK OF THE COVENANT

We find the earliest account of a code of law for Israel in Exodus xx–xxiii. Scholars can trace back the formulation given in these chapters to one of the two written collections of the earliest oral and written traditions, to which we referred on p. 29: this E collection was probably made about the eighth century before Christ. But how far back beyond the collection in which it appears this codified law goes, scholars cannot be certain. Until recently it was generally thought that, although Moses was probably the first to define clearly many of these laws, it was perhaps Solomon, the wise judge, with his interest in all phases of civilization, who arranged in this careful code the laws existing in his time. Thus the code would show us life as it was lived about the beginning of the kingdom, after the settlement in Canaan, in the centuries round about 1000 B.C. But recently scholars have begun to ascribe the greater part of this code to times before the early monarchy. The reason for this change is a new and interesting development in the material of modern scholarship.

Within the last fifty years men have learned much more about the ancient history of the nations which lived near Israel. Excavations have been made, old monuments have been discovered, ancient writings have been deciphered. In 1887, at Tel-el-Amarna, in Egypt, about 170 miles south of Cairo, a peasant woman discovered a collection of tablets on which were written the records of the reigns of two old Egyptian kings, including reports received by them from the Egyptian officials residing in Syria and Palestine. These tablets, which date back to about 1400 B.C., have taught us much of the kind of life lived in both Egypt and Canaan before the time of Moses. We also know much more about Babylon. In 1902 there was discovered at Susa, inscribed on three fragments of a large block of black stone, a code of law of Hammurabi, a king of Babylon who lived about 2000 B.C., or about a thousand years before King David. We have discovered other records which tell us more of this great ruler. He saved Babylon from her foes and built up the strength of his country by organizing its laws: on this old stone are preserved 248 separate laws!

But this is not all. The code of law of Hammurabi bears in places a very close resemblance to some of the Hebrew laws given in this Book of the Covenant. Either both Babylon and Israel inherited laws of this kind from a remote ancestor of both; or Abraham, when he first came to Canaan, brought with him from the East some knowledge of Hammurabi's Code; or, more probably, the Israelites learnt more of these laws after they had settled in Canaan from the Canaanites who knew a good deal of Babylonian civilization. At the same time we must note that much of the Book of the Covenant bears no resemblance to Babylonian law, and must be native to the Hebrews. Again, if about 2000 B.C. Hammurabi could

THE FIRST LITERATURE

have a code of law inscribed on a stone, could not Moses a few centuries later have had the Book of the Covenant inscribed on a stone? The truth is that we do not know the exact origin of these laws in the Covenant Book.

We give first some of the civil laws which bear a close resemblance to Babylonian law. We note how carefully they have been arranged.

LAWS ABOUT PERSONS

Slavery

If thou buy a Hebrew slave, six years he shall serve, and in the seventh he shall go out free for nothing.

If he came in by himself, he shall go out by himself: if he were married, then his wife shall go out with him.

If his master have given him a wife, and she have borne him sons or daughters; the wife and her children shall be her master's, and he shall go out by himself.

And if the servant shall plainly say, "I love my master, my wife, and my children; I will not go out free"; then his master shall bring him unto the judges; he shall also bring him unto the door, or unto the door post; and his master shall bore his ear through with an aul; and he shall serve him for ever.

Different laws are given for female slaves.

Capital Offences

He that smiteth a man, so that he die, shall be surely put to death.

And if a man lie not in wait, but God deliver him into his hand; then I will appoint thee a place whither he shall flee.

But if a man come presumptuously upon his neighbour, to slay him with guile; thou shalt take him from Mine altar, that he may die.

He that stealeth a man, and selleth him, or if he be found in his hand, he shall surely be put to death.

Bodily Injuries

And if men strive together, and one smite another with a stone, or with his fist, and he die not, but keepeth his bed: if he rise again, and walk abroad upon his staff, then shall he that smote him be quit: only he shall pay for the loss of his time, and shall cause him to be thoroughly healed.

If a man smite the eye of his servant, or the eye of his maid, that it perish, he shall let him go free for his eye's sake.

If an ox gore a man or a woman, that they die: then the ox shall be surely stoned, and his flesh shall be eaten; but the owner of the ox shall be quit.

But if the ox were wont to push with his horn in time past, and it hath been testified to his owner, and he hath not kept him in, but he hath killed a man or woman; the ox shall be stoned, and his owner also shall be put to death.

If there be laid on him a sum of money, then he shall give for the ransom of his life whatsoever is laid upon him.

[*From Exodus* xxi. 2–30

LAWS ABOUT PROPERTY

Accidents

If a man shall open a pit, or if a man shall dig a pit, and shall not cover it, and an ox or an ass fall therein; the owner of the pit shall make it good, and give money unto the owner of them; and the dead beast shall be his.

Theft

If a man shall steal an ox, or a sheep, and kill it, or sell it; he shall restore five oxen for an ox, and four sheep for a sheep.

Injury

If a man deliver unto his neighbour an ass, or an ox, or a sheep, or any beast, to keep; and it die, or be hurt, or driven away, no man seeing it: then shall an oath of the Lord be between them both, that he hath not put his hand upon his neighbour's goods; and the owner of it shall accept thereof, and he shall not make it good. If it be stolen from him, he shall make restitution to the owner thereof. If it be torn in pieces, let him bring it for witness, and he shall not make good that which was torn.

[*From Exodus* xxi. 33–xxii. 13

While such civil laws as those from which the above selection is made undoubtedly bear close kinship to the Code of Hammurabi, far different is it with the social and religious laws of the Book of the Covenant. Here we have the marks of the chosen people. There is little doubt that it is Moses to whom we owe the emphasis on the fundamental principles which underlie all the laws of Israel:—Jehovah alone is to be worshipped as Israel's one and only God; to Jehovah are due the people's first and best gifts; Jehovah's will for His people is social morality—the doing, that is, of what contributes to the welfare of the whole community.

SOCIAL LAWS

Justice to the Defenceless

Thou shalt neither vex a stranger, nor oppress him: for ye know the heart of a stranger, seeing ye were strangers in Egypt.

Ye shall not afflict any widow, or fatherless child. If thou afflict them in any wise, and they cry at all unto Me, I will surely hear their cry; and My wrath shall wax hot, and I will kill you with the sword; and your wives shall be widows and your children fatherless.

The Debtor

If thou lend money to any of My people that is poor by thee, thou shalt not be to him as an usurer, neither shalt thou lay upon him usury.

The Animals of an Enemy

If thou meet thine enemy's ox or his ass going astray, thou shalt surely bring it back to him again.

If thou see the ass of him that hateth thee lying under his burden and wouldest forbear to help him, thou shalt surely help with him.

Honest Justice

Thou shalt not raise a false report: put not thine hand with the wicked to be an unrighteous witness.

Thou shalt not wrest the judgment of thy poor in his cause.

And thou shalt take no gift: for the gift blindeth the wise, and perverteth the words of the righteous.

[*From Exodus* xxii. 21–xxiii. 8

RELIGIOUS LAWS AND THE CANAANITES

Moses died before the settlement in Canaan among the heathen Canaanites led to new conditions of life and to new difficulties. From being a nomadic people, wandering from place to place with their tents, with communal possessions rather than individual wealth, Israel became an agricultural people settled in villages and even in towns, with individual possessions, dwelling beside the heathen Canaanites, who were as religious in their own way as the Israelites, and in some respects more definitely civilized.

The Canaanites built elaborate altars to their gods, and worshipped idols; they paid, in particular, great respect to Baal, the god of fertility, who, as they believed, blessed the growth of their crops, and gave increase to their flocks and herds. They celebrated great agricultural feasts in connection with the harvests. Feasts like theirs the Israelites adopted, but in the worship of Jehovah—the feast of unleavened bread at the beginning of the grain harvest and the feast of weeks at the end of the grain harvest, two feasts in spring or early summer; also the feast of tabernacles at the end of the vintage and fruit harvest in the autumn, a great harvest thanksgiving festival.

In these early days of settlement in Canaan, long before Jerusalem became the centre of the religious life of the community, Israel worshipped in small local sanctuaries, called "high places", near their homes. These had before been the sacred places of the Canaanites, where they had worshipped their gods with foul rites and even with human sacrifice. Now they became the high places and sanctuaries of Israel, the places where Jehovah was worshipped.

How natural a development it all was! But we see the dangers. In assimilating the high places and the altars, and in caring much for agricultural prosperity and the fertility of their crops and herds, Israel was coming perilously near to the outlook of the heathen among whom they dwelt. The religious laws found beside the civil and social laws in the Book of the Covenant (Exod. xx. 23–xxiii. 19) would be much needed in these early days of the settlement in Canaan. Thus it is easy to understand why the existing laws would be likely to be codified in the early monarchy. But probably the laws themselves are considerably earlier.

Images and Altars
Ye shall not make with Me gods of silver, neither shall ye make unto you gods of gold.
An altar of earth shalt thou make unto Me, and shalt sacrifice thereon thy burnt offerings, and thy peace offerings, thy sheep and thine oxen.
If thou wilt make Me an altar of stone, thou shalt not build it of hewn stone.

Jehovah Alone
He that sacrificeth unto any god, save the Lord alone, he shall be utterly destroyed.

THE FIRST LITERATURE

Years and Days of Rest

Six years shalt thou sow thy land, and shalt gather in the fruits thereof: but the seventh year thou shalt let it rest and lie still; that the poor of thy people may eat: and what they leave the beasts of the field shall eat. In like manner thou shalt deal with thy vineyard, and with thy oliveyard.

Six days shalt thou do thy work, and on the seventh day thou shalt rest: that thine ox and thine ass may rest, and the son of thy handmaid, and the stranger, may be refreshed.

Firstfruits for Jehovah

Thou shalt not delay to offer the first of thy ripe fruits: the firstborn of thy sons shalt thou give unto Me. Likewise shalt thou do with thine oxen and with thy sheep: seven days shall it be with its dam; on the eighth day thou shalt give it Me.

Three Feasts

Three times shalt thou keep a feast unto Me in the year.

Thou shalt keep the feast of unleavened bread: (thou shalt eat unleavened bread seven days, as I commanded thee, in the time appointed of the month Abib; for in it thou camest out of Egypt: and none shall appear before Me empty:)

And the feast of harvest, the firstfruits of thy labours, which thou hast sown in the field:

And the feast of ingathering, which is in the end of the year, when thou hast gathered in thy labours out of the field.

Three times in the year all thy males shall appear before the Lord God.

[*From Exodus* xx. 23–xxiii. 17

THE TEN COMMANDMENTS

But the supreme brief expression of the religious and social laws of early Israel is that which is familiar to all of us, the Decalogue, or "Ten Words of Moses". One account of this is found, just before the Book of the Covenant, in Exodus xx. 2–17; another account is given in Deuteronomy v. 6–22. There are slight differences in these two accounts due to the fact that they are given by two different authors. The differences lie not in the meaning of the commandments themselves, but in the additional matter used to commend or expand them. The early Decalogue of which we have these two accounts must itself have been brief and emphatic; but later writers incorporating it in longer works, added such material as would be used by leaders of the people teaching the Ten Words to the common folk and the young people. Probably by the time of the early monarchy such additional teaching had itself become systematized. At any rate, the original commandments, scholars tell us, must have read something like this selection from the account in Exodus.

> Thou shalt have no other gods before Me.
> Thou shalt not make unto thee any graven image.
> Thou shalt not take the name of the Lord thy God in vain.
> Remember the sabbath day, to keep it holy.
> Honour thy father and thy mother.
> Thou shalt not kill.
> Thou shalt not commit adultery.
> Thou shalt not steal.
> Thou shalt not bear false witness against thy neighbour.
> Thou shalt not covet thy neighbour's house.
> [*From Exodus* xx. 2-17]

Perhaps in the earliest days, the positive commands were also prohibitions, such as "Thou shalt not profane the sabbath", "Thou shalt not injure thy father and mother".

We are pretty well agreed that these Ten Words were most likely given by Moses himself to the people. Similar brief ethical summaries have been found in old Egyptian and Babylonian documents. For instance, in an Egyptian "Book of the Dead", dating about 1500 B.C., a dead Egyptian is supposed to make to his god a list of denials that he has committed certain sins. This document is really a collection of magic formulae, as different in spirit from the religion of Israel as it well could be, but it contains this list:

> I have not killed.
> I have not committed adultery.
> . . . .
> I have not stolen.
> . . . .
> I have given bread to the hungry.
> I have given water to the thirsty.
> I have given clothes to the naked.

If Egypt could produce this kind of thing about 1500 B.C., those who deny that Moses could have compressed high religious and ethical teaching into the Ten Commandments are in a difficulty. On the other hand, the Words about graven images, the Sabbath, and the neighbour's *house*, as we now have them, come closer to the conditions of life after the settlement in Canaan than to the life of wanderers in the wilderness.

In spite of all argument, Moses stands out as the greatest law-giver of Israel, as the first great human personality through whom God revealed to men His will for the ordering of their lives.

ANOTHER ACCOUNT OF EARLY LAWS

In Exodus xxxiv. 10–28 is yet another record of early laws. But if this passage is read after studying both the Book of the Covenant and the Decalogue, it will all seem strangely familiar. The reason for this is that it is a different writer's account of these same laws. The author of Exodus as we now have it has incorporated two different earlier accounts of the same laws:—the full account from the E Document made by a writer much interested in God's education of His people, and this shorter account from the J Document made by a writer whose supreme genius it was to tell a story. See p. 178 for fuller information about these writers and their work.

II

DEUTERONOMY—A REMARKABLE LAW-BOOK

THE BEGINNINGS OF OLD TESTAMENT LITERATURE

IN Section I we have considered various aspects of the earliest literature found in the Old Testament:—primitive poetry such as the Song of Deborah, vivid written narrative such as the story of David and Absalom, messages of deep religious and moral value from such prophets as Amos and Isaiah, and a code of civil and religious law with the Ten Commandments as its highest ethical expression.

As we read this literature, we made for ourselves a rough outline of the history of the Hebrew people after they had settled in Palestine. We saw how at first they lived in scattered groups surrounded by heathen foes, and how from time to time they were delivered from deadly peril by great warrior leaders or "Judges", such as Deborah or Gideon. We found references in poetry and narrative to the first two Hebrew kings, Saul and David, while in the Court History of King David we noted the lack of good feeling between the men of Israel and the men of Judah. Even under King David the union of North and South under one monarch was more nominal than real; in the time of his grandson Rehoboam the division into two separate kingdoms became an accomplished fact.

From this time onward North and South had different kings and different histories. In studying the messages of the first prophets we saw how wicked ways, oppression of poor and defenceless persons, and disloyalty to Jehovah began to eat away the vitality of both kingdoms. In 722 B.C. Samaria, the capital of the North, was captured by the Assyrians and the Northern kingdom disappeared for ever. Jerusalem, for various reasons, but mainly because of the strong religious faith of

Isaiah and his Remnant of godly men, survived the attack of the Assyrians and entered on another century of independent existence.

DEUTERONOMY, THE BOOK OF THE SECOND LAW-CODE

With the life of this century the next piece of Old Testament literature is closely connected, although the roots of its being go farther back into the history of the people of Israel. This Book of Deuteronomy is akin to the work of the four prophets, Amos, Hosea, Isaiah, and Micah, being written very much in the style of their addresses and containing a message in many ways similar to their messages.

"Deuteronomy" is the Greek expression for "Second Law". We have seen how the first code of law (the Book of the Covenant) was probably formulated in the earlier years of the monarchy from laws already in existence. We now meet these questions:—How did this second code of law come into existence? Why is its style so much like that of the prophets, and why is its point of view so much like theirs?

Hezekiah was king of Judah when the Assyrians attacked Jerusalem. Later, moved by the memory of this great deliverance and influenced strongly by the faith of Isaiah, this king became a religious reformer and strove to lead his people back to whole-hearted loyalty to Jehovah. But a sad time of reaction followed under his successors, Manasseh and Amon. For about sixty years all that the prophets had urged suffered a serious eclipse: the reforming party was persecuted, even unto death. The gods of the Assyrians were worshipped along with Jehovah and much of the old Canaanite worship was revived in the high places throughout the land. Even the worship of the Temple was polluted, and in places human sacrifices were made. It seemed as if the South must follow the North into utter destruction for their lack of true religion and social righteousness.

But hope remained because Isaiah's Remnant remained. A little band of religious men fed their souls in secret on the written words of the prophets, keeping their loyalty to Jehovah and living devout lives. Being refused the expression of this loyalty in speech, they were driven to writing, and scholars tell us that what was written was most probably the main part of this Book of Deuteronomy, or Book of the Second Code of Law. Now undoubtedly, as with the first law-code, much of what is written as law in this book was already in existence in some form or other. Many of the laws fit in best with what we know of conditions of life earlier in the monarchy, not too long after the division of the kingdom, and in particular with what we know from Amos and Hosea of the circumstances of the Northern kingdom in the eighth century before Christ. At that time the people needed to purify the services at the local sanctuaries, to worship only Jehovah, to put Him first in every respect; they needed too to cleanse their personal lives, in particular avoiding oppression of the poor and injustice. It seems as if in Deuteronomy we have laws which came into existence to meet these needs.

But as these disciples of Isaiah in Jerusalem mused in secret on the special needs of their own time, they felt that one way to abolish for ever this corrupt worship and idolatry and horror of human sacrifice which polluted Judah, one way to reinstate Jehovah permanently in the first place in the life of their people, was to abolish entirely the old local sanctuaries, to tear down all the altars and high places, and to legislate that only in Jerusalem should be an altar to Jehovah, that only the Temple should be a sanctuary to the Jews.

As the minds of the Remnant became clearer, one of them, perhaps helped by others, *wrote* a new code of law, embodying laws already in existence which still fitted their own immediate situation, but introducing this new idea of making Jerusalem the one place where men should worship. They framed also new laws to cope with the difficulties involved in bringing all sacrifices to Jerusalem, and they expressed the best they knew as definite laws to safeguard the poor, the slaves and the administration of justice. They ascribed all to Moses for the reasons which we have indicated on p. 18. And with their whole hearts, in most moving and eloquent words, they urged on the people a fresh devotion to Jehovah: the force and beauty of their appeal was something entirely new in Hebrew writing. The style of the book is most impressive, akin to the style of the great prophets, the style of a "Preacher". The author of Deuteronomy was in truth a great preacher of the Reformation, although for a time his work lay hid. Later we shall see how it became public and what its effect was, both immediate and lasting.

1. INTRODUCTION AS FROM MOSES

And Moses called all Israel, and said unto them, "Hear, O Israel, the statutes and judgments which I speak in your ears this day, that ye may learn them, and keep, and do them.

"Now these are the commandments, the statutes, and the judgments, which the Lord your God commanded to teach you, that ye might do them in the land whither ye go to possess it:

"Hear, O Israel: The Lord our God is one Lord: and thou shalt love the Lord thy God with all thine heart, and with all thy soul, and with all thy might. And these words, which I command thee this day, shall be in thine heart: and thou shalt teach them diligently unto thy children, and shalt talk of them when thou sittest in thine house, and when thou walkest by the way, and when thou liest down, and when thou risest up. And thou shalt bind them for a sign upon thine hand, and they shall be as frontlets between thine eyes. And thou shalt write them upon the posts of thy house, and on thy gates.
[*Deuteronomy* v. 1, vi. 1, 4–9

"Beware that thou forget not the Lord thy God, in not keeping His commandments, and His judgments, and His statutes, which I command thee this day: lest when thou hast eaten and art full, and hast built goodly houses, and dwelt therein; and when thy herds and thy flocks multiply, and thy silver and thy gold is multiplied, and all that thou hast is multiplied; then thine heart be lifted up, and thou forget the Lord thy God, which brought thee forth out of the land of Egypt, from the house of bondage; who led thee through that great and terrible wilderness, wherein were fiery serpents, and scorpions, and drought, where there was no water; who brought thee forth water out of the rock of flint; who fed thee in the wilderness with manna, which thy fathers knew not, that He might humble thee, and that He might prove thee, to do thee good at thy latter end; and thou say in thine heart, 'My power and the might of mine hand hath gotten me this wealth.' But thou shalt remember the Lord thy

God: for it is He that giveth thee power to get wealth, that He may establish His covenant which He sware unto thy fathers, as it is this day.

"And it shall be, if thou do at all forget the Lord thy God, and walk after other gods, and serve them, and worship them, I testify against you this day that ye shall surely perish. As the nations which the Lord destroyeth before your face, so shall ye perish; because ye would not be obedient unto the voice of the Lord your God.

[*Deuteronomy* viii. 11–20

"And now, Israel, what doth the Lord thy God require of thee, but to fear the Lord thy God, to walk in all His ways, and to love Him, and to serve the Lord thy God with all thy heart and with all thy soul, to keep the commandments of the Lord, and His statutes, which I command thee this day for thy good? Behold, the heaven and the heaven of heavens is the Lord's thy God, the earth also, with all that therein is. Only the Lord had a delight in thy fathers to love them, and He chose their seed after them, even you above all people, as it is this day. The Lord your God is God of gods, and Lord of lords, a great God, a mighty, and a terrible, which regardeth not persons, nor taketh reward: He doth execute the judgment of the fatherless and widow, and loveth the stranger, in giving him food and raiment. Love ye therefore the stranger: for ye were strangers in the land of Egypt. Thou shalt fear the Lord thy God; Him shalt thou serve, and to Him shalt thou cleave, and swear by His name. He is thy praise, and He is thy God, that hath done for thee these great and terrible things, which thine eyes have seen. Thy fathers went down into Egypt with threescore and ten persons; and now the Lord thy God hath made thee as the stars of heaven for multitude."

[*Deuteronomy* x. 12–22

2. LAWS OF SOCIAL RIGHTEOUSNESS

The Poor

If there be among you a poor man of one of thy brethren within any of thy gates in thy land which the Lord thy God giveth thee, thou shalt not harden thine heart, nor shut thine hand from thy poor brother: but thou shalt open thine hand wide unto him, and shalt surely lend him sufficient for his need, in that which he wanteth.

[*Deuteronomy* xv. 7, 8

Release from Slavery

And if thy brother, an Hebrew man, or an Hebrew woman, be sold unto thee, and serve thee six years; then in the seventh year thou shalt let him go free from thee. And when thou sendest him out free from thee, thou shalt not let him go away empty: thou shalt furnish him liberally out of thy flock, and out of thy floor, and out of thy winepress: of that wherewith the Lord thy God hath blessed thee thou shalt give unto him. And thou shalt remember that thou wast a bondman in the land of Egypt, and the Lord thy God redeemed thee: therefore I command thee this thing to-day.

[Deuteronomy xv. 12–15]

Justice without Bribes or Respect of Persons

Judges and officers shalt thou make thee in all thy gates, which the Lord thy God giveth thee, throughout thy tribes: and they shall judge the people with just judgment. Thou shalt not wrest judgment; thou shalt not respect persons, neither take a gift: for a gift doth blind the eyes of the wise, and pervert the words of the righteous. That which is altogether just shalt thou follow, that thou mayest live, and inherit the land which the Lord thy God giveth thee.

[Deuteronomy xvi. 18–20]

Care for the Property of Others

Thou shalt not see thy brother's ox or his sheep go astray, and hide thyself from them: thou shalt in any case bring them again unto thy brother. And if thy brother be not nigh unto thee, or if thou know him not, then thou shalt bring it unto thine own house, and it shalt be with thee until thy brother seek after it, and thou shalt restore it to him again. In like manner shalt thou do with his ass; and so shalt thou do with his raiment; and with all lost thing of thy brother's, which he hath lost, and thou hast found, shalt thou do likewise: thou mayest not hide thyself. Thou shalt not see thy brother's ass or his ox fall down by the way, and hide thyself from them: thou shalt surely help him to lift them up again.

[Deuteronomy xxii. 1–4]

Regular Pay for Hired Servants

Thou shalt not oppress an hired servant that is poor and needy, whether he be of thy brethren, or of thy strangers that are in thy land within thy gates: at his day thou shalt give him his hire, neither shall the sun go down upon it; for he is poor, and setteth his heart upon it: lest he cry against thee unto the Lord, and it be sin unto thee.

[Deuteronomy xxiv. 14, 15]

Gleanings for the Needy

When thou cuttest down thine harvest in thy field, and hast forgot a sheaf in the field, thou shalt not go again to fetch it: it shall be for the stranger, for the fatherless, and for the widow: that the Lord thy God may bless thee in all the work of thine hands. When thou beatest thine olive tree, thou shalt not go over the boughs again: it shall be for the stranger, for the fatherless, and for the widow. When thou gatherest the grapes of thy vineyard, thou shalt not glean it afterward: it shall be for the stranger, for the fatherless, and for the widow. And thou shalt remember that thou wast a bondman in the land of Egypt: therefore I command thee to do this thing.

[Deuteronomy xxiv. 19–22]

3. LAWS CONCERNING RELIGION

Destruction of the High Places

These are the statutes and judgments, which ye shall observe to do in the land, which the Lord God of thy fathers giveth thee to possess it, all the days that ye live upon the earth. Ye shall utterly destroy all the places, wherein the nations which ye shall possess served their gods, upon the high mountains, and upon the hills, and under every green tree: and ye shall overthrow their altars, and break their pillars, and burn their groves with fire; and ye shall hew down the graven images of their gods, and destroy the names of them out of that place. Ye shall not do so unto the Lord your God. But unto the place which the Lord your God shall choose out of all your tribes to put His name there, even unto His habitation shall ye seek, and thither thou shalt come: and thither ye shall bring your burnt offerings, and your sacrifices, and your tithes, and heave offerings of your hand, and your vows, and your freewill offerings, and the firstlings of your herds and of your flocks: and there ye shall eat before the Lord your God, and ye shall rejoice in all that ye put your hand unto, ye and your households, wherein the Lord thy God hath blessed thee. [*Deuteronomy* xii. 1–7]

Following other Gods

If there arise among you a prophet, or a dreamer of dreams, and giveth thee a sign or a wonder, and the sign or the wonder come to pass, whereof he spake unto thee, saying, "Let us go after other gods, which thou hast not known, and let us serve them"; thou shalt not hearken unto the words of that prophet, or that dreamer of dreams: for the Lord your God proveth you, to know whether ye love the Lord your God with all your heart and with all your soul. Ye shall walk after the Lord your God, and fear Him, and keep His commandments, and obey His voice, and ye shall serve Him, and cleave unto Him. And that prophet, or that dreamer of dreams, shall be put to death; because he hath spoken to turn you away from the Lord your God, which brought you out of the land of Egypt, and redeemed you out of the house of bondage, to thrust thee out of the way which the Lord thy God commanded thee to walk in. So shalt thou put the evil away from the midst of thee. [*Deuteronomy* xiii. 1–5]

Abominations of other Nations

When thou art come into the land which the Lord thy God giveth thee, thou shalt not learn to do after the abominations of those nations. There shall not be found among you any one that maketh his son or his daughter to pass through the fire, or that useth divination, or an observer of times, or an enchanter, or a witch, or a charmer, or a consulter with familiar spirits, or a wizard, or a necromancer. For all that do these things are an abomination unto the Lord.

[*Deuteronomy* xviii. 9–12]

First and Best for Jehovah

All the firstling males that come of thy herd and of thy flock thou shalt sanctify unto the Lord thy God: thou shalt do no work with the firstling of thy bullock, nor shear the firstling of thy sheep. Thou shalt eat it before the Lord thy God year by year in the place which the Lord shall choose, thou and thy household. And if there be any blemish therein, as if it be lame, or blind, or have any ill blemish, thou shalt not sacrifice it into the Lord thy God.

[*Deuteronomy* xv. 19–21]

The following passage deals with the three great annual feasts of the Jews. They are interesting because they were the feasts observed by Jesus himself as a Jew, and are feasts which our modern Jewish friends keep unto this day. This is the passage which changed them from local feasts into feasts to be kept at Jerusalem.

The feast of tabernacles or booths, the great thanksgiving festival at the end of the vintage and fruit harvests in the fall of the year, presents no difficulties. Nor does the feast of weeks, kept seven weeks after the first grain was cut, a smaller harvest feast at the end of the grain harvest, which came earlier in the year. But the first feast, celebrating the cutting of the first grain, needs a word of explanation.

Why should the bread made from the new grain be unleavened? It is because the leaven represents the previous year, and the new harvest is to be partaken of in all the joy of a *new* harvest, untainted by any leaven from the old. Later, as we have it here, this feast was given added importance by being fused with the Passover Feast which celebrated the deliverance from Egypt.

The Passover Feast at the Beginning of Harvest

Observe the month of Abib, and keep the passover unto the Lord thy God: for in the month of Abib the Lord thy God brought thee forth out of Egypt by night. Thou shalt therefore sacrifice the passover unto the Lord thy God, of the flock and the herd, in the place which the Lord shall choose to place His name there. Thou shalt eat no leavened bread with it; seven days shalt thou eat unleavened bread therewith, even the bread of affliction; for thou camest forth out of the land of Egypt in haste: that thou mayest remember the day when thou camest forth out of the land of Egypt all the days of thy life. And there shall be no leavened bread seen with thee in all thy coast seven days; neither shall there any thing of the flesh, which thou sacrificedst the first day at even, remain all night until the morning. Thou mayest not sacrifice the passover within any of thy gates, which the Lord thy God giveth thee: but at the place which the Lord thy God shall choose to place His name in, there thou shalt sacrifice the passover at even, at the going down of the sun, at the season that thou camest forth out of Egypt. And thou shalt roast and eat it in the place which the Lord thy God shall choose: and thou shalt turn in the morning, and go unto thy tents. Six days thou shalt eat unleavened bread: and on the seventh day shall be a solemn assembly to the Lord thy God: thou shalt do no work therein.

[*Deuteronomy* xvi. 1–8

The Feast of Weeks at the Close of Grain Harvest

Seven weeks shalt thou number unto thee: begin to number the seven weeks from such time as thou beginnest to put the sickle to the corn. And thou shalt keep the feast of weeks unto the Lord thy God with a tribute of a freewill offering of thine hand, which thou shalt give unto the Lord thy God, according as the Lord thy God hath blessed thee: and thou shalt rejoice before the Lord thy God, thou, and thy son, and thy daughter, and thy manservant, and thy maidservant, and the Levite that is within thy gates, and the stranger, and the fatherless, and the widow, that are among you, in the place which the Lord thy God hath chosen to place His name there. And thou shalt remember that thou wast a bondman in Egypt: and thou shalt observe and do these statutes. [*Deuteronomy* xvi. 9–12

The Feast of Tabernacles as a Harvest Thanksgiving

Thou shalt observe the feast of tabernacles seven days, after that thou hast gathered in thy corn and thy wine: and thou shalt rejoice in thy feast, thou, and thy son, and thy daughter, and thy manservant, and thy maidservant, and the Levite, the stranger, and the fatherless, and the widow, that are within thy gates. Seven days shalt thou keep a solemn feast unto the Lord thy God in the place which the Lord shall choose: because the Lord thy God shall bless thee in all thine increase, and in all the works of thine hands, therefore thou shalt surely rejoice. [*Deuteronomy* xvi. 13–15

Feasts in Jerusalem

Three times in a year shall all thy males appear before the Lord thy God in the place which He shall choose; in the feast of unleavened bread, and in the feast of weeks, and in the feast of tabernacles: and they shall not appear before the Lord empty: every man shall give as he is able, according to the blessing of the Lord thy God which He hath given thee. [*Deuteronomy* xvi. 16, 17

DEUTERONOMY

4. CONCLUSION AS FROM MOSES

The statement of the Law is concluded by an eloquent appeal put into the mouth of Moses, in which with the utmost moral zeal are set forth the consequences of obedience and of disobedience to the new laws. The belief that good fortune always accompanies good conduct, bad fortune bad conduct, is typical of Deuteronomy.

Rewards

And it shall come to pass, if thou shalt hearken diligently unto the voice of the Lord thy God, to observe and to do all His commandments which I command thee this day, that the Lord thy God will set thee on high above all nations of the earth: and all these blessings shall come on thee, and overtake thee, if thou shalt hearken unto the voice of the Lord thy God. Blessed shalt thou be in the city, and blessed shalt thou be in the field. Blessed shall be the fruit of thy body, and the fruit of thy ground, and the fruit of thy cattle, the increase of thy kine, and the flocks of thy sheep. Blessed shall be thy basket and thy store. Blessed shalt thou be when thou comest in, and blessed shalt thou be when thou goest out. The Lord shall cause thine enemies that rise up against thee to be smitten before thy face: they shall come out against thee one way, and flee before thee seven ways. The Lord shall command the blessing upon thee in thy storehouses, and in all that thou settest thine hand unto; and He shall bless thee in the land which the Lord thy God giveth thee. The Lord shall establish thee an holy people unto Himself, as He hath sworn unto thee, if thou shalt keep the commandments of the Lord thy God and walk in His ways.

[*Deuteronomy* xxviii. 1–9]

Punishments

But it shall come to pass, if thou wilt not hearken unto the voice of the Lord thy God, to observe to do all His commandments and His statutes which I command thee this day; that all these curses shall come upon thee, and overtake thee: cursed shalt thou be in the city, and cursed shalt thou be in the field. Cursed shall be thy basket and thy store. Cursed shall be the fruit of thy body, and the fruit of thy land, the increase of thy kine, and the flocks of thy sheep. Cursed shalt thou be when thou comest in, and cursed shalt thou be when thou goest out. The Lord shall send upon thee cursing, vexation, and rebuke, in all that thou settest thine hand unto for to do, until thou be destroyed, and until thou perish quickly; because of the wickedness of thy doings, whereby thou hast forsaken Me. The Lord shall make the pestilence cleave unto thee, until He have consumed thee from off the land, whither thou goest to possess it. The Lord shall smite thee with a consumption, and with a fever, and with an inflammation, and with an extreme burning, and with the sword, and with blasting, and with mildew; and they shall pursue thee until thou perish. And thy heaven that is over thy head shall be brass, and the earth that is under thee shall be iron. The Lord shall make the rain of thy land powder and dust: from heaven shall it come down upon thee, until thou be destroyed. The Lord shall cause thee to be smitten before thine enemies: thou shalt go out one way against them, and flee seven ways before them; and shalt be removed into all the kingdoms of the earth.

[*Deuteronomy* xxviii. 15-25]

LATER EDITIONS OF DEUTERONOMY

Scholars tell us that in later centuries editors gathered together for the building up of the religious life of the Jews other material which we find at the beginning and end of the Book of Deuteronomy printed in our Bibles. Evidently at some period two editions of the original law-code were in existence furnished with different introductions: for besides the introduction in chapters v to xi, from which we made a selection, there is another separate introduction in chapters i to iv. 40. Amongst the material following the law-code, in chapter xxxiii, we find the old poem, "The Blessing of Moses", to which reference was made on p. 17.

III

JEREMIAH—A PERSECUTED PROPHET OF JUDAH

REVISION

IN connection with the prophet Isaiah, we noted the great religious reformation to which his teaching led in the reign of King Hezekiah, and the deepening knowledge of Jehovah which grew in the Remnant of Judah. Manasseh, the succeeding king, quickly undid the good work of Hezekiah, persecuting the prophetic party even unto death. Those who held fast to the religious ideas emphasized by Isaiah—one God Jehovah and Israel His people: the iniquity of idol worship and the futility of all heathen gods: Jehovah a righteous God demanding righteousness from His people; Jehovah a living wise God playing a vital part in the history of the world—the men who held such views were compelled to quietness and secrecy during the reigns of Manasseh and his son Amon. But in the quiet darkness some man or men among them began to formulate in writing a set of definite laws which would express these new ideas about Jehovah. They saw that, to reach the masses, these abstract lofty conceptions must be embodied in definite concrete commandments. So, guided by His Spirit, they composed this code of law, giving their new laws in addition to many of the older laws.

But for a time no one knew of the existence of this book. Even now it has taken scholars much study and research to understand what is not so much explicitly contained in the Bible narrative as to be gathered from it.

THE PUBLICATION OF DEUTERONOMY

At last the darkest days passed. The young King Josiah came to the throne full of good will towards Jehovah and the prophetic party. The most important event of his reign was the publication of the hidden law-book. Now, felt religious men, was the time to bring before the king and the people the new book of the law. So in 2 Kings xxii and xxiii (see p. 143) we may read of its "discovery" in the temple, of its delivery to King Josiah, and of its immediate practical effect in a religious reformation of the national life. The book which was discovered was most probably the main part of what in the Old Testament is called Deuteronomy.

JEREMIAH AND THE DESTRUCTION OF JERUSALEM

As we read the story of the prophet Jeremiah, we shall catch a glimpse of the life of Judah during the closing years of the kingdom: we shall discern something of the tragedy of its moral and political collapse. In the book called "Jeremiah" we have both the messages of the prophet given to the Jewish nation through a series of diverse situations, and a narrative account of these situations as they affected the life of the prophet. The narrative tells us, as we shall read on p. 76, that Jeremiah at one period of his work dictated to his secretary Baruch an account of his prophetic messages as he remembered them; also how, when this first account had been destroyed by an angry king, a second one of greater length was dictated to Baruch. Thus we have the prophetic message in the prophet's own words. As for the narrative account of Jeremiah's life, most probably we owe that to Baruch. In the selections which follow, prophetic and narrative passages are intermingled as the one sheds light on the other. Meantime let us look for a moment at the position of Judah in the closing years of the Kingdom, as it is indicated to us in the Book of Jeremiah.

Seventy years after Isaiah's victory over the Assyrians, in the middle of the reign of King Josiah, about 625 B.C., Jeremiah was called to the work of a prophet. He appears to have been descended from a family of priests who lived in Anathoth, a small village near Jerusalem. Jeremiah began his work in days of peace, for in Josiah's reign the prophetic party had gained the upper hand. Peace, however, was but brief, for at the close of the seventh century B.C. Josiah, meeting the Egyptians in battle, was defeated and killed.

The people again veered round. Josiah had had a tragic end. Surely he had made some terrible mistake in his religious reforms: bad fortune, they were certain, went with bad conduct. So his son Jehoiakim ruled, not as his father, but as Manasseh and Amon, the earlier persecutors of the prophets. Wickedness flourished; worship again became corrupt. Jeremiah, declaring God's message, was threatened with imprisonment, but succeeded in lying hid for a time. For a Jerusalem so wicked the prophet could see no future but utter destruction.

Nineveh, the great Assyrian capital in the East, had fallen before the conquering hordes of the Medes and Chaldeans, or Babylonians: thus Babylon became the new centre of Eastern power. Judah did not long escape attention. In 597 B.C. Jehoiakim's son, the youthful King Jehoiachin (or "Coniah"), together with the most able and intelligent dart of the nation, was deported to Babylon by Nebuchadrezzar (sometimes spelt Nebuchadnezzar); the people appear to have been settled in colonies near Babylon. Nebuchadrezzar put Zedekiah over Judah as king, subject to his own supreme power.

But after a few years Zedekiah became involved in a futile rebellion against Babylon, with the result that in 586 B.C., after a long siege, Jerusalem was captured. Both temple and city were utterly destroyed and the great bulk of the people carried off to captivity in the East. Through all this period Jeremiah lived and suffered. At first Zedekiah had favoured Jeremiah's advice, but when, after the first few years of the reign, the prophet was again compelled to preach unpopular and unpalatable words, he was beaten and imprisoned, spending, before the final destruction of Jerusalem, weeks and months of unspeakable misery.

Not even then was the end for Jeremiah. The Babylonians left him undisturbed among friends in Judah, but he became involved in a minor rebellion. The people, afraid of Nebuchadrezzar's wrath, hurried to Egypt, carrying off with them by force the aged prophet. There, in a foreign country, steadfastly to the end preaching the truth as God gave to him, died in utter loneliness the saddest of all the Hebrew prophets.

We may summarize this section in a table of dates:—

Kings of Judah.	Main Events.	The Ministry of Jeremiah.
Josiah: 638–608	Law-Book published: 621 Fall of Nineveh: 612	Ministry begun: about 625
Jehoahaz: 608		
Jehoiakim: 608–597		Preaches repentance, threatens destruction, persecuted Dictates to Baruch: c. 603
Jehoiachin: 597	First exiles go to Babylon: 597	
Zedekiah: 597–586	Siege begun: 588 Jerusalem destroyed, second captivity: 586	Sends letter to exiles Beaten and imprisoned as traitor Remains in Judah: 586
		Died in Egypt some time after 586

THE RELIGION OF JEREMIAH

We see then that Jeremiah's whole life was linked with the coming of the Exile and with its results. Thus we find in his work an expression of a new and deeper acceptance of Jehovah and of intimacy with Him, standing out against a background of weakness, misery and wickedness. Since by his suffering and loneliness this prophet was for fellowship driven in upon God, it is not surprising to find that his greatest contribution to the development of religion is the stress he lays on the need for an inward spiritual relationship between the individual soul and God. That in men's hearts God will write His law, is the hope of Jeremiah in the midst of apparent chaos.

The Prophet and his Times

The words of Jeremiah the son of Hilkiah, of the priests that were in Anathoth in the land of Benjamin: to whom the word of the Lord came in the days of Josiah the son of Amon king of Judah, in the thirteenth year of his reign. It came also in the days of Jehoiakim the son of Josiah king of Judah, unto the end of the eleventh year of Zedekiah the son of Josiah king of Judah, unto the carrying away of Jerusalem captive in the fifth month.

[*Jeremiah* i. 1-3

Jeremiah's Call and Commission

Then the word of the Lord came unto me, saying, "Before I formed thee in the belly I knew thee; and before thou camest forth out of the womb I sanctified thee, and I ordained thee a prophet unto the nations." Then said I, "Ah, Lord God! behold, I cannot speak: for I am a child." But the Lord said unto me, "Say not, 'I am a child': for thou shalt go to all that I shall send thee, and whatsoever I command thee thou shalt speak. Be not afraid of their faces: for I am with thee to deliver thee," saith the Lord. Then the Lord put forth his hand, and touched my mouth. And the Lord said unto me, "Behold, I have put my words in thy mouth. See, I have this day set thee over the nations and over the kingdoms, to root out, and to pull down, and to destroy, and to throw down, to build, and to plant."

And the word of the Lord came unto me, saying, "What seest thou?" And I said, "I see a seething pot; and the face thereof is toward the north." Then the Lord said unto me, "Out of the north an evil shall break forth upon all the inhabitants of the land. For, lo, I will call all the families of the kingdoms of the north; and they shall come, and they shall set every one his throne at the entering of the gates of Jerusalem, and against all the walls thereof round about, and against all the cities of Judah. And I will utter My judgments against them touching all their wickedness, who have forsaken Me and have burned incense unto other gods, and worshipped the works of their own hands. Thou therefore gird up thy loins, and arise, and speak unto them all that I command thee: be not dismayed at their faces, lest I confound thee before them. For, behold, I have made thee this day a defenced city, and an iron pillar, and brasen walls against the whole land, against the kings of Judah, against the princes thereof, against the priests thereof, and against the people of the land. And they shall fight against thee; but they shall not prevail against thee; for I am with thee," saith the Lord, "to deliver thee."

[*Jeremiah* i. 4-10, 13-19

Jeremiah's Grief over the Wickedness of Jerusalem

O Jerusalem, wash thine heart from wickedness, that thou mayest be saved. How long shall thy vain thoughts lodge within thee? For a voice declareth from Dan, and publisheth affliction from mount Ephraim. Make ye mention to the nations; behold, publish against Jerusalem, that watchers come from a far country, and give out their voice against the cities of Judah. As keepers of a field, are they against her round about; because she hath been rebellious against Me, saith the Lord. Thy way and thy doings have procured these things unto thee; this is thy wickedness, because it is bitter, because it reacheth unto thine heart.

I am pained at my very heart; my heart maketh a noise in me; I cannot hold my peace, because thou hast heard, O my soul, the sound of the trumpet, the alarm of war. Destruction upon destruction is cried; for the whole land is spoiled: suddenly are my tents spoiled, and my curtains in a moment. How long shall I see the standard, and hear the sound of the trumpet? For my people is foolish, they have not known me; they are sottish children, and they have none understanding: they are wise to do evil, but to do good they have no knowledge.

[*Jeremiah* iv. 14–22

A Vision of the Wrath of God

> I beheld the earth, and, lo, it was without form, and void,
> And the heavens, and they had no light.
> I beheld the mountains, and, lo, they trembled,
> And all the hills moved lightly.
> I beheld, and, lo, there was no man,
> And all the birds of the heavens were fled.
> I beheld, and, lo, the fruitful place was a wilderness,
> And all the cities thereof were broken down at the presence of the Lord, by His fierce anger.

[*Jeremiah* iv. 23–36

Jeremiah's Sermon at the Temple Gate

The word that came to Jeremiah from the Lord, saying, "Stand in the gate of the Lord's house, and proclaim there this word, and say, 'Hear the word of the Lord, all ye of Judah, that enter in at these gates to worship the Lord. Thus saith the Lord of hosts, the God of Israel, Amend your ways and your doings, and I will cause you to dwell in this place. Trust ye not in lying words, saying, "The temple of the Lord, the temple of the Lord, the temple of the Lord, are these." Behold, ye trust in lying words, that cannot profit. Will ye steal, murder, and commit adultery, and swear falsely, and burn incense unto Baal, and walk after other gods whom ye know not; and come and stand before Me in this house, which is called by My name, and say, "We are delivered to do all these abominations?" Is this house, which is called by My name, become a den of robbers in your eyes? Behold, even I have seen it, saith the Lord.

"'But go ye now unto My place which was in Shiloh, where I set My name at the first, and see what I did to it for the wickedness of My people Israel. And now, because ye have done all these works, saith the Lord, and I spake unto you, rising up early and speaking, but ye heard not; and I called you, but ye answered not; therefore will I do unto this house, which is called by My name, wherein ye trust, and unto the place which I gave you and to your fathers, as I have done to Shiloh. And I will cast you out of My sight, as I have cast out all your brethren, even the whole seed of Ephraim.'"

[*From Jeremiah* vii. 1-15

The Prophet's Sorrow for the People

When I would comfort myself against sorrow, my heart is faint in me. Behold the voice of the cry of the daughter of my people because of them that dwell in a far country: "Is not the Lord in Zion? is not her king in her?" Why have they provoked me to anger with their graven images, and with strange vanities? The harvest is past, the summer is ended, and we are not saved. For the hurt of the daughter of my people am I hurt; I am black; astonishment hath taken hold on me. Is there no balm in Gilead; is there no physician there? Why then is not the health of the daughter of my people recovered? Oh that my head were waters, and mine eyes a fountain of tears, that I might weep day and night for the slain of the daughter of my people!

[*Jeremiah* viii. 18-22, ix. 1

The above passages give the prophet's account of his work in his own words as he dictated it to his secretary Baruch. Below, for the sake of comparison, is the narrative account of the same event, composed by Baruch or some other disciple of Jeremiah.

Jeremiah threatened with Death for his Temple Sermon

In the beginning of the reign of Jehoiakim the son of Josiah king of Judah came this word from the Lord, saying, "Thus saith the Lord; Stand in the court of the Lord's house, and speak unto all the cities of Judah, which come to worship in the Lord's house, all the words that I command thee to speak unto them; diminish not a word." So the priests and the prophets and all the people heard Jeremiah speaking these words in the house of the Lord.

Now it came to pass, when Jeremiah had made an end of speaking all that the Lord had commanded him to speak unto all the people, that the priests and the prophets and all the people took him, saying, "Thou shalt surely die. Why hast thou prophesied in the name of the Lord, saying, 'This house shall be like Shiloh, and this city shall be desolate without an inhabitant'?" And all the people were gathered against Jeremiah in the house of the Lord. When the princes of Judah heard these things, then they came up from the king's house unto the house of the Lord, and sat down in the entry of the new gate of the Lord's house. Then spake the priests and the prophets unto the princes and to all the people, saying, "This man is worthy to die; for he hath prophesied against this city, as ye have heard with your ears."

Then spake Jeremiah unto all the princes and to all the people, saying, "The Lord sent me to prophesy against this house and against this city all the words that ye have heard. Therefore now amend your ways and your doings, and obey the voice of the Lord your God; and the Lord will repent Him of the evil that He hath pronounced against you. As for me, behold, I am in your hand: do with me as seemeth good and meet unto you. But know ye for certain, that if ye put me to death, ye shall surely bring innocent blood upon yourselves, and upon this city, and upon the inhabitants thereof: for of a truth the Lord hath sent me unto you to speak all these words in your ears." Then said the princes and all the people unto the priests and to the prophets; "This man is not worthy to die: for he hath spoken to us in the name of the Lord our God."

Then rose up certain of the elders of the land, and spake to all the assembly of the people, saying, "Micah the Morasthite prophesied in the days of Hezekiah king of Judah, and spake to all the people of Judah, saying, 'Thus saith the Lord of hosts; Zion shall be plowed like a field, and Jerusalem shall become heaps, and the mountain of the house as the high places of a forest.' Did Hezekiah king of Judah and all Judah put him at all to death? Did he not fear the Lord, and besought the Lord, and the Lord repented Him of the evil which He had pronounced against them? Thus might we procure great evil against our souls."

[*Jeremiah* xxvi. 1–19

Another Sermon and its Sequel

Thus saith the Lord, "Go and get a potter's earthen bottle, and take of the ancients of the people, and of the ancients of the priests; and go forth unto the valley of the son of Hinnom, which is by the entry of the east gate, and proclaim there the words that I shall tell thee. Then shalt thou break the bottle in the sight of the men that go with thee, and shalt say unto them, 'Thus saith the Lord of hosts; Even so will I break this people and this city, as one breaketh a potter's vessel, that cannot be made whole again: and they shall bury them in Tophet, till there be no place to bury. Thus will I do unto this place, saith the Lord, and to the inhabitants thereof, and even make this city as Tophet: and the houses of Jerusalem, and the houses of the kings of Judah, shall be defiled as the place of Tophet, because of all the houses upon whose roofs they have burned incense unto all the host of heaven, and have poured out drink offerings unto other gods.'"

Then came Jeremiah from Tophet, whither the Lord had sent him to prophesy; and he stood in the court of the Lord's house; and said to all the people, "Thus saith the Lord of hosts, the God of Israel; Behold, I will bring upon this city and upon all her towns all the evil that I have pronounced against it, because they have hardened their necks, that they might not hear My words."

Now Pashur the son of Immer the priest, who was also chief governor in the house of the Lord, heard that Jeremiah prophesied these things. Then Pashur smote Jeremiah the prophet, and put him in the stocks that were in the high gate of Benjamin which was by the house of the Lord. And it came to pass on the morrow, that Pashur brought forth Jeremiah out of the stocks.

[*Jeremiah* xix. 1, 2, 10–15, xx. 1–3

Jeremiah's Intense Suffering

Then said Jeremiah; "O Lord, Thou hast deceived me, and I was deceived: Thou art stronger than I, and hast prevailed: I am in derision daily, every one mocketh me. For since I spake, I cried out, I cried violence and spoil; because the word of the Lord was made a reproach unto me, and a derision, daily. Then I said, 'I will not make mention of Him, nor speak any more in His name.' But His word was in mine heart as a burning fire shut up in my bones, and I was weary with forbearing, and I could not stay. For I heard the defaming of many, fear on every side. All my familiars watched for my halting, saying, 'Peradventure he will be enticed, and we shall prevail against him, and we shall take our revenge on him.' But the Lord is with me as a mighty terrible one: therefore my persecutors shall stumble, and they shall not prevail: they shall be greatly ashamed; for they shall not prosper: their everlasting confusion shall never be forgotten.

"Cursed be the day wherein I was born: let not the day wherein my mother bare me be blessed. Cursed be the man who brought tidings to my father, saying, 'A man child is born unto thee': making him very glad. Wherefore came I forth out of the womb to see labour and sorrow, that my days should be consumed with shame?"

[*From Jeremiah* xx. 7–18

Writing of Jeremiah's Messages

And it came to pass in the fourth year of Jehoiakim the son of Josiah king of Judah, that this word came unto Jeremiah from the Lord, saying, "Take thee a roll of a book, and write therein all the words that I have spoken unto thee against Israel, and against Judah, and against all the nations, from the day I spake unto thee, from the days of Josiah, even unto this day. It may be that the house of Judah will hear all the evil which I purpose to do unto them; that they may return every man from his evil way; that I may forgive their iniquity and their sin." Then Jeremiah called Baruch the son of Neriah: and Baruch wrote from the mouth of Jeremiah all the words of the Lord, which he had spoken unto him, upon a roll of a book.

And Jeremiah commanded Baruch, saying, "I am shut up; I cannot go into the house of the Lord: therefore go thou, and read in the roll, which thou hast written from my mouth, the words of the Lord in the ears of the people in the Lord's house upon the fasting day: and also thou shalt read them in the ears of all Judah that come out of their cities. It may be they will present their supplication before the Lord, and will return every one from his evil way: for great is the anger and the fury that the Lord hath pronounced against this people." And Baruch the son of Neriah did according to all that Jeremiah the prophet commanded him, reading in the book the words of the Lord in the Lord's house.

And it came to pass in the fifth year of Jehoiakim the son of Josiah king of Judah, in the ninth month, that they proclaimed a fast before the Lord to all the people in Jerusalem, and to all the people that came from the cities of Judah unto Jerusalem. Then read Baruch in the book the words of Jeremiah in the house of the Lord, in the chamber of Gemariah at the entry of the new gate of the Lord's house, in the ears of all the people.

When Michaiah the son of Gemariah had heard out of the book all the words of the Lord, then he went down into the king's house, into the scribe's chamber: and, lo, all the princes sat there. Then Michaiah declared unto them all the words that he had heard, when Baruch read the book in the ears of the people. Therefore all the princes sent unto Baruch, saying, "Take in thine hand the roll wherein thou hast read in the ears of the people, and come." So Baruch the son of Neriah took the roll in his hand, and came unto them. And they said unto him, "Sit down now, and read it in our ears." So Baruch read it in their ears. Now it came to pass, when they had heard all the words, they were afraid both one and other, and said unto Baruch, "We will surely tell the king of all these words." And they asked Baruch, saying, "Tell us now, How didst thou write all these words at his mouth?" Then Baruch answered them, "He pronounced all these words unto me with his mouth, and I wrote them with ink in the book." Then said the princes unto Baruch, "Go, hide thee, thou and Jeremiah; and let no man know where ye be."

And they went in to the king into the court, but they laid up the roll in the chamber of Elishama the scribe, and told all the words in the ears of the king. So the king sent Jehudi to fetch the roll: and he took it out of Elishama the scribe's chamber. And Jehudi read it in the ears of the king, and in the ears of all the princes which stood beside the king. Now the king sat in the winterhouse in the ninth month: and there was a fire on the hearth burning before him. And it came to pass, that when Jehudi had read three or four leaves, he cut it with the penknife, and cast it into the fire that was on the hearth, until all the roll was consumed in the fire that was on the hearth. Yet they were not afraid, nor rent their garments, neither the king, nor any of his servants that heard all these words. Nevertheless Elnathan and Delaiah and Gemariah had made intercession to the king that he would not burn the roll: but he would not hear them. But the king commanded Shelemiah to take Baruch the scribe and Jeremiah the prophet: but the Lord hid them.

Then the word of the Lord came to Jeremiah, after that the king had burned the roll, and the words which Baruch wrote at the mouth of Jeremiah, saying, "Take thee again another roll, and write in it all the former words that were in the first roll, which Jehoiakim the king of Judah hath burned." Then took Jeremiah another roll, and gave it to Baruch the scribe, the son of Neriah; who wrote therein from the mouth of Jeremiah all the words of the book which Jehoiakim king of Judah had burned in the fire: and there were added besides unto them many like words.

[*From Jeremiah* xxxvi. 1–32]

Before the time to which the next passage refers, what the prophet had foretold had come to pass. Nebuchadrezzar had come, and had taken to exile in Babylon King Jehoiakin (Coniah) and the best of the nation. But Jerusalem was given yet another chance. Note that "seventy" is a round number with the Jews, so that "seventy years" means "in about two or three generations".

Jeremiah's Letter to the Exiles

Now these are the words of the letter that Jeremiah the prophet sent from Jerusalem unto the residue of the elders which were carried away captives, and to the priests, and to the prophets, and to all the people whom Nebuchadrezzar had carried away captive from Jerusalem to Babylon; by the hand of Elasah and Gemariah (whom Zedekiah king of Judah sent unto Babylon to Nebuchadrezzar king of Babylon) saying, "Thus saith the Lord of hosts, the God of Israel, unto all that are carried away captives, whom I have caused to be carried away from Jerusalem unto Babylon; build ye houses, and dwell in them; and plant gardens, and eat the fruit of them; take ye wives, and beget sons and daughters; and take wives for your sons, and give your daughters to husbands, that they may bear sons and daughters; that ye may be increased there, and not diminished. And seek the peace of the city whither I have caused you to be carried away captives, and pray unto the Lord for it: for in the peace thereof shall ye have peace. For thus saith the Lord, After seventy years be accomplished at Babylon I will visit you, and perform My good word toward you, in causing you to return to this place. For I know the thoughts that I think toward you, saith the Lord, thoughts of peace, and not of evil, to give you an expected end. Then shall ye call upon Me, and ye shall go and pray unto Me, and I will hearken unto you. And ye shall seek Me, and find Me, when ye shall search for Me with all your heart. And I will be found of you."

[*From Jeremiah* xxix. 1–14]

Siege of Jerusalem begun

The word which came unto Jeremiah from the Lord, when King Zedekiah sent unto him Pashur the son of Melchiah, and Zephaniah the son of Maaseiah the priest, saying, "Enquire, I pray thee, of the Lord for us; for Nebuchadrezzar king of Babylon maketh war against us; if so be that the Lord will deal with us according to all His wondrous works that He may go up from us."

Then said Jeremiah unto them, "Thus shall ye say to Zedekiah: 'Thus saith the Lord God of Israel; Behold, I will turn back the weapons of war that are in your hands, wherewith ye fight against the king of Babylon, and against the Chaldeans, which besiege you without the walls, and I will assemble them into the midst of this city. And I myself will fight against you with an outstretched hand and with a strong arm, even in anger, and in fury, and in great wrath. And I will smite the inhabitants of this city, both man and beast: they shall die of a great pestilence. And afterward, saith the Lord, I will deliver Zedekiah king of Judah, and his servants, and the people, and such as are left in this city from the pestilence, from the sword, and from the famine, into the hand of Nebuchadrezzar king of Babylon, and into the hand of their enemies, and into the hand of those that seek their life: and he shall smite them with the edge of the sword; he shall not spare them, neither have pity, nor have mercy.'" And Zedekiah the king sent to the prophet Jeremiah, saying, "Pray now unto the Lord our God for us."

Pharaoh's army was come forth out of Egypt: and when the Chaldeans that besieged Jerusalem heard tidings of them, they departed from Jerusalem.

Then came the word of the Lord unto the prophet Jeremiah, saying, "Thus saith the Lord, the God of Israel; Thus shall ye say to the king of Judah, that sent you unto me to enquire of me; 'Behold, Pharaoh's army, which is come forth to help you, shall return to Egypt into their own land. And the Chaldeans shall come again, and fight against this city, and take it, and burn it with fire. Thus saith the Lord; Deceive not yourselves, saying, "The Chaldeans shall surely depart from us:" for they shall not depart. For though ye had smitten the whole army of the Chaldeans that fight against you, and there remained but wounded men among them, yet should they rise up every man in his tent, and burn this city with fire.'"

[*From Jeremiah* xxi. 1–7, xxxvii. 3–10]

JEREMIAH

Jeremiah beaten and imprisoned as a Traitor

And it came to pass, that when the army of the Chaldeans was broken up from Jerusalem for fear of Pharaoh's army, then Jeremiah went forth out of Jerusalem to go into the land of Benjamin, to separate himself thence in the midst of the people. And when he was in the gate of Benjamin, a captain of the ward was there, whose name was Irijah, and he took Jeremiah the prophet, saying, "Thou fallest away to the Chaldeans." Then said Jeremiah, "It is false; I fall not away to the Chaldeans." But he hearkened not to him: so Irijah took Jeremiah, and brought him to the princes. Wherefore the princes were wroth with Jeremiah, and smote him, and put him in prison in the house of Jonathan the scribe: for they had made that the prison.

When Jeremiah was entered into the dungeon, and into the cabins, and Jeremiah had remained there many days; then Zedekiah the king sent, and took him out: and the king asked him secretly in his house, and said, "Is there any word from the Lord?" And Jeremiah said, "There is: for," said he, "thou shalt be delivered into the hand of the king of Babylon." Moreover Jeremiah said unto King Zedekiah, "What have I offended against thee, or against thy servants, or against this people, that ye have put me in prison? Where are now your prophets which prophesied unto you, saying, 'The king of Babylon shall not come against you, nor against this land?' Therefore hear now, I pray thee, O my lord the king: let my supplication, I pray thee, be accepted before thee; that thou cause me not to return to the house of Jonathan the scribe, lest I die there." Then Zedekiah the king commanded that they should commit Jeremia hinto the court of the prison, and that they should give him daily a piece of bread out of the bakers' street, until all the bread in the city were spent. Thus Jeremiah remained in the court of the prison.

[*Jeremiah* xxxvii. 11–21

Jerusalem taken

So Jeremiah abode in the court of the prison until the day that Jerusalem was taken: and he was there when Jerusalem was taken. And all the princes of the king of Babylon came in, and sat in the middle gate, even Nergal-sharezer, Samgar-nebo, Sarsechim, Rab-saris, Nergal-sharezer, Rab-mag, with all the residue of the princes of the king of Babylon. They sent, and took Jeremiah out of the court of the prison, and committed him unto Gedaliah the son of Ahikam the son of Shaphan, that he should carry him home: so he dwelt among the people.

[*Jeremiah* xxxviii. 28, xxxix. 3, 14

When the destruction of Jerusalem had become an inescapable fact, Jeremiah turned his face towards the dawning of a better day. The old covenant or agreement between Jehovah and His people had clearly come to an end: the prophet has a vision of a new one, involving a more spiritual relationship between men and God. Jeremiah's unique contribution to Old Testament prophecy lies in his teaching that religion depends neither on Temple nor on Holy City, but on each individual's personal communion with the Spirit of God.

The New Covenant

"Behold, the days come," saith the Lord, "that I will make a new covenant with the house of Israel, and with the house of Judah: not according to the covenant that I made with their fathers in the day that I took them by the hand to bring them out of the land of Egypt; which My covenant they brake, although I was an husband unto them," saith the Lord: "but this shall be the covenant that I will make with the house of Israel; after those days," saith the Lord, "I will put My law in their inward parts, and write it in their hearts; and will be their God, and they shall be My people. And they shall teach no more every man his neighbour, and every man his brother, saying, 'Know the Lord': for they shall all know Me, from the least of them unto the greatest of them: for I will forgive their iniquity, and I will remember their sin no more."

[*Jeremiah* xxxi. 31–34

Gedaliah, to whom the Babylonians entrusted Jeremiah, was left as Governor of Judah, subject to Babylon. But when Ishmael, a member of the royal house, assassinated Gedaliah, Judah feared the displeasure of Nebuchadrezzar. This last selection from the Book of Jeremiah tells of the prophet's position in connection with a proposed flight to Egypt to escape from the wrath of Babylon.

Appeal to Jeremiah for Guidance

Then all the captains of the forces, and Johanan the son of Kareah, and all the people from the least even unto the greatest, came near, and said unto Jeremiah the prophet, "Let, we beseech thee, our supplication be accepted before thee, and pray for us unto the Lord thy God, even for all this remnant; (for we are left but a few of many, as thine eyes do behold us:) that the Lord thy God may shew us the way wherein we may walk, and the thing that we may do." Then Jeremiah the prophet said unto them, "I have heard you; behold I will pray unto the Lord your God according to your words; and it shall come to pass, that whatsoever thing the Lord shall answer you, I will declare it unto you; I will keep nothing back from you."

JEREMIAH

After Ten Days came the Word of the Lord

And it came to pass after ten days, that the word of the Lord came unto Jeremiah. Then called he Johanan the son of Kareah, and all the captains of the forces which were with him, and all the people from the least even to the greatest, and said unto them, "Thus saith the Lord, the God of Israel, unto whom ye sent me to present your supplication before Him; 'If ye will still abide in this land, then will I build you, and not pull you down, and I will plant you, and not pluck you up: for I repent Me of the evil that I have done unto you. Be not afraid of the king of Babylon, of whom ye are afraid; be not afraid of him,' saith the Lord: 'for I am with you to save you, and to deliver you from his hand. And I will shew mercies unto you, that he may have mercy upon you, and cause you to return to your own land.' But if ye say, 'We will not dwell in this land, neither obey the voice of the Lord your God,' saying, 'No; but we will go into the land of Egypt, where we shall see no war, nor hear the sound of the trumpet, nor have hunger of bread; and there will we dwell': now therefore hear the word of the Lord, ye remnant of Judah; go ye not into Egypt, know certainly that I have admonished you this day. For ye dissembled in your hearts, when ye sent me unto the Lord your God, saying, 'Pray for us unto the Lord our God; and according unto all that the Lord our God shall say, so declare unto us, and we will do it.' And now I have this day declared it to you; but ye have not obeyed the voice of the Lord your God, nor anything for the which He hath sent me unto you."

The Flight to Egypt

Johanan the son of Kareah, and all the captains of the forces, and all the people, obeyed not the voice of the Lord, to dwell in the land of Judah. But Johanan the son of Kareah, and all the captains of the forces, took all the remnant of Judah, and Jeremiah the prophet, and Baruch the son of Neriah. So they came into the land of Egypt: for they obeyed not the voice of the Lord: thus came they even to Tahpanhes.

[*From Jeremiah* xlii and xliii

IV

OTHER PROPHETS
ZEPHANIAH, NAHUM, HABAKKUK

ZEPHANIAH AND THE DAY OF THE LORD

ZEPHANIAH, a man apparently descended from kings, prophesied in the earlier part of the reign of King Josiah, in the time before the reformation which followed the discovery of the law-book in the temple in 621 B.C. We know from Herodotus, the Greek historian, of hordes of uncivilized Scythians from the North, who, about 630 B.C., overran Western Asia, burning and destroying even as far as Palestine. The likelihood of an attack by these Scythians gave vivid reality to Zephaniah's warning that Jehovah must punish Jerusalem and Judah for their wickedness. Yet this prophet retains a modest hope for a Remnant of godly men in his nation.

A painter of the Middle Ages depicted Zephaniah as the man with the lantern of the Lord, searching for sinners to bring them forth to the destruction of the judgment of Jehovah. The prophet was far from the New Testament revelation of God as our Father in Heaven, a God who loves sinners while hating sin: to Zephaniah He is a God of righteous wrath, interfering even with the natural order of events to punish the wicked. But his message seems to have been revised by some later editor, who, with a strong desire to make the message of Zephaniah more suitable for religious teaching, added to it from some other unknown source a cheerful song of hope in God (Zeph. iii. 14).

The rhythmic beat in the passage about "the day of the Lord" is so marked that we set it out in verse form. See p. 29 for a note about the *form* of the prophetic messages.

OTHER PROPHETS

The Day of the Lord

The word of the Lord which came unto Zephaniah, in the days of Josiah, the son of Amon, king of Judah.

> The great day of the Lord is near;
> It is near and hasteth greatly,
> The voice of the day of the Lord:
> The mighty man shall cry there bitterly.
>
> That day is a day of wrath,
> A day of trouble and distress,
> A day of wasteness and desolation,
> A day of darkness and gloominess,
> A day of clouds and thick darkness,
> A day of the trumpet and alarm,
> Against the fenced cities,
> And against the high towers.

And I will bring distress upon men, that they shall walk like blind men, because they have sinned against the Lord: and their blood shall be poured out as dust, and their flesh as the dung. Neither their silver nor their gold shall be able to deliver them in the day of the Lord's wrath; but the whole land shall be devoured by the fire of his jealousy: for He shall make even a speedy riddance of all them that dwell in the land. "I will utterly consume all things from off the land," saith the Lord. "I will consume man and beast; I will consume the fowls of the heaven, and the fishes of the sea, and the stumbling-blocks with the wicked; and I will cut off man from off the land," saith the Lord. Hold thy peace at the presence of the Lord God: for the day of the Lord is at hand.

[*Zephaniah* i. 1, 14–18, 2, 3, and 7

Religious and Social Conditions in Judah

I will also stretch out Mine hand upon Judah, and upon all the inhabitants of Jerusalem; and I will cut off the remnant of Baal from this place. And them that worship the host of heaven upon the house-tops; and them that worship and that swear by the Lord, and that swear by Malcham; and them that are turned back from the Lord; and those that have not sought the Lord, nor enquired for Him. And it shall come to pass in the day of the Lord's sacrifice, that I will punish the princes, and the king's children, and all such as are clothed with strange apparel. In the same day also will I punish all those that leap on the threshold, which fill their masters' houses with violence and deceit. And it shall come to pass in that day, saith the Lord, that there shall be the noise of a cry from the fish gate, and an howling from the second, and a great crashing from the hills. Howl, ye inhabitants of Maktesh, for all the merchant people are cut down; all they that bear silver are cut off.

And it shall come to pass at that time, that I will search Jerusalem with candles, and punish the men that are settled on their lees: that say in their heart, "The Lord will not do good, neither will He do evil." Therefore their goods shall become a booty, and their houses a desolation: they shall also build houses, but not inhabit them; and they shall plant vineyards, but not drink the wine thereof.

[*Zephaniah* i. 4–6, 8–13

Hope for the Remnant

Gather yourselves together, yea, gather together, O nation not desired; before the decree bring forth, before the day pass as the chaff, before the fierce anger of the Lord come upon you, before the day of the Lord's anger come upon you. Seek ye the Lord, all ye meek of the earth, which have wrought His judgment; seek righteousness, seek meekness: it may be ye shall be hid in the day of the Lord's anger. "Therefore wait ye upon Me", saith the Lord, "until the day that I rise up to the prey: for My determination is to gather the nations, that I may assemble the kingdoms, to pour upon them Mine indignation, even all My fierce anger: for all the earth shall be devoured with that fire of My jealousy. Then I will take away out of the midst of thee them that rejoice in thy pride, and thou shalt no more be haughty because of My holy mountain. I will also leave in the midst of thee an afflicted and poor people, and they shall trust in the name of the Lord. The remnant of Israel shall not do iniquity, nor speak lies; neither shall a deceitful tongue be found in their mouth: for they shall feed and lie down, and none shall make them afraid."

[*Zephaniah* ii. 1–3, iii. 8, 11–13

NAHUM, THE NATIONALIST

Nahum was a great poet and a master of vivid imagery, but certainly the least religious of the Hebrew prophets. He appears to have been a contemporary of Jeremiah, and to have prophesied in the later years of Josiah's reign, just before the fall of Nineveh in 612 B.C. His position is, however, entirely different from Jeremiah's. Nahum is certain that Nineveh must fall because the Assyrians are the foes of the Jews, and, under Sennacherib, once dared to attack Jerusalem: Jeremiah is certain that Jerusalem must fall because of the wickedness of its inhabitants. Nahum says not one word of the sin of the Jews: they are his own people. In fact, apart from the introductory poem in Nahum i. 1–8, the only religious utterance is the reason given for the woe of Assyria, "Behold, I am against thee, saith the Lord of Hosts."

We must notice, however, the compression of meaning and the splendid imagery in his description of the sorrow of Nineveh. It is easy to read this as free verse: the rhythm is so well marked.

The Sorrow of Nineveh

Behold upon the mountains the feet of him that bringeth good tidings, that publisheth peace! O Judah, keep thy solemn feasts, perform thy vows: for the wicked shall no more pass through thee; he is utterly cut off.

Woe to the bloody city! it is all full of lies and robbery; the prey departeth not; the noise of a whip, and the noise of the rattling of the wheels, and of the pransing horses, and of the jumping chariots. The horseman lifteth up both the bright sword and the glittering spear: and there is a multitude of slain, and a great number of carcases; and there is none end of their corpses; they stumble upon their corpses.

Thy crowned are as the locusts, and thy captains as the great grasshoppers, which camp in the hedges in the cold day, but when the sun ariseth they flee away, and their place is not known where they are. Thy shepherds slumber, O king of Assyria: thy nobles shall dwell in the dust: thy people is scattered upon the mountains, and no man gathereth them. There is no healing of thy bruise; thy wound is grievous: all that hear the bruit of thee shall clap the hands over thee: for upon whom hath not thy wickedness passed continually?

[*Nahum* i. 15, iii. 1–3, 17–19]

Scholars have worked hard to understand the relation of the description of the sorrow of Nineveh to the above-mentioned introductory poem, i. 1–8 (in Hebrew an acrostic poem), which contains the familiar words (Nahum i. 7):—

The Lord is good, a strong hold in the day of trouble;
He knoweth them that trust in Him.

Some think that a later editor, anxious to make Nahum's message more suitable for reading for religious teaching, inserted this poem from another unknown source. Others think that Nahum himself composed it, in order to justify his hatred of Nineveh by his ideas of Jehovah. To Nahum the Jews are not sinners: they are "them that trust in Him", and to the Jews "the Lord is good". This book shows the extent to which it is possible to ignore the beam in one's own eye when trying to take the mote out of a brother's eye!

HABAKKUK UPON THE WATCH TOWER

A third short prophetic book of the Old Testament comes most probably from the same period as Jeremiah, the closing years of the seventh century before Christ: this is the Book of Habakkuk. Hebrew scholars are diligently seeking to understand exactly how and when this book was written, how much of it comes direct from the prophet himself, and how much may be due to later editors working to improve it for purposes of religious education. No definite decision has been reached. As the book is translated in the Authorized Version, it refers to the "Chaldeans" (i.e. Babylon) as coming to overrun Judah: which places the prophet as a contemporary of Jeremiah. But some scholars think that the Hebrew word translated "Chaldeans" should be translated "Kittim", which means "Greeks": this would alter, of course, the whole historical background, and bring the book down to the time of the amazing conquests of Alexander the Great, 250 years later.

Fortunately for the ordinary reader, the real meaning of the message of Habakkuk depends not at all on the history of any one period: his cry is not to a sinning people living at a certain time, seeking their repentance and salvation: his cry is to Jehovah Himself, in utter weariness of the wickedness of those around him and the still greater wickedness of those who come from afar to overwhelm them. The great lesson of the book is a message of patience, of the need of waiting for God to declare Himself; a message that the one permanent thing in human life is the just (righteous) man and his faith (rather faithfulness or moral steadfastness); that, whatever be the outward circumstances of life, such a man lives by his vision of God and the calm faith given to his soul by his vision.

The Prophet Weary of Wickedness

The burden which Habakkuk the prophet did see. O Lord, how long shall I cry, and Thou wilt not hear? Even cry out unto Thee of violence, and Thou wilt not save? Why dost Thou shew me iniquity, and cause me to behold grievance? For spoiling and violence are before me: and there are that raise up strife and contention. Therefore the law is slacked, and judgment doth never go forth: for the wicked doth compass about the righteous; therefore wrong judgment proceedeth.

Art thou not from everlasting, O Lord my God, mine Holy One? We shall not die. O Lord, Thou hast ordained them for judgment; and, O mighty God, Thou hast established them for correction. Thou art of purer eyes than to behold evil, and canst not look on iniquity: wherefore lookest Thou upon them that deal treacherously, and holdest Thy tongue when the wicked devoureth the man that is more righteous than he? And makest men as the fishes of the sea, as the creeping things, that have no ruler over them? They take up all of them with the angle, they catch them in their net, and gather them in their drag: therefore they rejoice and are glad. Therefore they sacrifice unto their net, and burn incense unto their drag; because by them their portion is fat, and their meat plenteous. Shall they therefore empty their net, and not spare continually to slay the nations?

[*Habakkuk* i. 1–4, 12–17

The Answer of Jehovah

I will stand upon my watch, and set me upon the tower, and will watch to see what He will say unto me, and what I shall answer when I am reproved. And the Lord answered me, and said, "Write the vision, and make it plain upon tables, that he may run that readeth it. For the vision is yet for an appointed time, but at the end it shall speak, and not lie: though it tarry, wait for it; because it will surely come, it will not tarry. Behold, his soul which is lifted up is not upright in him: but the just shall live by his faith."

[*Habakkuk* ii. 1–4

The third chapter of this book expands this key-phrase of the prophet's message, "The just shall live by his faith", by showing Jehovah still going forth to save His people as in days of old. Very probably another bard has added the beautiful verses 17–19 quoted here, verses which voice the same note of patience and hope as the kernel of Habakkuk's message (ii. 3, 4).

A Song of Confidence

> Although the fig tree shall not blossom,
> Neither shall fruit be in the vines;
> The labour of the olive shall fail,
> And the flocks shall yield no meat;
> The flock shall be cut off from the fold,
> And there shall be no herd in the stalls:

Yet I will rejoice in the Lord,
I will joy in the God of my salvation.
The Lord God is my strength,
And He will make my feet like hinds' feet,
And will make me to walk upon mine high places.

[*Habakkuk* iii. 17-19

V

THE BOOK OF KINGS—A HISTORY FROM DAVID'S DEATH TO THE EXILE

1. INTRODUCTION

REVISION

IN Jeremiah's story, we have seen how in 586 B.C. the Southern kingdom of Judah came to an end by the attacks of the Babylonians, as in 722 B.C. the Northern kingdom of Israel had come to an end by the attacks of the Assyrians. We have seen how, to men of insight, the doom of each kingdom had come to appear unavoidable because of the iniquity of the people. We have seen how, while Israel as a separate people passes for ever from the stage of history as a more or less homogeneous mass of corruption, Judah was sharply divided between the small but virile party of the Reformation and the great majority of the nation. Isaiah's Remnant, both by what they were and by what they accomplished during the last century before the Exile, provided a nucleus round which in time grew up a new national life of sufficient force to rebuild Jerusalem and the Temple, to hold fast to Jehovah through centuries of subjection and even persecution, until in fullness of time came the first Day of the Christ Child.

We must look now more closely at the activities of this Remnant, although owing to lack of knowledge of individual men and exact dates, it is impossible to be precise in our statements. Yet the rough truth about their saving actions is now well known to us through the work of many students of the Scriptures. By what means did the Remnant prevent Judah from being swallowed up by Babylon and disappearing altogether, as Israel had already completely disappeared?

THE VALUE OF BOOKS

To a very great extent, Judah was saved by its literature. Men are born and die; books remain. A man can be in but one place at a time; in many places can be copies of a book even when these have had to be laboriously copied by hand in a roll. A leader of any authority in Babylon could gather round him a small company of Jews and read to them from one of these much-prized rolls; this was the beginning of the custom which Jesus followed in the Synagogues of Galilee, and of the custom of reading from the Bible which we follow even until now. At this time religion began to be the religion of a Book: the Bible began to be. Probably the writing most appreciated was the book of Deuteronomy, or, at any rate, the greater part of it: we know too of other writings already in existence, the messages of Amos, Hosea, Isaiah, Micah, and the words and life of Jeremiah.

A NEW INTEREST IN HISTORY

But by 586 B.C. Judah had already literary possessions of another kind. We have mentioned on p. 11 the stories and poems handed on orally from generation to generation, gradually gathered together and written down, and finally incorporated in the historical books of the Bible as we now have them. By the time of the Exile a certain amount of compilation of this kind had already been undertaken, so that there was a collection of narratives which could be read in public and used by the exiles for spiritual nourishment, while, as ever, parents had many stories almost by heart to tell to their children. There were also various annals and chronicles, such as the Annals of the Temple, kept much as men keep diaries, very accurate and valuable as historical documents, but too dull in themselves to be used largely by the common folk.

The Remnant, or the "Deuteronomic School", as scholars call the literary men amongst the Remnant, had begun to have larger ideas about history. They were deeply conscious that Jehovah had a special concern for their nation, and in those years of bewilderment and approaching desolation just before the Exile they began to muse on the centuries before, trying to see in them more of the ways of Jehovah. They were sure that worship of idols was wrong, that worship in high places was inferior to worship in the Temple at Jerusalem, that the Temple worship mattered vitally to the nation; they were certain too that God always rewarded goodness with prosperity and wickedness with misfortune. This last idea of theirs, that suffering was always due to wrongdoing, was, of course, mistaken; it marks the stage of religious development reached by these men. This common idea of the time must have hurt Jeremiah deeply. He suffered intensely, not for his own wrongdoing.

HISTORY WITH A MORAL

At any rate, these Deuteronomic historians saw all the past in this way, and they began to write history books from this point of view. They did not set out to write history as we know it, but to teach religion through history. Even children know the difference between a story told for the sake of the story and a story told for the sake of the lesson behind it. These unknown historians set out to write history for the sake of the lesson behind it. As a matter of fact, they themselves did very little actual writing. They wrote introductions and connecting links for what had already been compiled in more scattered forms: or they collected in writing what had been told orally. Either just before or during the Exile these Deuteronomic historians had in this way told the story of the people of Israel from the Exodus from Egypt down to the Departure into Exile.

THE FIRST PROPHETIC HISTORY BOOK

The first section of this story to be tackled was the part nearest to the lives of the historians, telling of the period from David's death to the Exile. Fortunately the construction of this part is also the simplest to follow: it is contained in the first and second books of Kings.

It is most probable that these books received what is practically their present form during the last years before the Exile—sometime round about 600 B.C. The reign of Jehoiakin or the reign of Zedekiah is a likely time. But the concluding chapters of the Book of Kings, which tell of the fall of Jerusalem and later of Jehoiakin's release from his Babylonian prison, must be exilic additions to the main history. There are also signs that the whole work was revised during the Exile and turned into what has been well described as a "great confession of sin". Some scholars even think that no part of the work received its present form until during the years of exile, but the majority attribute the main part of the compilation to the years just preceding the fall of Jerusalem. For ordinary readers it makes little difference which is the correct account of this matter.

The main points for us are these. This history was written with a strong religious purpose; for instance, the great King Omri who built Samaria as a capital for the Northern kingdom was scarcely mentioned because the religious value of his story was negligible. While this history was based on chronicles and annals of the Temple and of various kings, most accurate historical sources, it also incorporated with practically no editorial care the oral traditions about Elijah and Elisha, because of the religious value of the stories. The reading of this history during the Exile served to impress on the hearts of the people the fact that their own sin and the sin of their forefathers had brought them into their present troubles, so developing in them a broken and contrite spirit which was the first precursor of brighter days.

This first Deuteronomic History Book falls naturally into three parts:—

(*a*) The Building of the Temple and the Division of the Kingdom (1 Kings i. 1–xii. 20).

(*b*) The History of both Kingdoms from the Division to the Fall of Samaria (1 Kings xii. 21–2 Kings xvii. 41).

(*c*) The History of Judah alone from the Fall of Samaria to the Fall of Jerusalem (2 Kings xviii. 1–xxv. 30).

2. A WISE KING AND A DIVIDED KINGDOM

To understand the character and work of Solomon, we must "look before and after". This story of the Wise King begins at the close of the reign of his father David, and extends after his own death into the reign of his son Rehoboam. On one hand we may see, even when King David was an aged man, the strife in his family coming once more to an open crisis over the succession: Solomon was the son of the beloved woman Bath-sheba. On the other hand we may see the next king, Rehoboam, losing far more than half his kingdom, as the result not only of his own foolish conceit, but also of his father's excessive wealth and tyranny.

David chooses his Successor

Now King David was old and stricken in years; and they covered him with clothes, but he gat no heat. Wherefore his servants said unto him, "Let there be sought for my lord the king a young virgin: and let her stand before the king, and let her cherish him, and let her lie in thy bosom, that my lord the king may get heat." So they sought for a fair damsel throughout all the coasts of Israel, and found Abishag a Shunammite, and brought her to the king. And the damsel was very fair, and cherished the king, and ministered to him.

Then Adonijah the son of Haggith exalted himself, saying, "I will be king": and he prepared him chariots and horsemen, and fifty men to run before him. And his father had not displeased him at any time in saying, "Why hast thou done so?" and he also was a very goodly man; and his mother bare him after Absalom. And he conferred with Joab the son of Zeruiah, and with Abiathar the priest: and they following Adonijah helped him. But Zadok the priest, and Benaiah the son of Jehoiada, and Nathan the prophet, and Shimei, and Rei, and the mighty men which belonged to David, were not with Adonijah.

Wherefore Nathan spake unto Bath-sheba the mother of Solomon, saying, "Hast thou not heard that Adonijah the son of Haggith doth reign, and David our lord knoweth it not? Now therefore come, let me, I pray thee, give thee counsel, that thou mayest save thine own life, and the life of thy son Solomon. Go and get thee in unto King David, and say unto him, 'Didst not thou, my lord, O king, swear unto thine handmaid, saying, Assuredly Solomon thy son shall reign after me, and he shall sit upon my throne? Why then doth Adonijah reign?' Behold, while thou yet talkest there with the king, I also will come in after thee, and confirm thy words."

And Bath-sheba went in unto the king into the chamber: and the king was very old; and Abishag the Shunammite ministered unto the king. And Bath-sheba bowed, and did obeisance unto the king. And the king said, "What wouldest thou?" And she said unto him, "My lord, thou swarest by the Lord thy God unto thine handmaid, saying, 'Assuredly Solomon thy son shall reign after me, and he shall sit upon my throne.' And now, behold, Adonijah reigneth; and now, my lord the king, thou knowest it not: and he hath slain oxen and fat cattle and sheep in abundance, and hath called all the sons of the king, and Abiathar the priest, and Joab the captain of the host: but Solomon thy servant hath he not called. And thou, my lord, O king, the eyes of all Israel are upon thee, that thou shouldest tell them who shall sit on the throne of my lord the king after him. Otherwise it shall come to pass, when my lord the king shall sleep with his fathers, that I and my son Solomon shall be counted offenders."

And lo, while she yet talked with the king, Nathan the prophet also came in. And they told the king, saying, "Behold Nathan the prophet." And when he was come in before the king, he bowed himself before the king with his face to the ground. And Nathan said, "My lord, O king, hast thou said, 'Adonijah shall reign after me, and he shall sit upon my throne'? For he is gone down this day, and hath slain oxen and fat cattle and sheep in abundance, and hath called all the king's sons, and the captains of the host, and Abiathar the priest; and, behold, they eat and drink before him, and say, 'God save king Adonijah.' But me, even me thy servant, and Zadok the priest, and Benaiah the son of Jehoiada, and thy servant Solomon, hath he not called. Is this thing done by my lord the king, and thou hast not shewed it unto thy servant, who should sit on the throne of my lord the king after him?"

Then King David answered and said, "Call me Bath-sheba." And she came into the king's presence, and stood before the king. And the king sware, and said, "As the Lord liveth, that hath redeemed my soul out of all distress, even as I sware unto thee by the Lord God of Israel, saying, 'Assuredly Solomon thy son shall reign after me, and he shall sit upon my throne in my stead'; even so will I certainly do this day." Then Bath-sheba bowed with her face to the earth, and did reverence to the king, and said, "Let my lord King David live for ever."

And King David said, "Call me Zadok the priest, and Nathan the prophet, and Benaiah the son of Jehoiada." And they came before the king. The king also said unto them, "Take with you the servants of your lord, and cause Solomon my son to ride upon mine own mule, and bring him down to Gihon: and let Zadok the priest and Nathan the prophet anoint him there king over Israel: and blow ye with the trumpet, and say, 'God save King Solomon.' Then ye shall come up after him, that he may come and sit upon my throne; for he shall be king in my stead: and I have appointed him to be ruler over Israel and over Judah." And Benaiah the son of Jehoiada answered the king, and said, "Amen: the Lord God of my lord the king say so too.

As the Lord hath been with my lord the king, even so be He with Solomon, and make his throne greater than the throne of my lord King David."

[1 *Kings* i. 1-37

The narrative goes on in 1 Kings i to tell how Solomon was anointed king over Israel, and how he made peace with Adonijah, his disappointed brother.

Death of King David
  Now the days of David drew nigh that he should die; and he charged Solomon his son, saying, "I go the way of all the earth: be thou strong therefore, and shew thyself a man; and keep the charge of the Lord thy God, to walk in His ways, to keep His statutes, and His commandments, and His judgments, and His testimonies, as it is written in the law of Moses, that thou mayest prosper in all that thou doest, and whithersoever thou turnest thyself: that the Lord may continue His word which He spake concerning me, saying, 'If thy children take heed to their way, to walk before Me in truth with all their heart and with all their soul, there shall not fail thee' (said He) 'a man on the throne of Israel.' " So David slept with his fathers, and was buried in the city of David. And the days that David reigned over Israel were forty years: seven years reigned he in Hebron, and thirty and three years reigned he in Jerusalem. Then sat Solomon upon the throne of David his father.

[1 *Kings* ii. 1-4, 10-12

In the above passages we can see the Deuteronomic writers at work. To selections from the Court History of King David (see p. 21), or a similar work, they have added David's charge to Solomon, introducing not David's ideas but their own. The words bring to our memories words from the Book of Deuteronomy.

A PROSPEROUS REIGN

Solomon was a great king and had a most prosperous reign. His humility before God at the beginning is in sad contrast to his spiritual blindness and exalted despotism at the end. We note that God is said to have spoken to this king directly in a dream and not indirectly through prophets. His friendly alliances with heathen potentates led him to take many wives including foreign princesses, one, at least, of whom he kept in magnificence to correspond with her exalted position in her native land. Solomon, it is true, built for Jehovah a beautiful Temple, but he also built for himself a magnificent palace, and amongst other buildings a house for the Pharaoh's daughter: he appears to have had a passion for building.

It was a great achievement to begin to centralize the worship of Jehovah in Jerusalem by building the Temple. In time Jerusalem became the religious heart of the nation, with most important results in Hebrew history. Naturally at the time this was less palatable to Israel than to Judah. But this achievement, along with Solomon's other building, was only carried through by the use of forced labour: compulsory toil at a distance from their homes was not likely to endear Solomon to those subjects whose lot it was. We see too the wealth of the whole land beginning to pour itself into Jerusalem. The king's hand was stretched out to other lands. He acquired a navy from King Hiram of Tyre, which brought to Jerusalem the treasures of the East. Ophir may have been either India or Arabia; it is uncertain which. Sheba, from which came the stranger queen, is known to have been in South Arabia.

Here we see the beginning of the chasm between the luxurious, idle rich and the oppressed and overworked poor, of which we have heard so much from the prophets of rather later times.

Solomon's Vision of Jehovah

And Solomon made affinity with Pharaoh king of Egypt, and took Pharaoh's daughter, and brought her into the city of David, until he had made an end of building his own house, and the house of the Lord, and the wall of Jerusalem round about. Only the people sacrificed in high places, because there was no house built unto the name of the Lord, until those days. And Solomon loved the Lord, walking in the statutes of David his father: only he sacrificed and burnt incense in high places. And the king went to Gibeon to sacrifice there; for that was the great high place: a thousand burnt offerings did Solomon offer upon that altar.

In Gibeon the Lord appeared to Solomon in a dream by night: and God said, "Ask what I shall give thee." And Solomon said, "Thou hast shewed unto Thy servant David my father great mercy, according as he walked before Thee in truth, and in righteousness, and in uprightness of heart with Thee; and Thou hast kept for him this great kindness, that Thou hast given him a son to sit on his throne, as it is this day. And now, O Lord my God, Thou hast made Thy servant king instead of David my father: and I am but a little child: I know not how to go out or come in. And thy servant is in the midst of Thy people which Thou hast chosen, a great people, that cannot be numbered nor counted for multitude. Give therefore Thy servant an understanding heart to judge Thy people, that I may discern between good and bad: for who is able to judge this Thy so great a people?" And the speech pleased the Lord, that Solomon had asked this thing.

And God said unto him, "Because thou hast asked this thing, and hast not asked for thyself long life; neither hast asked riches for thyself, nor hast asked the life of thine enemies, but hast asked for thyself understanding to discern judgment; behold, I have done according to thy words: lo, I have given thee a wise and an understanding heart; so that there was none like thee before thee, neither after thee shall any arise like unto thee. And I have also given thee that which thou hast not asked, both riches, and honour: so that there shall not be any among the kings like unto thee all thy days. And if thou wilt walk in My ways, to keep My statutes and My commandments, as thy father David did walk, then I will lengthen thy days." And Solomon awoke; and, behold, it was a dream. And he came to Jerusalem, and stood before the ark of the covenant of the Lord, and offered up burnt offerings, and offered peace offerings, and made a feast to all his servants.

[1 *Kings* iii. 1–15

Solomon's Success, his Wealth and Knowledge

So King Solomon was king over all Israel. Judah and Israel were many, as the sand which is by the sea in multitude, eating and drinking, and making merry. And Solomon reigned over all kingdoms from the river unto the land of the Philistines, and unto the border of Egypt: they brought presents, and served Solomon all the days of his life.

And Solomon's provision for one day was thirty measures of fine flour, and threescore measures of meal, ten fat oxen, and twenty oxen out of the pastures, and an hundred sheep, beside harts, and roebucks, and fallowdeer, and fatted fowl. For he had dominion over all the region on this side the river: and he had peace on all sides round about him. And Judah and Israel dwelt safely, every man under his vine and under his fig tree, from Dan even to Beer-sheba, all the days of Solomon.

And Solomon had forty thousand stalls of horses for his chariots, and twelve thousand horsemen. And those officers provided victual for King Solomon, and for all that came unto King Solomon's table, every man in his month: they lacked nothing. Barley also and straw for the horses and dromedaries brought they unto the place where the officers were, every man according to his charge.

And God gave Solomon wisdom and understanding exceeding much, and largeness of heart, even as the sand that is on the sea shore. And Solomon's wisdom excelled the wisdom of all the children of the east country, and all the wisdom of Egypt. For he was wiser than all men; than Ethan the Ezrahite, and Heman, and Chalcol, and Darda, the sons of Mahol: and his fame was in all nations round about. And he spake three thousand proverbs: and his songs were a thousand and five. And he spake of trees, from the cedar tree that is in Lebanon even unto the hyssop that springeth out of the wall: he spake also of beasts, and of fowl, and of creeping things, and of fishes. And there came of all people to hear the wisdom of Solomon, from all kings of the earth, which had heard of his wisdom.

[1 *Kings* iv. 1, 20–34

Cedar Wood for the Temple from Lebanon

And Hiram king of Tyre sent his servants unto Solomon; for he had heard that they had anointed him king in the room of his father: for Hiram was ever a lover of David. And Solomon sent to Hiram, saying, "Thou knowest how that David my father could not build an house unto the name of the Lord his God for the wars which were about him on every side, until the Lord put them under the soles of his feet. But now the Lord my God hath given me rest on every side, so that there is neither adversary nor evil occurrent. And, behold, I purpose to build an house unto the name of the Lord my God, as the Lord spake unto David my father, saying, 'Thy son, whom I will set upon thy throne in thy room, he shall build an house unto My name.' Now therefore command thou that they hew me cedar trees out of Lebanon; and my servants shall be with thy servants: and unto thee will I give hire for thy servants according to all that thou shalt appoint: for thou knowest that there is not among us any that can hew timber like unto the Sidonians."

And it came to pass when Hiram heard the words of Solomon, that he rejoiced greatly, and said, "Blessed be the Lord this day, which hath given unto David a wise son over this great people." And Hiram sent to Solomon, saying, "I have considered the things which thou sentest to me for: and I will do all thy desire concerning timber of cedar, and concerning timber of fir. My servants shall bring them down from Lebanon unto the sea: and I will convey them by sea in floats unto the place that thou shalt appoint me, and will cause them to be discharged there, and thou shalt receive them: and thou shalt accomplish my desire, in giving food for my household." So Hiram gave Solomon cedar trees and fir trees according to all his desire. And Solomon gave Hiram twenty thousand measures of wheat for food to his household, and twenty measures of pure oil: thus gave Solomon to Hiram year by year.

[1 *Kings* v. 1–11

Forced Labour for the Temple

And King Solomon raised a levy out of all Israel; and the levy was thirty thousand men. And he sent them to Lebanon, ten thousand a month by courses: a month they were in Lebanon, and two months at home: and Adoniram was over the levy. And Solomon had threescore and ten thousand that bare burdens, and fourscore thousand hewers in the mountains; beside the chief of Solomon's officers which were over the work, three thousand and three hundred, which ruled over the people that wrought in the work. And the king commanded, and they brought great stones, costly stones, and hewed stones, to lay the foundation of the house. And Solomon's builders and Hiram's builders did hew them, and the stonesquarers: so they prepared timber and stones to build the house. [1 *Kings* v. 13–18

The Temple built in Seven Years

And it came to pass in the four hundred and eightieth year after the children of Israel were come out of the land of Egypt, in the fourth year of Solomon's reign over Israel, in the month Ziv, which is the second month, that he began to build the house of the Lord. And the house which King Solomon built for the Lord, the length thereof was threescore cubits, and the breadth thereof twenty cubits, and the height thereof thirty cubits. And the porch before the temple of the house, twenty cubits was the length thereof, according to the breadth of the house; and ten cubits was the breadth thereof before the house. And for the house he made windows of narrow lights. And against the wall of the house he built chambers round about, against the walls of the house round about, both of the temple and of the oracle: and he made chambers round about: and the house, when it was in building, was built of stone made ready before it was brought thither: so that there was neither hammer nor axe nor any tool of iron heard in the house, while it was in building. So he built the house, and finished it, and covered the house with beams and boards of cedar. And then he built chambers against all the house, five cubits high: and they rested on the house with timber of cedar.

And the word of the Lord came to Solomon saying, "Concerning this house which thou art in building, if thou wilt walk in My statutes, and execute My judgments, and keep all My commandments to walk in them; then will I perform My word with thee, which I spake unto David thy father: and I will dwell among the children of Israel, and will not forsake My people Israel." So Solomon built the house, and finished it.

In the fourth year was the foundation of the house of the Lord laid, in the month Ziv: and in the eleventh year, in the month Bul which is the eighth month, was the house finished throughout all the parts thereof, and according to all the fashion of it. So was he seven years in building it. [1 *Kings* vi. 1–5, 7, 9–14, 37, 38

The Deuteronomic compilers took this account of the building of the Temple from a special Temple Source, probably written by a priest. This Temple Source continues with an elaborate description of the Temple (1 Kings vi. 15–36); a brief account of Solomon's other buildings (1 Kings vii. 1–12), in which doubtless a priest took little interest; and a full account of the metal work for the Temple, which was wrought by a skilled worker in brass from Tyre (1 Kings vii. 13–51).

THE DEDICATION OF THE TEMPLE

Here the Deuteronomic historians have combined material from an ancient source with their own deeply reverent prayer and exhortation, put into the mouth of Solomon on this occasion of intense religious significance to the nation.

The Removal of the Ark

Then Solomon assembled the elders of Israel, and all the heads of the tribes, the chief of the fathers of the children of Israel, unto King Solomon in Jerusalem, that they might bring up the ark of the covenant of the Lord out of the city of David, which is Zion. And all the men of Israel assembled themselves unto King Solomon at the feast in the month Ethanim, which is the seventh month. And all the elders of Israel came, and the priests took up the ark. And King Solomon and all the congregation of Israel, that were assembled unto him, were with him before the ark, sacrificing sheep and oxen, that could not be told nor numbered for multitude. And the priests brought in the ark of the covenant of the Lord unto his place, into the oracle of the house, to the most holy place, even under the wings of the cherubim. For the cherubim spread forth their two wings over the place of the ark, and the cherubim covered the ark and the staves thereof above. And they drew out the staves, that the ends of the staves were seen out in the holy place before the oracle, and they were not seen without: and there they are unto this day. There was nothing in the ark save the two tables of stone, which Moses put there at Horeb, when the Lord made a covenant with the children of Israel, when they came out of the land of Egypt. And it came to pass, when the priests were come out of the holy place, that the cloud filled the house of the Lord, so that the priests could not stand to minister because of the cloud: for the glory of the Lord had filled the house of the Lord.

[1 *Kings* viii. 1–11

THE BOOK OF KINGS

Words of Dedication (from early Source: see p. 17)

Then spake Solomon,
"The Lord said that He would dwell in the thick darkness.
I have surely built Thee an house to dwell in,
A settled place for Thee to abide in for ever."

[1 *Kings* viii. 12, 13

Acts and Words of Dedication (from Deuteronomic School—added to down to late period of Exile)

And Solomon stood before the altar of the Lord in the presence of all the congregation of Israel, and spread forth his hands toward heaven: and he said, "Lord God of Israel, there is no God like Thee, in heaven above, or on earth beneath, who keepest covenant and mercy with Thy servants that walk before Thee with all their heart: who hast kept with Thy servant David my father that Thou promisedst him: Thou spakest also with Thy mouth, and hast fulfilled it with Thine hand, as it is this day. Therefore now, Lord God of Israel, keep with Thy servant David my father that Thou promisedst him, saying, 'There shall not fail thee a man in my sight to sit on the throne of Israel; so that thy children take heed to their way, that they walk before Me as thou hast walked before Me.' And now, O God of Israel, let Thy word, I pray Thee, be verified, which Thou spakest unto Thy servant David my father.

"But will God indeed dwell on the earth? Behold, the heaven and heaven of heavens cannot contain Thee; how much less this house that I have builded? Yet have Thou respect unto the prayer of Thy servant, and to his supplication, O Lord my God, to hearken unto the cry and to the prayer, which Thy servant prayeth before Thee to-day: that Thine eyes may be open toward this house night and day, even toward the place of which Thou hast said, 'My name shall be there': that Thou mayest hearken unto the prayer which Thy servant shall make toward this place. And hearken Thou to the supplication of Thy servant, and of Thy people Israel, when they shall pray toward this place: and hear Thou in heaven Thy dwelling place: and when Thou hearest, forgive.

"When Thy people Israel be smitten down before the enemy, because they have sinned against Thee, and shall turn again to Thee, and confess Thy name, and pray, and make supplication unto Thee in this house: then hear Thou in heaven, and forgive the sin of Thy people Israel, and bring them again unto the land which Thou gavest unto their fathers.

"When heaven is shut up, and there is no rain, because they have sinned against Thee; if they pray toward this place, and confess Thy name, and turn from their sin, when Thou afflictest them: then hear Thou in heaven, and forgive the sin of Thy servants, and of Thy people Israel, that Thou teach them the good way wherein they should walk, and give rain upon Thy land, which Thou hast given to Thy people for an inheritance.

"Moreover concerning a stranger, that is not of Thy people Israel, but cometh out of a far country for Thy name's sake; (for they shall hear of Thy great name, and of Thy strong hand, and of Thy stretched out arm;) when he shall come and pray toward this house: hear Thou in heaven Thy dwelling place, and do according to all that the stranger calleth to Thee for: that all people of the earth may know Thy name, to fear Thee, as do Thy people Israel; and that they may know that this house, which I have builded, is called by Thy name.

"If Thy people go out to battle against their enemy, whithersoever Thou shalt send them, and shall pray unto the Lord toward the city which Thou hast chosen, and toward the house that I have built for Thy name: then hear Thou in heaven their prayer and their supplication, and maintain their cause. If they sin against Thee, (for there is no man that sinneth not,) and Thou be angry with them, and deliver them to the enemy, so that they carry them away captives unto the land of the enemy, far or near; yet if they shall bethink themselves in the land whither they were carried captives, and repent, and make supplication unto Thee in the land of them that carried them captives, saying, 'We have sinned, and have done perversely, we have committed wickedness'; and so return unto Thee with all their heart, and with all their soul, in the land of their enemies, which led them away captive, and pray unto Thee toward their land, which Thou gavest unto their fathers, the city which Thou hast chosen, and the house which I have built for Thy name: then hear Thou their prayer and their supplication in heaven Thy dwelling place, and maintain their cause, and forgive Thy people that have sinned against Thee, and all their transgressions wherein they have transgressed against Thee, and give them compassion before them who carried them captive, that they may have compassion on them; for they be Thy people, and Thine inheritance, which Thou broughtest forth out of Egypt, from the midst of the furnace of iron."

[*From* 1 *Kings* viii. 22–51

The Benediction (from Ancient Source)

And it was so, that when Solomon had made an end of praying all this prayer and supplication unto the Lord, he arose from before the altar of the Lord, from kneeling on his knees with his hands spread up to heaven. And he stood, and blessed all the congregation of Israel with a loud voice, saying, "Blessed be the Lord, that hath given rest unto His people Israel, according to all that He promised: there hath not failed one word of all His good promise, which He promised by the hand of Moses His servant. The Lord our God be with us, as He was with our fathers: let Him not leave us, nor forsake us: that He may incline our hearts unto Him, to walk in all His ways, and to keep His commandments, and His statutes, and His judgments, which He commanded our fathers. And let these my words, wherewith I have made supplication before the Lord, be nigh unto the Lord our God day and night, that He maintain the cause of His servant, and the cause of His people Israel at all times, as the matter shall require: that all the people of the earth may know that the Lord is God, and that there is none else. Let your heart therefore be perfect with the Lord our God, to walk in His statutes, and to keep his commandments, as at this day."

[1 *Kings* viii. 54–61

THE QUEEN OF SHEBA

And King Solomon made a navy of ships in Ezion-geber, which is beside Eloth, on the shore of the Red Sea, in the land of Edom. And Hiram sent in the navy his servants, shipmen that had knowledge of the sea, with the servants of Solomon. And they came to Ophir, and fetched from thence gold, four hundred and twenty talents, and brought it to King Solomon.

And when the queen of Sheba heard of the fame of Solomon concerning the name of the Lord, she came to prove him with hard questions. And she came to Jerusalem with a very great train, with camels that bare spices, and very much gold, and precious stones: and when she was come to Solomon, she communed with him of all that was in her heart. And Solomon told her all her questions: there was not any thing hid from the king, which he told her not. And when the queen of Sheba had seen all Solomon's wisdom, and the house that he had built, and the meat of his table, and the sitting of his servants, and the attendance of his ministers, and their apparel, and his cupbearers, and his ascent by which he went up unto the house of the Lord; there was no more spirit in her.

And she said to the king, "It was a true report that I heard in mine own land of thy acts and of thy wisdom. Howbeit I believed not the words, until I came, and mine eyes had seen it: and, behold, the half was not told me: thy wisdom and prosperity exceedeth the fame which I heard. Happy are thy men, happy are these thy servants, which stand continually before thee, and that hear thy wisdom. Blessed be the Lord thy God, which delighted in thee, to set thee on the throne of Israel: because the Lord loved Israel for ever, therefore made He thee king, to do judgment and justice." And she gave the king an hundred and twenty talents of gold, and of spices very great store, and precious stones: there came no more such abundance of spices as these which the queen of Sheba gave to King Solomon. And the navy also of Hiram, that brought gold from Ophir, brought in from Ophir great plenty of almug trees, and precious stones. And the king made of the almug trees pillars for the house of the Lord, and for the king's house, harps also and psalteries for singers: there came no such almug trees, nor were seen unto this day. And King Solomon gave unto the queen of Sheba all her desire, whatsoever she asked, beside that which Solomon gave her of his royal bounty. So she turned and went to her own country, she and her servants.

Moreover the king made a great throne of ivory, and overlaid it with the best gold. The throne had six steps, and the top of the throne was round behind: and there were stays on either side on the place of the seat, and two lions stood beside the stays. And twelve lions stood there on the one side and on the other upon the six steps: there was not the like made in any kingdom.

And all King Solomon's drinking vessels were of gold, and all the vessels of the house of the forest of Lebanon were of pure gold: none were of silver: it was nothing accounted of in the days of Solomon. For the king had at sea a navy of Tharshish with the navy of Hiram: once in three years came the navy of Tharshish, bringing gold and silver, ivory, and apes, and peacocks. So King Solomon exceeded all the kings of the earth for riches and for wisdom. And all the earth sought to Solomon, to hear his wisdom, which God had put in his heart. [1 Kings ix. 26–28, and *from* 1 Kings x

THE DIVISION OF THE KINGDOM

In fact, we have in this story the picture of a most prosperous reign: Solomon appeared to succeed in his attempt to serve both God and Mammon. All too soon, had things continued thus, would the Hebrews have become like to their neighbours and allies, and unfit for their high destiny. Thus we find the prophets approving of the division of the kingdom, realizing that peace and wealth, without honour toward God, were far worse than any ills of poverty and civil warfare. The result of the division was a speedy return in Judah and Jerusalem to a much simpler and more primitive life.

In connection with this, we see in the prophet Ahijah tearing his garment into twelve pieces, a first example of that dramatic action by a prophet, so common later. (Cp. Jeremiah breaking the potter's vessel; see p. 74.)

It is not difficult in the following passages to detect the Deuteronomic Compiler adding the moral to the old stories.

Solomon's Sin and Troubles

But King Solomon loved many strange women, together with the daughter of Pharaoh, women of the Moabites, Ammonites, Edomites,

Zidonians, and Hittites; of the nations concerning which the Lord said unto the children of Israel, "Ye shall not go in to them, neither shall they come in unto you: for surely they will turn away your heart after their gods": Solomon clave unto these in love. It came to pass, when Solomon was old, that his wives turned away his heart after other gods: and his heart was not perfect with the Lord his God, as was the heart of David his father. For Solomon went after Ashtoreth the goddess of the Zidonians, and after Milcom the abomination of the Ammonites. And Solomon did evil in the sight of the Lord, and went not fully after the Lord, as did David his father. Then did Solomon build an high place for Chemosh, the abomination of Moab, in the hill that is before Jerusalem, and for Molech, the abomination of the children of Ammon. And likewise did he do for all his strange wives, which burnt incense and sacrificed unto their gods.

And the Lord was angry with Solomon, because his heart was turned from the Lord God of Israel, which had appeared unto him twice, and had commanded him concerning this thing, that he should not go after other gods: but he kept not that which the Lord commanded. Wherefore the Lord said unto Solomon, "Forasmuch as this is done of thee, and thou hast not kept My covenant and My statutes, which I have commanded thee, I will surely rend the kingdom from thee, and will give it to thy servant. Notwithstanding in thy days I will not do it for David thy father's sake: but I will rend it out of the hand of thy son. Howbeit I will not rend away all the kingdom; but will give one tribe to thy son for David My servant's sake, and for Jerusalem's sake which I have chosen."

And the Lord stirred up an adversary unto Solomon, Hadad the Edomite. And God stirred him up another adversary, Rezon the son of Eliadah;—he was an adversary to Israel all the days of Solomon, beside the mischief that Hadad did: and he abhorred Israel, and reigned over Syria. And Jeroboam the son of Nebat, an Ephrathite of Zereda, Solomon's servant, whose mother's name was Zeruah, a widow woman, even he lifted up his hand against the king.

[1 *Kings* xi. 1–14, 23, 25, 26

Jeroboam and the Ten Tribes of the North

And this was the cause that he lifted up his hand against the king: Solomon built Millo, and repaired the breaches of the city of David his father. And the man Jeroboam was a mighty man of valour: and Solomon seeing the young man that he was industrious, made him ruler over all the charge of the house of Joseph. And it came to pass at that time when Jeroboam went out of Jerusalem, that the prophet Ahijah the Shilonite found him in the way; and he had clad himself with a new garment; and they two were alone in the field: and Ahijah caught the new garment that was on him, and rent it in twelve pieces: and he said to Jeroboam, "Take thee ten pieces: for thus saith the Lord, the God of Israel, 'Behold, I will rend the kingdom out of the hand of Solomon, and will give ten tribes to thee: (but he shall have one tribe for my servant David's sake, and for Jerusalem's sake, the city which I have chosen out of all the tribes of Israel:) because that they have forsaken Me, and have worshipped Ashtoreth, the goddess of the Zidonians, Chemosh the god of the Moabites, and Milcom the god of the children of Ammon, and have not walked in My ways, to do that which is right in Mine eyes, and to keep My statutes and My judgments, as did David his father. Howbeit I will not take the whole kingdom out of his hand: but I will make him a prince all the days of his life for David my servant's sake, whom I chose, because he kept My commandments and My statutes: but I will take the kingdom out of his son's hand, and will give it unto thee, even ten tribes. And unto his son will I give one tribe, that David My servant may have a light alway before Me in Jerusalem, the city which I have chosen Me to put My name there. And I will take thee, and thou shalt reign according to all that thy soul desireth, and shalt be king over Israel. And it shall be, if thou wilt hearken unto all that I command thee, and wilt walk in My ways, and do what is right in My sight, to keep My statutes and My commandments, as David My servant did; that I will be with thee, and build thee a sure house, as I built for David, and will give Israel unto thee. And I will for this afflict the seed of David, but not for ever.' " Solomon sought therefore to kill Jeroboam. And Jeroboam arose, and fled into Egypt, unto Shishak king of Egypt, and was in Egypt until the death of Solomon.

[1 *Kings* xi. 27-40

Death of King Solomon

And the rest of the acts of Solomon and all that he did, and his wisdom, are they not written in the Book of the Acts of Solomon? And the time that Solomon reigned in Jerusalem over all Israel was forty years. And Solomon slept with his fathers, and was buried in the city of David his father: and Rehoboam his son reigned in his stead.

[1 *Kings* xi. 41-43

King Rehoboam' Foolish Conceit

And Rehoboam went to Shechem: for all Israel were come to Shechem to make him king. And it came to pass, when Jeroboam the son of Nebat, who was yet in Egypt, heard of it, (for he was fled from the presence of King Solomon, and Jeroboam dwelt in Egypt;) that they sent and called him. And Jeroboam and all the congregation of Israel came, and spake unto Rehoboam, saying, "Thy father made our yoke grievous: now therefore make thou the grievous service of thy father, and his heavy yoke which he put upon us, lighter, and we will serve thee." And he said unto them, "Depart yet for three days, then come again to me." And the people departed.

And King Rehoboam consulted with the old men, that stood before Solomon his father while he yet lived, and said, "How do ye advise that I may answer this people?" And they spake unto him, saying, "If thou wilt be a servant unto this people this day, and wilt serve them, and answer them, and speak good words to them, then they will be thy servants for ever." But he forsook the counsel of the old men, which they had given him, and consulted with the young men that were grown up with him, and which stood before him: and he said unto them, "What counsel give ye that we may answer this people, who have spoken to me, saying, 'Make the yoke which thy father did put upon us lighter'?" And the young men that were grown up with him spake unto him, saying, "Thus shalt thou speak unto this people that spake unto thee, saying, 'Thy father made our yoke heavy, but make thou it lighter unto us'; thus shalt thou say unto them, 'My little finger shall be thicker than my father's loins. And now whereas my father did lade you with a heavy yoke, I will add to your yoke: my father hath chastised you with whips, but I will chastise you with scorpions.'"

So Jeroboam and all the people came to Rehoboam the third day, as the king had appointed, saying, "Come to me again the third day." And the king answered the people roughly, and forsook the old men's counsel that they gave him; and spake to them after the counsel of the young men, saying, "My father made your yoke heavy, and I will add to your yoke: my father also chastised you with whips, but I will chastise you with scorpions."

[1 *Kings* xii. 1–14

The Rebellion of Israel

So when all Israel saw that the king hearkened not unto them, the people answered the king, saying, "What portion have we in David? Neither have we inheritance in the son of Jesse: to your tents, O Israel: now see to thine own house, David." So Israel departed unto their tents. But as for the children of Israel which dwelt in the cities of Judah, Rehoboam reigned over them. Then King Rehoboam sent Adoram, who was over the tribute; and all Israel stoned him with stones, that he died. Therefore King Rehoboam made speed to get him up to his chariot, to flee to Jerusalem. So Israel rebelled against the house of David unto this day.

[1 *Kings* xii. 16–19

THE TWO KINGDOMS

Certain facts concerning the relative sizes, positions, and resources of the two kingdoms should be noted. In area, Judah was not more than half of Israel, while of arable land she possessed less than one quarter. Judah, however, had a very strong geographical position. To the East was the Dead Sea, a protection against Moabite and Ammonite. To the South stretched the desert (see Map), an effective barrier to all save wandering Arabs. The Philistines, to the West, had ceased to be troublesome. To the North lay Israel, and Israel for two centuries saved the Southern kingdom from the attacks of the two great military powers of the North, Syria and Assyria. Egypt was the only foe to affect Judah seriously, and for the most part Egypt troubled not herself with Canaan. Israel, on the other hand, was open to attack from all sides: her wide valleys led in the conquering hosts. Syria, and later Assyria, swept down upon her, and Egypt did not fail at times to penetrate beyond Judah.

In their occupations too we find a contrast between North and South. Judah was a very rocky country, with soil so poor that it took much labour to extract from it even a scanty livelihood. Water was scarce. There were no natural products which might have led to the development of commerce; the people thus became stay-at-home, hard-working, earnest and strong. Their only occupations were the growing of the vine and the keeping of flocks.

But Israel was much more "a land flowing with milk and honey", rich in springs and very fertile. This both led to commerce and made Israel worth invading. Its people became luxurious (see Amos, p. 32) and were much exposed to foreign influences. Their moral and religious ideals became corrupt. They had no Temple to unite them, no one hereditary line of rulers like the line of David, no great capital like Jerusalem. Finally, they were ten or eleven distinct tribes, some agriculturists, some shepherds, some fishermen, cut off from each other by the natural divisions of their territory. In nearly every way Israel and Judah formed a contrast. The wonder is not that they divided, but that they ever united under one authority.

When Judah lost the tribes of the North, her measure of political success had passed for ever from her grasp. But political success is not the highest good: Judah preserved a better thing. Poverty, tribulation, and the throb of the national love for Jerusalem and the Temple saved her from the corruption of heathendom. The lamp was kept burning even in the darkest hours of later centuries, until a star stood over the house where the young child Jesus was. From the glory and magnificence of Solomon the Great to the Babe lying in a manger, is a long leap: the one had to go before the other could come.

Jeroboam King of Israel

And it came to pass, when all Israel heard that Jeroboam was come again, that they sent and called him unto the congregation, and made him king over all Israel: there was none that followed the house of David, but the tribe of Judah only. And when Rehoboam was come to Jerusalem, he assembled all the house of Judah, with the tribe of Benjamin, an hundred and fourscore thousand chosen men, which were warriors, to fight against the house of Israel, to bring the kingdom again to Rehoboam the son of Solomon. But the word of God came unto Shemaiah the man of God, saying, "Speak unto Rehoboam, the son of Solomon, king of Judah, and unto all the house of Judah and Benjamin, and to the remnant of the people, saying, 'Thus saith the Lord, Ye shall not go up, nor fight against your brethren the children of Israel: return every man to his house; for this thing is from Me.'" They hearkened therefore to the word of the Lord, and returned to depart, according to the word of the Lord.

[1 *Kings* xii. 20-24

Jeroboam's Religious Problem

Then Jeroboam built Shechem in Mount Ephraim, and dwelt therein; and went out from thence, and built Penuel. And Jeroboam said in his heart, "Now shall the kingdom return to the house of David: if this people go up to do sacrifice in the house of the Lord at Jerusalem, then shall the heart of this people turn again unto their lord, even unto Rehoboam king of Judah, and they shall kill me, and go again to Rehoboam king of Judah." Whereupon the king took counsel, and made two calves of gold, and said unto them, "It is too much for you to go up to Jerusalem: behold thy gods, O Israel, which brought thee up out of the land of Egypt." And he set the one in Beth-el, and the other put he in Dan. And this thing became a sin: for the people went to worship before the one, even unto Dan. And he made an house of high places, and made priests of the lowest of the people, which were not of the sons of Levi. And Jeroboam ordained a feast in the eighth month, on the fifteenth day of the month, like unto the feast that is in Judah, and he offered upon the altar. So did he in

Beth-el, sacrificing unto the calves that he had made: and he placed in Beth-el the priests of the high places which he had made. So he offered upon the altar which he had made in Beth-el the fifteenth day of the eighth month, even in the month which he had devised of his own heart; and ordained a feast unto the children of Israel: and he offered upon the altar, and burnt incense.

[1 *Kings* xii. 25–33]

Death of King Jeroboam

And the rest of the acts of Jeroboam, how he warred, and how he reigned, behold, they are written in the Book of the Chronicles of the Kings of Israel. And the days which Jeroboam reigned were two and twenty years: and he slept with his fathers, and Nadab his son reigned in his stead.

[1 *Kings* xiv. 19, 20]

ANCIENT MONUMENTS

The Deuteronomic Compiler has here mentioned by name one of his historical sources, The Book of the Chronicles of the Kings of Israel. It is worth while noting that we have now reached a part of Hebrew history when the stories in the Bible are corroborated by the discoveries of recent excavations and research.

For instance, Gudea, a Babylonian ruler who lived about 2450 B.C., fifteen hundred years before King Solomon, in his account of his work in rebuilding a temple for a certain god, states that he obtained cedar wood from mountains belonging to the same general range as Lebanon. Evidently Solomon not only behaved like other monarchs in undertaking such building, but he obtained his building materials from the same sources. Gudea mentions great cut stones which he had brought from afar and made into pillars. A seal has been found in excavations at Megiddo, inscribed, "Belonging to Shema, servant of Jeroboam." We have no means of knowing whether the Jeroboam referred to is Jeroboam I of whom we have just read, who reigned about 925 B.C., or the wealthy Jeroboam II, in whose reign Amos prophesied, about 760 B.C.

Shishak I (see p. 111), the king of Egypt who invaded and plundered Jerusalem in the reign of Rehoboam, left a long inscription in Egyptian hieroglyphics on the wall of the temple at Karnak, telling of his invasion of Palestine. A most valuable document is the famous Moabite stone, discovered to the East of the Jordan, an inscribed monument of black basalt, now in the Louvre in Paris. It was erected by the Moabite King Mesha (see 2 Kings iii. 4), in commemoration of his victories over the Israelites: it refers to his previous defeats at their hands and corroborates marvellously the accounts given in the Bible. Here is a short quotation:—

I am Mesha, son of Chemoshmelok, king of Moab. My father ruled over Moab thirty years, and I ruled after my father. And I made this high place in Chemosh because of the deliverance of Mesha, because he saved me from all the kings and because he caused me to see (my desire) upon all who hated me. Omri, king of Israel,—he oppressed Moab many days, because Chemosh was angry with his land. And his son succeeded him, and he also said, "I will oppress Moab." In my day he spoke, but I saw (my desire) upon him and upon all his house, and Israel utterly perished for ever.

For other quotations from ancient inscriptions see pp. 114, 137, and 256.

King Rehoboam's Reign and Death

And Rehoboam the son of Solomon reigned in Judah. Rehoboam was forty and one years old when he began to reign, and he reigned seventeen years in Jerusalem, the city which the Lord did choose out of all the tribes of Israel, to put His name there. And his mother's name was Naamah an Ammonitess. And Judah did evil in the sight of the Lord, and they provoked Him to jealousy with their sins which they had committed, above all that their fathers had done. For they also built them high places, and images, and groves, on every high hill, and under every green tree. And they did according to all the abominations of the nations which the Lord cast out before the children of Israel.

And it came to pass in the fifth year of King Rehoboam, that Shishak king of Egypt came up against Jerusalem: and he took away the treasures of the house of the Lord, and the treasures of the king's house; he even took away all: and he took away all the shields of gold which Solomon had made. And King Rehoboam made in their stead brasen shields, and committed them unto the hands of the chief of the guard, which kept the door of the king's house. And it was so, when the king went into the house of the Lord, that the guard bare them, and brought them back into the guard chamber.

Now the rest of the acts of Rehoboam, and all that he did, are they not written in the Book of the Chronicles of the Kings of Judah? And there was war between Rehoboam and Jeroboam all their days. And Rehoboam slept with his fathers, and was buried with his fathers in the city of David. And his mother's name was Naamah an Ammonitess. And Abijam his son reigned in his stead.

[1 *Kings* xiv. 21–31

3. THE LAST TWO CENTURIES OF THE NORTHERN KINGDOM

SOURCES OF INFORMATION USED BY THE DEUTERONOMISTS

The Book of Kings, in recording the history of the next two centuries (the years between the death of Jeroboam in 912 B.C. and the fall of Samaria in 722 B.C.), has to deal with the parallel histories of the two kingdoms. By means of a rather complicated framework the Deuteronomic Compilers shift the stage from one kingdom to the other, describing king by king in turn, his right to the succession, his contemporary in the other kingdom, his attitude to religion, his death and successor. These facts were obtained from The Book of the Chronicles of the Kings of Judah and The Book of the Chronicles of the Kings of Israel, the official annals of the two kingdoms. The Compiler also passes judgment on each king, the nature of the judgment depending on the Deuteronomic views of history and religion.

The record is complicated by the obvious fact that reigns varied in length and a king in Judah did not die at the same moment as his contemporary in Israel: thus the Deuteronomist has to alternate between the two kingdoms. It has proved difficult for scholars to determine exact dates from the material in Kings, but the discovery of Assyrian inscriptions has settled many points. To us only the dates of the most important events matter: we refer the reader to any good modern Bible dictionary or one-volume commentary for a comprehensive article on the Chronology of the Old Testament; these will give the results of scholars' investigations into these matters.

But for intimate knowledge of the affairs of the Northern

THE BOOK OF KINGS

kingdom during the last two centuries of its existence, the Compiler depended on the more vivid, if less accurate, "Acts of Elijah" and "Acts of Elisha" in which an earlier compiler had gathered up the oral traditions about these two early prophets. Impressed by the deep religious value of these sources, the Deuteronomic Compiler has used them without criticism or comment. He had also a history of the Syrian wars. For further light on the period we should refer again to the prophets Amos and Hosea, whose lives fell within the latter half of this period (see p. 30).

THE FOREIGN AFFAIRS OF ISRAEL

The story of Israel's foreign politics lies in her ever-changing relationships with Judah on the South, Syria to the North-East, and, later, Assyria to the East. It is a mesh of war and truce, alliance and counter-alliance, victory and defeat. At one time Syria and Israel together attack Judah; at another, Judah and Israel together attack Syria; at yet another, Judah, Israel and Syria combine to attack Assyria.

Israel's lot was woe when Syria was strong in her attack, and Judah weak or negative in her help. Israel's lines fell in pleasant places when Judah was more or less friendly, Syria crippled by Assyria, and the Assyrians not yet free enough from nearer foes to attack the desirable land of Israel. Israel was laid desolate and her people carried into captivity when the hosts of the Assyrians were at last free for conquest, and not even Egypt could intervene to save. Such is the rough outline of the foreign affairs of Israel in the last decades of their existence as a separate people.

THE KINGS OF ISRAEL

The internal history of Israel we may regard first from a political standpoint and then from a religious one. The main fact, politically, is the instability of its royal line. Time after time the throne was wrested from its rightful successor and fell into the hands of one or other strong man of a different family. Only two houses of kings kept their royal power for any length of time. The one was the house of Omri, to which belongs Omri who built Samaria, a great capital for the Northern kingdom; and Ahab, who made himself strong by alliances with foreign princes and married the fierce Zidonian princess Jezebel. The other was the house of Jehu, who was called by Elisha to the kingdom, who destroyed the worship of Baal in the land, and of whose descendants by far the most prosperous was Jeroboam II. In his reign the Syrians were already crippled and Assyria still so much occupied nearer home as to leave Israel in peace. The dark clouds loomed on the far horizon, but it took a prophet like Amos to discern their meaning.

The last thirty years of the Northern kingdom saw the overthrow of the house of Jehu, and a perpetual story of changing kings, no one able to hold his own for long. Inside and outside, Israel was in deep distress, and her own prophet Hosea, sharing in these sufferings and knowing too the sorrows of his own heart, rose to a new vision of a God of Love, nearer by far to the Father of the Prodigal Son than comes any other vision of God in the Old Testament. And then came the end.

Assyria would have been content with submission and payment of tribute; but some, still seeing hope in Egypt's help, yielded to treachery, with the result that King Hoshea was carried away into captivity, and, after a siege of three years, Samaria fell to the Assyrian King Sargon in 722 B.C. In 2 Kings xvii (see p. 135) we may read the Hebrew account of this calamity. Here is Sargon's own account of the matter, as given in an Assyrian inscription:

At the beginning of my reign, in my first year, Samaria I besieged, I captured. 27,290 people from its midst I carried captive. 50 chariots I took there as an addition to my royal force.... I returned and made more than formerly to dwell. People from lands which my hands had captured I settled in the midst. My officers over them as governors I appointed. Tribute and taxes I imposed upon them after the Assyrian manner.

It appears then that many, but not nearly all of the people were taken away and settled in Assyria, while a mixed foreign population was brought to inhabit the land "flowing with milk and honey". The "ten tribes" were in no sense of the word "lost". Some became gradually embedded in the life of the land whither they went, just as the Normans became embedded in the life of our Saxon England; others intermarried with the foreign settlers brought to Israel and became the ancestors of the sect of Samaritans as known in the days of Christ.

THE RELIGION OF ISRAEL

But why did the Northern kingdom vanish in this way, while Judah maintained in exile a life of her own and returned again to Jerusalem? To answer this, we must study the religious development of Israel.

We have read how Jeroboam I, the first king of the separate Northern kingdom, being cut off from Jerusalem and the Temple worship there, set up high places at Dan and Bethel at which the people might worship, with golden calves as images of Jehovah, and a select circle of men as priests. Unfortunately the worship became contaminated with all sorts of sensual evils: days of sacrifice were an occasion for feasting and for riotous self-indulgence. See Amos for a picture of this.

This low level of worship worked itself out in a very low morality both individual and social. There was no vision of a righteous God to raise the people to the nobler things of which they were capable. Only Amos, the stranger prophet from Judah, pricked the bubble of their apparent prosperity and denounced the evil that is in idle luxury, and in the oppression of the poor by the rich. Not by these things do men and women live. They are the seeds of death wherever found, be it Palestine, Greece, Rome, or a modern state.

ELIJAH, AN OPPONENT OF BAAL

While this slow decadence of religious and moral life gradually undermined the strength of Israel, there came one period when still more dreadful things befel. Ahab married a pagan woman of very strong personality, the famous Queen Jezebel. The daughter of a king who was also a priest of Baal, she set herself to protect and extend the worship of Baal in her adopted land. Ahab himself worshipped both Baal and Jehovah. Even the old idea, one God Jehovah and Israel His chosen people, was in danger. Baal was the god of fertility. As Israel was an agricultural people, it was easy for this worship to become part of their scheme of life.

Then came there from the desert Elijah, the man of God, of whose struggle against Baal-worship we read in this story. He succeeded rather in encouraging the faithful than in exterminating Baal-worship. Not in one day nor by a great display of force are spiritual victories won. So was Elijah taught at Mount Horeb (Sinai) where he found God, not in earthquake or wind or fire, but in "the still small voice" or "voice of stillness". But Elijah accomplished a great work in the inner consciousness of the people. The continuation of that work depended on Elisha.

In conclusion, we may note the importance of the story of Naboth's vineyard. "By their fruits ye shall know them"; this was the fruit of the Baal-worshippers. Probably, as has been said, it did more to unseat the house of Omri than did all their actual worship of Baal.

In what follows, after the Compiler's short account of Omri's important reign (short because of its lack of religious significance) and his introduction of Ahab, note the absence of Deuteronomic comment or criticism in the vivid Elijah narratives.

Omri, King of Israel
Then were the people of Israel divided into two parts: half of the people followed Tibni the son of Ginath, to make him king; and half followed Omri. But the people that followed Omri prevailed against the people that followed Tibni the son of Ginath: so Tibni died, and Omri reigned. In the thirty and first year of Asa king of Judah began Omri to reign over Israel, twelve years: six years reigned he in Tirzah. And he bought the hill Samaria of Shemer for two

talents of silver, and built on the hill, and called the name of the city which he built, after the name of Shemer, owner of the hill, Samaria.

But Omri wrought evil in the eyes of the Lord, and did worse than all that were before him. For he walked in all the way of Jeroboam the son of Nebat, and in his sin wherewith he made Israel to sin, to provoke the Lord God of Israel to anger with their vanities. Now the rest of the acts of Omri which he did, and his might that he shewed, are they not written in the Book of the Chronicles of the Kings of Israel? So Omri slept with his fathers, and was buried in Samaria: and Ahab his son reigned in his stead.

[1 *Kings* xvi. 21–28]

Elijah's Message to the Wicked King Ahab

And in the thirty and eighth year of Asa king of Judah began Ahab the son of Omri to reign over Israel: and Ahab the son of Omri reigned over Israel in Samaria twenty and two years. And Ahab the son of Omri did evil in the sight of the Lord above all that were before him. And it came to pass, as if it had been a light thing for him to walk in the sins of Jeroboam the son of Nebat, that he took to wife Jezebel the daughter of Ethbaal king of the Zidonians, and went and served Baal, and worshipped him. And he reared up an altar for Baal in the house of Baal, which he had built in Samaria. And Ahab made a grove; and Ahab did more to provoke the Lord God of Israel to anger than all the kings of Israel that were before him. And Elijah the Tishbite, who was of the inhabitants of Gilead, said unto Ahab, "As the Lord God of Israel liveth, before whom I stand, there shall not be dew nor rain these years, but according to my word."

[1 *Kings* xvi. 29–33, xvii. 1]

Elijah's Experience during the Long Drought

And the word of the Lord came unto him, saying, "Get thee hence, and turn thee eastward, and hide thyself by the brook Cherith, that is before Jordan. And it shall be that thou shalt drink of the brook; and I have commanded the ravens to feed thee there." So he went and did according unto the word of the Lord: for he went and dwelt by the brook Cherith, that is before Jordan. And the ravens brought him bread and flesh in the morning, and bread and flesh in the evening; and he drank of the brook. And it came to pass after a while, that the brook dried up, because there had been no rain in the land.

And the word of the Lord came unto him, saying, "Arise, get thee to Zarephath, which belongeth to Zidon, and dwell there: behold, I have commanded a widow woman there to sustain thee." So he arose and went to Zarephath. And when he came to the gate of the city, behold, the widow woman was there gathering of sticks: and he called to her, and said, "Fetch me, I pray thee, a little water in a vessel, that I may drink." And as she was going to fetch it, he called to her, and said, "Bring me, I pray thee, a morsel of bread in thine hand." And she said, "As the Lord thy God liveth, I have not a cake, but an handful of meal in a barrel, and a little oil in a cruse: and, behold, I am gathering two sticks, that I may go in and dress it for me and my son, that we may eat it, and die." And Elijah said unto her, "Fear not; go and do as thou hast said: but make me thereof a little cake first, and bring it unto me, and after make for thee and for thy son. For thus saith the Lord God of Israel, 'The barrel of meal shall not waste, neither shall the cruse of oil fail, until the day that the Lord sendeth rain upon the earth.'" And she went and did according to the saying of Elijah: and she, and he, and her house, did eat many days. And the barrel of meal wasted not, neither did the cruse of oil fail, according to the word of the Lord, which he spake by Elijah.

And it came to pass after these things, that the son of the woman, the mistress of the house, fell sick; and his sickness was so sore, that there was no breath left in him. And she said unto Elijah, "What have I to do with thee, O thou man of God? Art thou come unto me to call my sin to remembrance, and to slay my son?" And he said unto her, "Give me thy son." And he took him out of her bosom, and carried him up into a loft, where he abode, and laid him upon his own bed. And he cried unto the Lord, and said, "O Lord my God, hast Thou also brought evil upon the widow with whom I sojourn, by slaying her son?" And he stretched himself upon the child three times, and cried unto the Lord, and said, "O Lord my God, I pray Thee, let this child's soul come into him again." And the Lord heard the voice of Elijah; and the soul of the child came into him again, and he revived. And Elijah took the child, and brought him down out of the chamber into the house, and delivered him unto his mother: and Elijah said, "See, thy son liveth." And the woman said to Elijah, "Now by this I know that thou art a man of God, and that the word of the Lord in thy mouth is truth."

[1 *Kings* xvii. 2–24

Elijah's Return to Samaria

And it came to pass after many days, that the word of the Lord came to Elijah in the third year, saying, "Go, shew thyself unto Ahab; and I will send rain upon the earth." And Elijah went to shew himself unto Ahab. And there was a sore famine in Samaria. And Ahab called Obadiah, which was the governor of his house. (Now Obadiah feared the Lord greatly: for it was so, when Jezebel cut off the prophets of the Lord, that Obadiah took an hundred prophets, and hid them by fifty in a cave, and fed them with bread and water.) And Ahab said unto Obadiah, "Go into the land, unto all fountains of water, and unto all brooks: peradventure we may find grass to save the horses and mules alive, that we lose not all the beasts." So they divided the land between them to pass throughout it: Ahab

went one way by himself, and Obadiah went another way by himself.
And as Obadiah was in the way, behold, Elijah met him: and he knew him, and fell on his face, and said, "Art thou that my lord Elijah?" And he answered him, "I am: go, tell thy lord, 'Behold, Elijah is here.' " And he said, "What have I sinned, that thou wouldest deliver thy servant into the hand of Ahab, to slay me? As the Lord thy God liveth, there is no nation or kingdom, whither my lord hath not sent to seek thee: and when they said, 'He is not there'; he took an oath of the kingdom and nation, that they found thee not. And now thou sayest, 'Go, tell thy lord, Behold, Elijah is here.' And it shall come to pass, as soon as I am gone from thee, that the Spirit of the Lord shall carry thee whither I know not; and so when I come and tell Ahab, and he cannot find thee, he shall slay me: but I thy servant fear the Lord from my youth. Was it not told my lord what I did when Jezebel slew the prophets of the Lord, how I hid an hundred men of the Lord's prophets by fifty in a cave, and fed them with bread and water? And now thou sayest, 'Go, tell thy lord, Behold, Elijah is here': and he shall slay me." And Elijah said, "As the Lord of hosts liveth, before whom I stand, I will surely shew myself unto him to-day." So Obadiah went to meet Ahab, and told him: and Ahab went to meet Elijah.

[1 *Kings* xviii. 1–16

Elijah's Victory on Mount Carmel

And it came to pass, when Ahab saw Elijah, that Ahab said unto him, "Art thou he that troubleth Israel?" And he answered, "I have not troubled Israel; but thou, and thy father's house, in that ye have forsaken the commandments of the Lord, and thou hast followed Baalim. Now therefore send, and gather to me all Israel unto Mount Carmel, and the prophets of Baal four hundred and fifty, and the prophets of the groves four hundred, which eat at Jezebel's table." So Ahab sent unto all the children of Israel, and gathered the prophets together unto Mount Carmel.

And Elijah came unto all the people, and said, "How long halt ye between two opinions? If the Lord be God, follow Him: but if Baal, then follow him." And the people answered him not a word. Then said Elijah unto the people, "I, even I, only remain a prophet of the Lord; but Baal's prophets are four hundred and fifty men. Let them therefore give us two bullocks; and let them choose one bullock for themselves, and cut it in pieces, and lay it on wood, and put no fire under: and I will dress the other bullock, and lay it on wood, and put no fire under: and call ye on the name of your gods, and I will call on the name of the Lord: and the God that answereth by fire, let Him be God." And all the people answered and said, "It is well spoken." And Elijah said unto the prophets of Baal, "Choose you one bullock for yourselves, and dress it first; for ye are many; and call on the name of your gods, but put no fire under."

And they took the bullock which was given them, and they dressed it, and called on the name of Baal from morning even until noon, saying, "O Baal, hear us." But there was no voice, nor any that answered. And they leaped upon the altar which was made. And it came to pass at noon, that Elijah mocked them, and said, "Cry aloud: for he is a god; either he is talking, or he is pursuing, or he is in a journey, or peradventure he sleepeth, and must be awaked." And they cried aloud, and cut themselves after their manner with knives and lancets, till the blood gushed out upon them. And it came to pass, when midday was past, and they prophesied until the time of the offering of the evening sacrifice, that there was neither voice, nor any to answer, nor any that regarded.

And Elijah said unto all the people, "Come near unto me." And all the people came near unto him. And he repaired the altar of the Lord that was broken down. And Elijah took twelve stones, according to the number of the tribes of the sons of Jacob, unto whom the word of the Lord came, saying, "Israel shall be thy name": and with the stones he built an altar in the name of the Lord: and he made a trench about the altar, as great as would contain two measures of seed. And he put the wood in order, and cut the bullock in pieces, and laid him on the wood, and said, "Fill four barrels with water, and pour it on the burnt sacrifice, and on the wood." And he said, "Do it the second time." And they did it the second time. And he said, "Do it the third time." And they did it the third time. And the water ran round about the altar; and he filled the trench also with water.

And it came to pass at the time of the offering of the evening sacrifice, that Elijah the prophet came near, and said, "Lord God of Abraham, Isaac, and of Israel, let it be known this day that Thou art God in Israel, and that I am Thy servant, and that I have done all these things at Thy word. Hear me, O Lord, hear me, that this people may know that Thou art the Lord God, and that Thou has turned their heart back again." Then the fire of the Lord fell, and consumed the burnt sacrifice, and the wood and the stones, and the dust, and licked up the water that was in the trench. And when all the people saw it, they fell on their faces: and they said, "The Lord, He is the God; the Lord, He is the God." And Elijah said unto them, "Take the prophets of Baal; let not one of them escape." And they took them: and Elijah brought them down to the brook Kishon, and slew them there.

And Elijah said unto Ahab, "Get thee up, eat and drink; for there is a sound of abundance of rain." So Ahab went up to eat and to drink. And Elijah went up to the top of Carmel; and he cast himself down upon the earth, and put his face between his knees, and said to his servant, "Go up now, look toward the sea." And he went up, and looked, and said, "There is nothing." And he said, "Go again seven times." And it came to pass at the seventh time, that he said, "Behold, there ariseth a little cloud out of the sea, like a man's hand." And he said, "Go up, say unto Ahab, 'Prepare thy chariot, and get thee down, that the rain stop thee not.' " And it came to pass in the meanwhile, that the heaven was black with clouds and wind, and there was a great rain. And Ahab rode, and went to Jezreel. And the hand of the Lord was on Elijah; and he girded up his loins, and ran before Ahab to the entrance to Jezreel.

[1 *Kings* xviii. 17–46

Elijah's Flight from Jezebel

And Ahab told Jezebel all that Elijah had done, and withal how he had slain all the prophets with the sword. Then Jezebel sent a messenger unto Elijah, saying, "So let the gods do to me, and more also, if I make not thy life as the life of one of them by to-morrow about this time." And when he saw that, he arose, and went for his life, and came to Beer-sheba, which belongeth to Judah, and left his servant there.

But he himself went a day's journey into the wilderness, and came and sat down under a juniper tree: and he requested for himself that he might die; and said, "It is enough; now, O Lord, take away my life; for I am not better than my fathers." And as he lay and slept under a juniper tree, behold, then an angel touched him, and said unto him, "Arise and eat." And he looked, and, behold, there was a cake baken on the coals, and a cruse of water at his head. And he did eat and drink, and laid him down again. And the angel of the Lord came again the second time, and touched him, and said, "Arise and eat; because the journey is too great for thee." And he arose, and did eat and drink, and went in the strength of that meat forty days and forty nights unto Horeb the mount of God.

And he came thither unto a cave, and lodged there; and, behold, the word of the Lord came to him, and He said unto him, "What doest thou here, Elijah?" And he said, "I have been very jealous for the Lord God of hosts: for the children of Israel have forsaken Thy covenant, thrown down Thine altars, and slain Thy prophets with the sword; and I, even I only, am left; and they seek my life, to take it away." And He said, "Go forth, and stand upon the mount before the Lord." And, behold, the Lord passed by, and a great and strong wind rent the mountains, and brake in pieces the rocks before the Lord; but the Lord was not in the wind: and after the wind an earthquake; but the Lord was not in the earthquake: and after the earthquake a fire; but the Lord was not in the fire: and after the fire a still small voice. And it was so, when Elijah heard it, that he wrapped his face in his mantle, and went out, and stood in the entering in of the cave.

And, behold, there came a voice unto him, and said, "What doest thou here, Elijah?" And he said, "I have been very jealous for the Lord God of hosts: because the children of Israel have forsaken Thy covenant, thrown down Thine altars, and slain Thy prophets with the sword; and I, even I only, am left; and they seek my life, to take it away." And the Lord said unto him, "Elisha the son of Shaphat of Abelmeholah shalt thou anoint to be prophet in thy room. Yet I have left me seven thousand in Israel, all the knees which have not bowed unto Baal, and every mouth which hath not kissed him."

[From 1 *Kings* xix. 1–18

The Call of Elisha

So he departed thence, and found Elisha the son of Shaphat, who was plowing with twelve yoke of oxen before him, and he with the twelfth: and Elijah passed by him, and cast his mantle upon him. And he left the oxen, and ran after Elijah, and said, "Let me, I pray thee, kiss my father and my mother, and then I will follow thee." And he said unto him, "Go back again: for what have I done to thee?" And he returned back from him, and took a yoke of oxen, and slew them, and boiled their flesh with the instruments of the oxen, and gave unto the people, and they did eat. Then he arose, and went after Elijah, and ministered unto him.

[1 *Kings* xix. 19–21

Naboth's Vineyard

And it came to pass after these things, that Naboth the Jezreelite had a vineyard, which was in Jezreel, hard by the palace of Ahab king of Samaria. And Ahab spake unto Naboth, saying, "Give me thy vineyard, that I may have it for a garden of herbs, because it is near unto my house: and I will give thee for it a better vineyard than it; or, if it seem good to thee, I will give the worth of it in money." And Naboth said to Ahab, "The Lord forbid it me, that I should give the inheritance of my fathers unto thee."

And Ahab came into his house heavy and displeased because of the word which Naboth the Jezreelite had spoken to him: for he had said, "I will not give thee the inheritance of my fathers." And he laid him down upon his bed, and turned away his face, and would eat no bread. But Jezebel his wife came to him, and said unto him, "Why is thy spirit so sad, that thou eatest no bread?" And he said unto her, "Because I spake unto Naboth the Jezreelite, and said unto him, 'Give me thy vineyard for money; or else, if it please thee, I will give thee another vineyard for it': and he answered, 'I will not give thee my vineyard.'" And Jezebel his wife said unto him, "Dost thou now govern the kingdom of Israel? Arise, and eat bread, and let thine heart be merry: I will give thee the vineyard of Naboth the Jezreelite."

So she wrote letters in Ahab's name, and sealed them with his seal, and sent the letters unto the elders and to the nobles that were in his city, dwelling with Naboth. And she wrote in the letters, saying, "Proclaim a fast, and set Naboth on high among the people: and set two men, sons of Belial, before him, to bear witness against him, saying, "Thou didst blaspheme God and the king.' And then carry him out, and stone him, that he may die." And the men of his city, even the elders and the nobles who were the inhabitants in his city, did as Jezebel had sent unto them, and as it was written in the letters which she had sent unto them.

They proclaimed a fast, and set Naboth on high among the people. And there came in two men, children of Belial, and sat before him: and the men of Belial witnessed against him, even against Naboth, in the presence of the people, saying, "Naboth did blaspheme God and the king." Then they carried him forth out of the city, and stoned him with stones, that he died. Then they sent to Jezebel, saying, "Naboth is stoned, and is dead."

And it came to pass, when Jezebel heard that Naboth was stoned, and was dead, that Jezebel said to Ahab, "Arise, take possession of the vineyard of Naboth the Jezreelite, which he refused to give thee for money, for Naboth is not alive, but dead." And it came to pass when Ahab heard that Naboth was dead, that Ahab rose up to go down to the vineyard of Naboth the Jezreelite, to take possession of it.

Now the rest of the acts of Ahab, and all that he did, and the ivory house which he made, and all the cities that he built, are they not written in the Book of the Chronicles of the Kings of Israel? So Ahab slept with his fathers; and Ahaziah his son reigned in his stead.

[1 *Kings* xxi. 1–16, xxii. 39, 40

The Passing of Elijah

And it came to pass, when the Lord would take up Elijah into heaven by a whirlwind, that Elijah went with Elisha from Gilgal. And Elijah said unto Elisha, "Tarry here, I pray thee; for the Lord hath sent me to Beth-el." And Elisha said unto him, "As the Lord liveth, and as thy soul liveth, I will not leave thee." So they went down to Beth-el. And the sons of the prophets that were at Beth-el came forth to Elisha, and said unto him, "Knowest thou that the Lord will take away thy master from thy head to-day?" And he said, "Yea, I know it; hold ye your peace." And Elijah said unto him, "Elisha, tarry here, I pray thee; for the Lord hath sent me to Jericho." And he said, "As the Lord liveth, and as thy soul liveth, I will not leave thee." So they came to Jericho. And the sons of the prophets that were at Jericho came to Elisha, and said unto him, "Knowest thou that the Lord will take away thy master from thy head to-day?" And he answered, "Yea, I know it; hold ye your peace." And Elijah said unto him, "Tarry, I pray thee, here; for the Lord hath sent me to Jordan." And he said, "As the Lord liveth, and as thy soul liveth, I will not leave thee." And they two went on. And fifty men of the sons of the prophets went, and stood to view afar off; and they two stood by Jordan. And Elijah took his mantle, and wrapped it together, and smote the waters, and they were divided hither and thither, so that they two went over on dry ground. And it came to pass, when they were gone over, that Elijah said unto Elisha, "Ask what I shall do for thee, before I be taken away from thee." And Elisha said, "I pray thee, let a double portion of thy spirit be upon me." And he said, "Thou hast asked a hard thing: nevertheless, if thou see me when I am taken from thee, it shall be so unto thee; but if not, it shall not be so." And it came to pass, as they still went on, and talked, that, behold, there appeared a chariot of fire, and horses of fire, and parted them both asunder; and Elijah went up by a whirlwind into heaven.

[2 *Kings* ii. 1–11

Elisha, the Prophet-Friend

Elisha was Elijah's successor in prophetic work for Israel. But the only likeness between the two men lay in their devotion to Jehovah, their insight into His ways with Israel, and their great faith in the Unseen which resulted, so these old stories tell us, in wonders of diverse kinds.

Elijah was a solitary, rugged figure who came from the wild lands to the East of the Jordan, and in days of stress retired South to the desert, even to Mount Sinai. His work for God was done by direct combat with the forces of evil, as summed up in the royal family and their Baal-priests. The woman whose oil and meal he replenished was not of his own people. Dignity and mystery surrounded him: he came and went in strange ways, and the close of his life was wrapt in mystery.

Elisha, on the other hand, is seldom found alone; either he is clinging to the company of Elijah, or dwelling with "the sons of the prophets", a reference to the guilds of prophets (see p. 212). He does not directly challenge the forces of evil in the land, but he deliberately plans for a change in the kingship to take from the family of Ahab its power for evil. To accomplish this, he both encourages an imminent revolution in Syria, under Hazael, and, by deputy, anoints Jehu as the new king of Israel. He is found helping the kings in their difficulties, as when he lets the king know of the places where the Syrians lie in wait. He works through other men rather than alone.

Throughout we see the humanity of the man and the friendliness of the prophet. His dealings with a woman in debt, a man in trouble over losing a borrowed axe, a mother of a sick child, a Syrian officer smitten with leprosy—these are instances of Elisha's response to all sorts and conditions of men.

It should be noted that it is no uncommon thing in the desert to secure water by digging holes in the sand. The Moabite King Mesha is he whose inscription was quoted on p. 111.

Jehoram King of Israel

Now Jehoram the son of Ahab began to reign over Israel in Samaria the eighteenth year of Jehoshaphat king of Judah, and reigned twelve years. And he wrought evil in the sight of the Lord; but not like his father, and like his mother: for he put away the image of Baal that his father had made. Nevertheless he cleaved unto the sins of Jeroboam the son of Nebat, which made Israel to sin; he departed not therefrom.

[2 *Kings* iii. 1-3

Israel, Judah and Edom war with Moab

And Mesha king of Moab was a sheepmaster, and rendered unto the king of Israel an hundred thousand lambs, and an hundred thousand rams, with the wool. But it came to pass, when Ahab was dead, that the king of Moab rebelled against the king of Israel. And King Jehoram went out of Samaria the same time, and numbered all Israel. And he went and sent to Jehoshaphat the king of Judah, saying, "The king of Moab hath rebelled against me: wilt thou go with me against Moab to battle?" And he said, "I will go up: I am as thou art, my people as thy people, and my horses as thy horses." And he said, "Which way shall we go up?" And he answered, "The way through the wilderness of Edom."

So the king of Israel went, and the king of Judah, and the king of Edom: and they fetched a compass of seven days' journey: and there was no water for the host, and for the cattle that followed them. And the king of Israel said, "Alas! that the Lord hath called these three kings together, to deliver them into the hand of Moab!" But Jehoshaphat said, "Is there not here a prophet of the Lord, that we may enquire of the Lord by him?" And one of the king of Israel's servants answered and said, "Here is Elisha the son of Shaphat, which poured water on the hands of Elijah." And Jehoshaphat said, "The word of the Lord is with him." So the king of Israel and Jehoshaphat and the kng of Edom went down to him. And Elisha said unto the king of Israel, "What have I to do with thee? Get thee to the prophets of thy father, and to the prophets of thy mother." And the king of Israel said unto him, "Nay: for the Lord hath called these three kings together, to deliver them into the hand of Moab." And Elisha said, "As the Lord of hosts liveth, before whom I stand, surely, were it not that I regard the presence of Jehoshaphat the king of Judah, I would not look toward thee, nor see thee. But now bring me a minstrel." And it came to pass, when the minstrel played, that the hand of the Lord came upon him. And he said, "Thus saith the Lord, 'Make this valley full of ditches.' For thus saith the Lord, 'Ye shall not see wind, neither shall ye see rain; yet that valley shall be filled with water, that ye may drink, both ye, and your cattle, and your beasts.' And this is but a light thing in the sight of the Lord: he will deliver the Moabites also into your hand. And ye shall smite every fenced city, and every choice city, and shall fell every good tree, and stop all wells of water, and mar every good piece of land with stones." And it came to pass in the morning, when the meat offering was offered, that, behold, there came water by the way of Edom, and the country was filled with water.

And when all the Moabites heard that the kings were come up to fight against them, they gathered all that were able to put on armour, and upward, and stood in the border. And they rose up early in the morning, and the sun shone upon the water, and the Moabites saw the water on the other side as red as blood: and they said, "This is blood: the kings are surely slain, and they have smitten one another: now therefore, Moab, to the spoil." And when they came to the camp of Israel, the Israelites rose up and smote the Moabites, so that they fled before them: but they went forward smiting the Moabites, even in their country.

[2 *Kings* iii. 4-24]

Help for a Woman in Debt

Now there cried a certain woman of the wives of the sons of the prophets unto Elisha, saying, "Thy servant my husband is dead; and thou knowest that thy servant did fear the Lord: and the creditor is come to take unto him my two sons to be bondmen." And Elisha said unto her, "What shall I do for thee? Tell me, what hast thou in the house?" And she said, "Thine handmaid hath not anything in the house, save a pot of oil." Then he said, "Go, borrow thee vessels abroad of all thy neighbours, even empty vessels; borrow not a few. And when thou art come in, thou shalt shut the door upon thee and upon thy sons, and shalt pour out into all those vessels, and thou shalt set aside that which is full." So she went from him, and shut the door upon her and upon her sons, who brought the vessels to her; and she poured out. And it came to pass, when the vessels were full, that she said unto her son, "Bring me yet a vessel." And he said unto her, "There is not a vessel more." And the oil stayed. Then she came and told the man of God. And he said, "Go, sell the oil, and pay thy debt, and live thou and thy children of the rest."

[2 *Kings* iv. 1-7]

Help for a Mother and her Child

And it fell on a day, that Elisha passed to Shunem, where was a great woman; and she constrained him to eat bread. And so it was, that as oft as he passed by, he turned in thither to eat bread. And she said unto her husband, "Behold now, I perceive that this is an holy man of God, which passeth by us continually. Let us make a little chamber, I pray thee, on the wall; and let us set for him there a bed, and a table, and a stool, and a candlestick: and it shall be, when he cometh to us, that he shall turn in thither." And it fell on a day, that he came thither, and he turned into the chamber, and lay there. And he said to Gehazi his servant, "Call this Shunammite." And when he had called her, she stood before him. And he said unto him, "Say now unto her, 'Behold, thou hast been careful for us with all this care; what is to be done for thee? Wouldest thou be spoken for to the king, or to the captain of the host?' " And she answered, "I dwell among mine own people." And he said, "What then is to be done for her?" And Gehazi answered, "Verily she hath no child, and her husband is old." And he said, "Call her." And when he had called her, she stood in the door. And he said, "About this season, according to the time of life, thou shalt embrace a son." And she said, "Nay, my lord, thou man of God, do not lie unto thine handmaid." And the woman bare a son at that season that Elisha had said unto her, according to the time of life.

And when the child was grown, it fell on a day, that he went out to his father to the reapers. And he said unto his father, "My head, my head." And he said to a lad, "Carry him to his mother." And when he had taken him, and brought him to his mother, he sat on her knees till noon, and then died. And she went up, and laid him on the bed of the man of God, and shut the door upon him, and went out. And she called unto her husband, and said, "Send me, I pray thee, one of the young men, and one of the asses, that I may run to the man of God, and come again." And he said, "Wherefore wilt thou go to him to-day? It is neither new moon, nor sabbath." And she said, "It shall be well." Then she saddled an ass, and said to her servant, "Drive, and go forward; slack not thy riding for me, except I bid thee."

So she went and came unto the man of God to Mount Carmel. And it came to pass, when the man of God saw her afar off, that he said to Gehazi his servant, "Behold, yonder is that Shunammite: run now, I pray thee, to meet her, and say unto her, 'Is it well with thee? Is it well with thy husband? Is it well with the child?' " And she answered, "It is well." And when she came to the man of God to the hill, she caught him by the feet: but Gehazi came near to thrust her away. And the man of God said, "Let her alone; for her soul is vexed within her: and the Lord hath hid it from me, and hath not told me." Then she said, "Did I desire a son of my lord? Did I not say, 'Do not deceive me'?" Then he said to Gehazi, "Gird up thy loins, and take my staff in thine hand, and go thy way: if thou meet any man, salute him not; and if any salute thee, answer him not again: and lay my staff upon the face of the child." And the mother of the child said, "As the Lord liveth, and as thy soul liveth, I will not leave thee." And he arose, and followed her.

And Gehazi passed on before them, and laid the staff upon the face of the child; but there was neither voice, nor hearing. Wherefore he went again to meet him, and told him, saying, "The child is not awaked." And when Elisha was come into the house, behold, the child was dead, and laid upon his bed. He went in therefore, and shut the door upon them twain, and prayed unto the Lord. And he went up, and lay upon the child, and put his mouth upon his mouth, and his eyes upon his eyes, and his hands upon his hands; and he stretched himself upon the child; and the flesh of the child waxed warm. Then he returned, and walked in the house to and fro; and went up, and stretched himself upon him: and the child sneezed seven times, and the child opened his eyes. And he called Gehazi, and said, "Call this Shunammite." So he called her. And when she was come in unto him, he said, "Take up thy son." Then she went in, and fell at his feet, and bowed herself to the ground, and took up her son, and went out.

[2 *Kings* iv. 8–37

Help for a Woodman in Trouble

And the sons of the prophets said unto Elisha, "Behold now, the place where we dwell with thee is too strait for us. Let us go, we pray thee, unto Jordan, and take thence every man a beam, and let us make us a place there, where we may dwell." And he answered, "Go ye." And one said, "Be content, I pray thee, and go with thy servants." And he answered, "I will go." So he went with them. And when they came to Jordan, they cut down wood. But as one was felling a beam, the axe head fell into the water: and he cried, and said, "Alas, master! for it was borrowed." And the man of God said, "Where fell it?" And he shewed him the place. And he cut down a stick, and cast it in thither; and the iron did swim. Therefore said he, "Take it up to thee." And he put out his hand, and took it.

[2 *Kings* vi. 1–7

Help for a Syrian Leper

Now Naaman, captain of the host of the king of Syria, was a great man with his master, and honourable, because by him the Lord had given deliverance unto Syria: he was also a mighty man in valour, but he was a leper. And the Syrians had gone out by companies, and had brought away captive out of the land of Israel a little maid; and she waited on Naaman's wife. And she said unto her mistress, "Would God my lord were with the prophet that is in Samaria! He would recover him of his leprosy." And one went in, and told his lord, saying, "Thus and thus said the maid that is of the land of Israel."

And the king of Syria said, "Go to, go, and I will send a letter unto the king of Israel." And he departed, and took with him ten talents of silver, and six thousand pieces of gold, and ten changes of raiment. And he brought the letter to the king of Israel, saying, "Now when this letter is come unto thee, behold, I have therewith sent Naaman my servant to thee, that thou mayest recover him of his leprosy." And it came to pass, when the king of Israel had read the letter, that he rent his clothes, and said, "Am I God, to kill and to make alive, that this man doth send unto me to recover a man of his leprosy? Wherefore consider, I pray you, and see how he seeketh a quarrel against me."

And it was so, when Elisha the man of God had heard that the king of Israel had rent his clothes, that he sent to the king, saying, "Wherefore hast thou rent thy clothes? Let him come now to me, and he shall know that there is a prophet in Israel." So Naaman came with his horses and with his chariot, and stood at the door of the house of Elisha. And Elisha sent a messenger unto him, saying, "Go and wash in Jordan seven times, and thy flesh shall come again to thee, and thou shalt be clean."

But Naaman was wroth, and went away, and said, "Behold, I thought, he will surely come out to me, and stand, and call on the name of the Lord his God, and strike his hand over the place, and recover the leper. Are not Abana and Pharpar, rivers of Damascus, better than all the waters of Israel? May I not wash in them, and be clean?" So he turned and went away in a rage. And his servants came near and spake unto him, and said, "My father, if the prophet had bid thee do some great thing, wouldest thou not have done it? How much rather then, when he saith to thee, 'Wash, and be clean'?" Then went he down, and dipped himself seven times in Jordan, according to the saying of the man of God: and his flesh came again like unto the flesh of a little child, and he was clean.

And he returned to the man of God, he and all his company, and came, and stood before him: and he said, "Behold, now I know that there is no God in all the earth, but in Israel: now therefore, I pray thee, take a blessing of thy servant." But he said, "As the Lord liveth, before whom I stand, I will receive none." And he urged him to take it, but he refused. And Naaman said, "Shall there not then, I pray thee, be given to thy servant two mules' burden of earth? Thy servant will henceforth offer neither burnt offering nor sacrifice unto other gods, but unto the Lord. In this thing the Lord pardon thy servant, that when my master goeth into the house of Rimmon to worship there, and he leaneth on my hand, and I bow myself in the house of Rimmon: when I bow down myself in the house of Rimmon, the Lord pardon thy servant in this thing." And he said unto him, "Go in peace." So he departed from him a little way.

But Gehazi, the servant of Elisha, the man of God, said, "Behold, my master hath spared Naaman this Syrian, in not receiving at his hands that which he brought: but, as the Lord liveth, I will run after him, and take somewhat of him." So Gehazi followed after Naaman. And when Naaman saw him running after him, he lighted down from the chariot to meet him, and said, "Is all well?" And he said, "All is well. My master hath sent me, saying, 'Behold, even now there be come to me from Mount Ephraim two young men of the sons of the prophets: give them, I pray thee, a talent of silver, and two changes of garments.'" And Naaman said, "Be content, take two talents." And he urged him, and bound two talents of silver in two bags, with two changes of garments, and laid them upon two of his servants; and they bare them before him. And when he came to the tower, he took them from their hand, and bestowed them in the house: and he let the men go, and they departed.

But he went in and stood before his master. And Elisha said unto him, "Whence comest thou, Gehazi?" And he said, "Thy servant went no whither." And he said unto him, "Went not mine heart with thee, when the man turned again from his chariot to meet thee? Is it a time to receive money, and to receive garments, and oliveyards, and vineyards, and sheep, and oxen, and menservants, and maidservants? The leprosy therefore of Naaman shall cleave unto thee, and unto thy seed for ever." And he went out from his presence a leper as white as snow.

[2 *Kings* v. 1–27

Elisha in Danger from the Syrians

Then the king of Syria warred against Israel, and took counsel with his servants, saying, "In such and such a place shall be my camp." And the man of God sent unto the king of Israel, saying, "Beware that thou pass not such a place; for thither the Syrians are come down." And the king of Israel sent to the place which the man of God told him and warned him of, and saved himself there, not once nor twice.

Therefore the heart of the king of Syria was sore troubled for this thing; and he called his servants, and said unto them, "Will ye not shew me which of us is for the king of Israel?" And one of his servants said, "None, my lord, O king: but Elisha, the prophet that is in Israel, telleth the king of Israel the words that thou speakest in thy bedchamber." And he said, "Go and spy where he is, that I may send and fetch him." And it was told him, saying, "Behold, he is in Dothan." Therefore sent he thither horses, and chariots, and a great host: and they came by night, and compassed the city about.

And when the servant of the man of God was risen early, and gone forth, behold, an host compassed the city both with horses and chariots. And his servant said unto him, "Alas, my master! How shall we do?" And he answered, "Fear not: for they that be with us are more than they that be with them." And Elisha prayed, and said, "Lord, I pray Thee, open his eyes, that he may see." And the Lord opened the eyes of the young man; and he saw: and behold, the mountain was full of horses and chariots of fire round about Elisha.

And when they came down to him, Elisha prayed unto the Lord, and said, "Smite this people, I pray thee, with blindness." And He smote them with blindness according to the word of Elisha. And Elisha said unto them, "This is not the way, neither is this the city: follow me, and I will bring you to the man whom ye seek." But he led them to Samaria. And it came to pass, when they were come into Samaria, that Elisha said, "Lord, open the eyes of these men, that they may see." And the Lord opened their eyes, and they saw; and, behold, they were in the midst of Samaria. And the king of Israel said unto Elisha, when he saw them, "My father, shall I smite them? Shall I smite them?" And he answered, "Thou shalt not smite them: wouldest thou smite those whom thou hast taken captive with thy sword and with thy bow? Set bread and water before them, that they may eat and drink, and go to their master." And he prepared great provision for them: and when they had eaten and drunk, he sent them away, and they went to their master. So the bands of Syria came no more into the land of Israel.

[2 *Kings* vi. 8–23

The narrative goes on to tell of the siege of Samaria by the Syrians and of its deliverance by reason of a panic that fell upon the foe (2 Kings vi. 24 to vii. 20); of Elisha visiting Damascus and coming into contact with the Syrian King Hazael (2 Kings viii. 7–15); of the Syrians wounding in battle Joram king of Israel, and of the visit to the wounded king of Ahaziah king of Judah, himself a descendant of Omri on his mother's side (2 Kings viii. 25–29). Then follows this vivid narrative which tells of the rise of Jehu and the fall of the house of Omri. We note how, for the sake of vengeance, the corpse of Joram is thrown on to the plot of land that once was the vineyard of Naboth.

Jehu seizes the Throne of Israel

And Elisha the prophet called one of the children of the prophets, and said unto him, "Gird up thy loins, and take this box of oil in thine hand, and go to Ramoth-gilead: and when thou comest thither, look out there Jehu the son of Jehoshaphat the son of Nimshi, and go in, and make him arise up from among his brethren, and carry him to an inner chamber; then take the box of oil, and pour it on his head, and say, 'Thus saith the Lord, I have anointed thee king over Israel.' Then open the door, and flee, and tarry not."

So the young man, even the young man the prophet, went to Ramoth-gilead. And when he came, behold, the captains of the host were sitting; and he said, "I have an errand to thee, O captain." And Jehu said, "Unto which of all of us?" And he said, "To thee, O captain." And he arose, and went into the house; and he poured the oil on his head, and said unto him, "Thus saith the Lord God of Israel, 'I have anointed thee king over the people of the Lord, even over Israel. And thou shalt smite the house of Ahab thy master, that I may avenge the blood of My servants the prophets, and the blood of all the servants of the Lord, at the hand of Jezebel.' "

Then Jehu came forth to the servants of his lord: and one said unto him, "Is all well? Wherefore came this mad fellow to thee?" And he said unto them, "Ye know the man, and his communication." And they said, "It is false; tell us now." And he said, "Thus and thus spake he to me, saying, 'Thus saith the Lord, I have anointed thee king over Israel.' " Then they hasted, and took every man his garment, and put it under him on the top of the stairs, and blew with trumpets, saying, "Jehu is king." So Jehu the son of Jehoshaphat the son of Nimshi conspired against Joram. (Now Joram had kept Ramoth-gilead, he and all Israel, because of Hazael king of Syria. But King Joram was returned to be healed in Jezreel of the wounds which the Syrians had given him, when he fought with Hazael king of Syria.) And Jehu said, "If it be your minds, then let none go forth nor escape out of the city to go to tell it in Jezreel."

So Jehu rode in a chariot, and went to Jezreel; for Joram lay there. And Ahaziah king of Judah was come down to see Joram. And there stood a watchman on the tower in Jezreel, and he spied the company of Jehu as he came, and said, "I see a company." And Joram said, "Take an horseman, and send to meet them, and let him say, 'Is it peace?' " So there went one on horseback to meet him, and said, "Thus saith the king, 'Is it peace?' " And Jehu said, "What hast thou to do with peace? Turn thee behind me." And the watchman told, saying, "The messenger came to them, but he cometh not again." Then he sent out a second on horseback, which came to them, and said, "Thus saith the king, 'Is it peace?' " And Jehu answered, "What hast thou to do with peace? Turn thee behind me." And the watchman told, saying, "He came even unto them, and cometh not again: and the driving is like the driving of Jehu the son of Nimshi; for he driveth furiously." And Joram said, "Make ready." And his chariot was made ready. And Joram king of Israel and Ahaziah king of Judah went out, each in his chariot, and they went out against Jehu, and met him in the portion of Naboth the Jezreelite. And it came to pass, when Joram saw Jehu, that he said, "Is it peace, Jehu?" And he answered, "What peace, so long as the whoredoms of thy mother Jezebel and her witchcrafts are so many?" And Joram turned his hands, and fled, and said to Ahaziah, "There is treachery, O Ahaziah." And Jehu drew a bow with his full strength and smote Joram between his arms, and the arrow went out at his heart, and he sunk down in his chariot. Then said Jehu to Bidkar his captain, "Take up, and cast him in the portion of the field of Naboth the Jezreelite: for remember how that, when I and thou rode together after Ahab his father, the Lord laid this burden upon him; 'Surely I have seen yesterday the blood of Naboth, and the blood of his sons,' saith the Lord; 'and I will requite thee in this plat,' saith the Lord. Now therefore take and cast him into the plat of ground, according to the word of the Lord."

But when Ahaziah the king of Judah saw this, he fled by the way of the garden house. And Jehu followed after him, and said, "Smite him also in the chariot." And they did so at the going up to Gur, which is by Ibleam. And he fled to Megiddo, and died there.

[2 *Kings* ix. 1–27

The old story goes on to tell of the death of Jezebel, followed by the massacre of all Ahab's descendants, and, by a stratagem, of all the worshippers of Baal (2 Kings ix. 30–35 and x. 17–28). "Thus," it ends, "Jehu destroyed Baal out of Israel." The narrative does not tell us whether Elisha did or did not approve of Jehu's wholesale extermination of the house of Ahab and the Baal-worshippers. On the one hand, Israel was thus rid of a great abomination: on the other, the method used so exhausted the life-blood of the nobles of Israel that never again did she rally her strength. We may admire Jehu's loyalty to Jehovah while we deplore his cruelty and short-sighted belief that might is right.

The Death of Elisha

Now Elisha was fallen sick of his sickness whereof he died. And Joash the king of Israel came down unto him, and wept over his face, and said, "O my father, my father, the chariot of Israel, and the horsemen thereof." And Elisha said unto him, "Take bow and arrows." And he took unto him bow and arrows. And he said to the king of Israel, "Put thine hand upon the bow." And he put his hand upon it: and Elisha put his hands upon the king's hands. And he said "Open the window eastward." And he opened it. Then Elisha said, "Shoot." And he shot. And he said, "The arrow of the Lord's deliverance, and the arrow of deliverance from Syria: for thou shalt smite the Syrians in Aphek, till thou have consumed them." And he said, "Take the arrows." And he took them. And he said unto the king of Israel, "Smite upon the ground." And he smote thrice, and stayed. And the man of God was wroth with him, and said, "Thou shouldest

have smitten five or six times; then hadst thou smitten Syria till thou hadst consumed it: whereas now thou shalt smite Syria but thrice."
And Elisha died, and they buried him.

[2 *Kings* xiii. 14-20

The Deuteronomic Historians now lead us in the Book of Kings, through brief record of king after king both in Israel and in Judah. They use no longer oral tradition as in the case of the Elijah and Elisha stories, but base their own comments and judgments on bald extracts from the annals and chronicles kept throughout this period. Here, for instance, is their brief account of the reign of that great and prosperous Jeroboam II, of whom we learnt much more from Amos.

Jeroboam II

In the fifteenth year of Amaziah the son of Joash king of Judah Jeroboam the son of Joash king of Israel began to reign in Samaria, and reigned forty and one years. And he did that which was evil in the sight of the Lord: he departed not from all the sins of Jeroboam the son of Nebat, who made Israel to sin. He restored the coast of Israel from the entering of Hamath unto the sea of the plain, according to the word of the Lord God of Israel, which he spake by the hand of his servant Jonah, the son of Amittai, the prophet, which was of Gath-hepher. For the Lord saw the affliction of Israel, that it was very bitter: for there was not any shut up, nor any left, nor any helper for Israel. And the Lord said not that he would blot out the name of Israel from under heaven: but he saved them by the hand of Jeroboam the son of Joash.

Now the rest of the acts of Jeroboam, and all that he did, and his might, how he warred, and how he recovered Damascus, and Hamath, which belonged to Judah, for Israel, are they not written in the Book of the Chronicles of the Kings of Israel? And Jeroboam slept with his fathers, even with the kings of Israel; and Zechariah his son reigned in his stead.

[2 *Kings* xiv. 23-29

THE FALL OF SAMARIA

Soon after Jeroboam's death, the house of Jehu followed the house of Omri into oblivion. Conspiracy followed conspiracy: men who made themselves kings by force ruled for short periods and were killed in the next rising. No longer could Assyria be resisted. Great tribute had to be paid, wrung by the king from the mighty men of wealth in Israel. Here is an account of the closing days of Israel, a statement of facts intermingled with moral and religious reflections as to the cause and meaning of this overwhelming calamity, very clearly the writing of the Deuteronomic Reformers. Compare Sargon's inscription quoted on p. 114.

The First Coming of the Assyrians

In the two and fiftieth year of Azariah king of Judah Pekah the son of Remaliah began to reign over Israel in Samaria, and reigned twenty years. And he did that which was evil in the sight of the Lord: he departed not from the sins of Jeroboam the son of Nebat, who made Israel to sin. In the days of Pekah king of Israel came Tiglath-pileser king of Assyria, and took Ijon, and Abelbeth-maachah, and Janoah, and Kedesh, and Hazor, and Gilead, and Galilee, all the land of Naphtali, and carried them captive to Assyria. And Hoshea the son of Elah made a conspiracy against Pekah the son of Remaliah, and smote him, and slew him, and reigned in his stead, in the twentieth year of Jotham the son of Uzziah.

[2 *Kings* xv. 27–30

The Fall of Samaria

In the twelfth year of Ahaz king of Judah began Hoshea the son of Elah to reign in Samaria over Israel nine years. And he did that which was evil in the sight of the Lord, but not as the kings of Israel that were before him. Against him came up Shalmaneser king of Assyria; and Hoshea became his servant, and gave him presents. And the king of Assyria found conspiracy in Hoshea: for he had sent messengers to So king of Egypt, and brought no present to the king of Assyria, as he had done year by year: therefore the king of Assyria shut him up, and bound him in prison. Then the king of Assyria came up throughout all the land, and went up to Samaria, and besieged it three years. In the ninth year of Hoshea the king of Assyria took Samaria, and carried Israel away into Assyria, and placed them in Halah and in Habor by the river of Gozan, and in the cities of the Medes.

[2 *Kings* xvii. 1–6

Calamity caused by Wickedness

For so it was, that the children of Israel had sinned against the Lord their God, which had brought them up out of the land of Egypt, from under the hand of Pharaoh king of Egypt, and had feared other gods, and walked in the statutes of the heathen, whom the Lord cast out from before the children of Israel, and of the kings of Israel, which they had made. And the children of Israel did secretly those things that were not right against the Lord their God, and they built them high places in all their cities, from the tower of the watchmen to the fenced city. And they set them up images and groves in every high hill, and under every green tree: and there they burnt incense in all the high places, as did the heathen whom the Lord carried away before them; and wrought wicked things to provoke the Lord to anger.

And they left all the commandments of the Lord their God, and made them molten images, even two calves, and made a grove, and worshipped all the host of heaven, and served Baal. And they caused their sons and their daughters to pass through the fire, and used divination and enchantments, and sold themselves to do evil in the sight of the Lord, to provoke Him to anger. Therefore the Lord was very angry with Israel, and removed them out of His sight: there was none left but the tribe of Judah only. Also Judah kept not the commandments of the Lord their God, but walked in the statutes of Israel which they made. And the Lord rejected all the seed of Israel, and afflicted them, and delivered them into the hand of the spoilers, until He had cast them out of His sight. For He rent Israel from the house of David; and they made Jeroboam the son of Nebat king: and Jeroboam drave Israel from following the Lord, and made them sin a great sin. For the children of Israel walked in all the sins of Jeroboam which he did; they departed not from them; until the Lord removed Israel out of His sight, as He had said by all His servants the prophets. So was Israel carried away out of their own land to Assyria unto this day.

[2 *Kings* xvii. 7–11, 16–23

Samaria colonized by Foreigners

And the king of Assyria brought men from Babylon, and from Cuthah, and from Ava, and from Hamath, and from Sepharvaim, and placed them in the cities of Samaria instead of the children of Israel: and they possessed Samaria, and dwelt in the cities thereof.

[2 *Kings* xvii. 24

4. JERUSALEM ATTACKED BY THE ASSYRIANS

The Book of Kings now carries us to the kingdom of Judah, and shows how, by Jehovah's help, given through the prophet Isaiah (see p. 36), the Assyrians failed to crown their victory in the North with any comparable success in the South. The Deuteronomic Compiler first gives the bald facts as obtained from a Chronicle, but in 2 Kings xviii. 17 he passes into vivid description of the kind we have met in the Court History of David and in the "Acts" of Elijah and Elisha. It is almost certain that he is using here a similar "Acts" or Biography of Isaiah.

Hezekiah King of Judah when Samaria fell

Now it came to pass in the third year of Hoshea king of Israel, that Hezekiah the son of Ahaz king of Judah began to reign. Twenty and five years old was he when he began to reign; and he reigned twenty and nine years in Jerusalem. And he did that which was right in the sight of the Lord, according to all that David his father did. He removed the high places, and brake the images, and cut down the groves, and brake in pieces the brasen serpent that Moses had made: for unto those days the children of Israel did burn incense to it: and he called it Nehushtan. He trusted in the Lord God of Israel; so that after him was none like him among all the kings of Judah, nor any that were before him. For he clave to the Lord, and departed not from following Him, but kept His commandments, which the Lord commanded Moses. And the Lord was with him; and he prospered whithersoever he went forth: and he rebelled against the king of Assyria, and served him not. He smote the Philistines even unto Gaza, and the borders thereof, from the tower of the watchmen to the fenced city.

And it came to pass in the fourth year of King Hezekiah, which was the seventh year of Hoshea son of Elah king of Israel, that Shalmaneser king of Assyria came up against Samaria and besieged it. And at the end of three years they took it: even in the sixth year of Hezekiah, that is the ninth year of Hoshea king of Israel, Samaria was taken. And the king of Assyria did carry away Israel unto Assyria and put them in Halah and in Habor by the river of Gozan, and in the cities of the Medes.

[2 *Kings* xviii. 1–11

Hezekiah and Sennacherib

Now in the fourteenth year of King Hezekiah did Sennacherib king of Assyria come up against all the fenced cities of Judah, and took them. And Hezekiah king of Judah sent to the king of Assyria to Lachish, saying, "I have offended; return from me: that which thou puttest on me will I bear." And the king of Assyria appointed unto Hezekiah king of Judah three hundred talents of silver and thirty talents of gold. And Hezekiah gave him all the silver that was found in the house of the Lord, and in the treasures of the king's house. At that time did Hezekiah cut off the gold from the doors of the temple of the Lord, and from the pillars which Hezekiah king of Judah had overlaid, and gave it to the king of Assyria.

[2 *Kings* xviii. 13–16

Sennacherib's own inscription in Assyria reads thus:

As to Hezekiah, the Judaean, who had not submitted to my yoke, 46 of his strongholds, fortified cities, and smaller cities of their environs without number, with the onset of battering rams and the attack of engines, mines, breaches. . . . I besieged, I captured. 200,150 people, small and great, male and female, horses, mules, asses, camels, oxen, and sheep without number I brought out of their midst and counted as booty. He himself I shut up like a caged bird in Jerusalem, his capital city; I erected beleaguering works against him, and turned back by command every one who came out of his city gate. . . . As to Hezekiah himself, the fear of the lustre of my lordship overcame him. . . . With 30 talents of gold, 800 talents of silver, precious stones, rouge, . . . beds of ivory, stationary ivory thrones, elephants' hide, ivory, . . . all sorts of objects, a heavy treasure; also his daughters, the women of his palace, male and female musicians he sent after me to Nineveh, my capital city, and sent his messenger to present the gift and to do homage.

But Sennacherib is silent with regard to his defeat next recorded in Kings. An interesting passage from the Greek Historian, Herodotus, however, confirms this account probably taken from a Biography of Isaiah.

The Assyrians at Jerusalem

And the king of Assyria sent Tartan and Rabsaris and Rab-shakeh from Lachish to King Hezekiah with a great host against Jerusalem. And they went up and came to Jerusalem. And when they were come up, they came and stood by the conduit of the upper pool, which is in the highway of the fullers' field. And when they had called to the king, there came out to them Eliakim, which was over the household, and Shebna the scribe, and Joah the recorder. And Rab-shakeh said unto them, "Speak ye now to Hezekiah, Thus saith the great king, the king of Assyria, What confidence is this wherein thou trustest? Thou sayest, (but they are but vain words,) 'I have counsel and strength for the war.' Now on whom dost thou trust, that thou rebellest against me? Now, behold, thou trustest upon the staff of this bruised reed, even upon Egypt, on which if a man lean, it will go into his hand, and pierce it: so is Pharaoh king of Egypt unto all that trust on him. But if ye say unto me, 'We trust in the Lord our God': is not that He, whose high places and whose altars Hezekiah hath taken away, and hath said to Judah and Jerusalem, 'Ye shall worship before this altar in Jerusalem'? Now therefore, I pray thee, give pledges to my lord the king of Assyria, and I will deliver thee two thousand horses if thou be able on thy part to set riders upon them. How then wilt thou turn away the face of one captain of the least of my master's servants, and put thy trust on Egypt for chariots and for horsemen? Am I now come up without the Lord against this place to destroy it? The Lord said to me, 'Go up against this land, and destroy it.'"

Then said Eliakim the son of Hilkiah, and Shebna, and Joah, unto Rab-shakeh, "Speak, I pray thee, to thy servants in the Syrian

language; for we understand it: and talk not with us in the Jews' language in the ears of the people that are on the wall." But Rab-shakeh said unto them, "Hath my master sent me to thy master, and to thee, to speak these words? Hath he not sent me to the men which sit on the wall." Then Rab-shakeh stood and cried with a loud voice in the Jews' language, and spake, saying, "Hear the word of the great king, the king of Assyria: Thus saith the king, 'Let not Hezekiah deceive you:' for he shall not be able to deliver you out of his hand: neither let Hezekiah make you trust in the Lord, saying, 'The Lord will surely deliver us, and this city shall not be delivered into the hand of the king of Assyria.' Hearken not to Hezekiah: for thus saith the king of Assyria, 'Make an agreement with me by a present, and come out to me, and then eat ye every man of his own vine, and every one of his fig tree, and drink ye every one the waters of his cistern: until I come and take you away to a land like your own land, a land of corn and wine, a land of bread and vineyards, a land of oil olive and of honey, that ye may live and not die: and hearken not unto Hezekiah, when he persuadeth you, saying, "The Lord will deliver us." Hath any of the gods of the nations delivered at all his land out of the hand of the king of Assyria? Where are the gods of Hamath, and of Arpad? Where are the gods of Sepharvaim, Hena, and Ivah? Have they delivered Samaria out of mine hand? Who are they among all the gods of the countries, that have delivered their country out of mine hand, that the Lord should deliver Jerusalem out of mine hand?'" But the people held their peace, and answered him not a word: for the king's commandment was, saying, "Answer him not."
[2 *Kings* xviii. 17–36

Hezekiah sends unto Isaiah

Then came Eliakim, and Shebna, and Joah, to Hezekiah with their clothes rent, and told him the words of Rab-shakeh. And it came to pass, when King Hezekiah heard it, that he rent his clothes, and covered himself with sackcloth, and went into the house of the Lord. And he sent Eliakim, Shebna, and the elders of the priests covered with sackcloth, unto Isaiah the prophet. And they said unto him, "Thus saith Hezekiah, 'This day is a day of trouble, and of rebuke, and of blasphemy: for the children are come to the birth, and there is not strength to bring forth. It may be the Lord thy God will hear the words of Rab-shakeh, whom the king of Assyria his master hath sent to reproach the living God, and will reprove the words which the Lord thy God hath heard: wherefore lift up thy prayer for the remnant that is left.'" So the servants of King Hezekiah came to Isaiah.

And Isaiah said unto them, "Thus shall ye say unto your master 'Thus saith the Lord, Be not afraid of the words that thou hast heard, wherewith the servants of the king of Assyria have blasphemed Me. Behold, I will send a blast upon him, and he shall hear a rumour, and return to his own land; and I will cause him to fall by the sword in his own land.'"

[2 *Kings* xviii. 37, xix. 1–7]

Hezekiah's Prayer

So Rab-shakeh returned, and found the king of Assyria warring against Libnah: for he had heard that he was departed from Lachish. And he heard say concerning Tirhakah king of Ethiopia, "He is come forth to make war with thee." And when he heard it, he sent messengers to Hezekiah, saying, "Thus shall ye speak to Hezekiah king of Judah, saying, 'Let not thy God, in whom thou trustest, deceive thee, saying, "Jerusalem shall not be given into the hand of the king of Assyria." Behold, thou hast heard what the kings of Assyria have done to all lands by destroying them utterly; and shalt thou be delivered? Have the gods of the nations delivered them which my fathers have destroyed, as Gozan, and Haran, and Rezeph, and the children of Eden which were in Telassar? Where is the king of Hamath, and the king of Arpad, and the king of the city of Sepharvaim, Hena, and Ivah?'"

And Hezekiah received the letter from the hand of the messengers, and read it: and Hezekiah went up unto the house of the Lord, and spread it before the Lord. And Hezekiah prayed unto the Lord, saying, "O Lord of hosts, God of Israel, that dwellest between the cherubims, Thou art the God, even Thou alone, of all the kingdoms of the earth: Thou hast made heaven and earth. Incline Thine ear, O Lord, and hear; open Thine eyes, O Lord, and see: and hear all the words of Sennacherib, which hath sent to reproach the living God. Of a truth, Lord, the kings of Assyria have laid waste all the nations, and their countries, and have cast their gods into the fire: for they were no gods, but the work of men's hands, wood and stone: therefore they have destroyed them. Now therefore, O Lord our God, save us from his hand, that all the kingdoms of the earth may know that Thou art the Lord, even Thou only."

[2 *Kings* xix. 8–19]

Jerusalem delivered from the Assyrians

Then Isaiah sent unto Hezekiah, saying, "Thus saith the Lord God of Israel, Whereas thou hast prayed to Me against Sennacherib king of Assyria: this is the word which the Lord hath spoken concerning him; 'The virgin, the daughter of Zion, hath despised thee, and laughed thee to scorn; the daughter of Jerusalem hath shaken her head at thee. Whom hast thou reproached and blasphemed? And against whom hast thou exalted thy voice, and lifted up thine eyes on high? Even against the Holy One of Israel. By thy messengers thou hast reproached the Lord.' Therefore thus saith the Lord concerning the king of Assyria, He shall not come into this city, nor shoot an arrow there, nor come before it with shields, nor cast a bank against it. By the way that he came, by the same shall he return, and shall not come into this city, saith the Lord. For I will defend this city to save it for Mine own sake, and for My servant David's sake."

Then the angel of the Lord went forth, and smote in the camp of the Assyrians a hundred and fourscore and five thousand: and when they arose early in the morning, behold, they were all dead corpses. So Sennacherib king of Assyria departed, and went and returned, and dwelt at Nineveh.

[2 *Kings* xix. 20–23, 32–36

For the great importance of this deliverance in the development of Jewish religion, see Isaiah, p. 42. As for the exact method of deliverance, it should be noted that the Hebrews regarded the attack of a plague as a smiting by the angel of God. (Compare the descriptions of the pestilence in the time of David in 2 Samuel xxiv. 16, and of the sudden sickness of Herod in Acts xii. 23.)

Is there any clue to the nature of the plague? Not in the Book of Kings, but the passage from Herodotus to which we referred above may furnish such a clue. Here is a quotation from it:

After this the next king (of Egypt) was a priest, called Sethos. He held the warrior class of the Egyptians in contempt as though he had no need of them. He did them dishonour and deprived them of the arable lands which had been granted to them by previous kings, twelve acres to each soldier. And afterwards Sennacherib, king of the Arabians and Assyrians, marched a great army into Egypt.

Then the soldiers of Egypt would not help him; whereupon the priest went into the inner sanctuary to the image of the god and bewailed the things which he was in danger of suffering. As he wept, he fell asleep, and there appeared to him in a vision the god standing over him to encourage him, saying that, when he went forth to meet the Arabian army he would suffer no harm, for he himself would send him helpers. Trusting to his dream he collected those Egyptians who were willing to follow him ... traders, artisans and market men.

Then, as the two armies lay opposite to each other, there came in the night a multitude of field mice, which ate up all the quivers and bowstrings of the enemy, and the thongs of their shields. In consequence, on the next day they fled, and, being deprived of their arms, many of them fell. And there stands now in the temple a statue of this king holding a mouse in his hand, bearing an inscription which says, "Let any who look on me reverence the gods!"

From this scholars draw the conclusion that the Assyrian army was destroyed by bubonic plague. In modern times we read, "This plague first attacks rats and mice, which in their sufferings swarm the dwellings of men and spread the disease." Whatever it was, a mighty deliverance was wrought for Judah.

5. THE REFORMATION IN JUDAH

Wickedness of King Manasseh

Manasseh was twelve years old when he began to reign, and reigned fifty and five years in Jerusalem. And he did that which was evil in the sight of the Lord, after the abominations of the heathen, whom the Lord cast out before the children of Israel. For he built up again the high places which Hezekiah his father had destroyed; and he reared up altars for Baal, and made a grove, as did Ahab king of Israel; and worshipped all the host of heaven, and served them. And he built altars in the house of the Lord, of which the Lord said, "In Jerusalem will I put My name." And he built altars for all the host of heaven in the two courts of the house of the Lord. And he made his son pass through the fire, and observed times, and used enchantments, and dealt with familiar spirits and wizards: he wrought much wickedness in the sight of the Lord, to provoke Him to anger.

And the Lord spake by His servants the prophets, saying, "Because Manasseh king of Judah hath done these abominations, and hath done wickedly above all that the Amorites did, which were before him, and hath made Judah also to sin with his idols: therefore thus saith the Lord God of Israel, Behold, I am bringing such evil upon Jerusalem and Judah, that whosoever heareth of it, both his ears shall tingle. And I will stretch over Jerusalem the line of Samaria, and the plummet of the house of Ahab: and I will wipe Jerusalem as a man wipeth a dish, wiping it, and turning it upside down. And I will forsake the remnant of Mine inheritance, and deliver them into the hand of their enemies; and they shall become a prey and a spoil to all their enemies; because they have done that which was evil in My sight, and have provoked Me to anger, since the day their fathers came forth out of Egypt, even unto this day."

Moreover Manasseh shed innocent blood very much, till he had filled Jerusalem from one end to another; beside his sin wherewith he made Judah to sin, in doing that which was evil in the sight of the Lord. Now the rest of the acts of Manasseh, and all that he did, and his sin that he sinned, are they not written in the Book of the Chronicles of the Kings of Judah? And Manasseh slept with his fathers, and was buried in the garden of his own house, in the garden of Uzza: and Amon his son reigned in his stead.

[2 *Kings* xxi. 1–6, 10–18

King Amon

Amon was twenty and two years old when he began to reign, and he reigned two years in Jerusalem. And he did that which was evil in the sight of the Lord, as his father Manasseh did. And he walked in all the way that his father walked in, and served the idols that his father served, and worshipped them: and he forsook the Lord God of his fathers, and walked not in the way of the Lord. And the servants of Amon conspired against him, and slew the king in his own house. And the people of the land slew all them that had conspired against king Amon; and the people of the land made Josiah his son king in his stead. Now the rest of the acts of Amon which he did, are they not written in the Book of the Chronicles of the Kings of Judah? And he was buried in his sepulchre in the garden of Uzza: and Josiah his son reigned in his stead.

[2 *Kings* xxi. 19–26

King Josiah desires to repair the Temple

Josiah was eight years old when he began to reign, and he reigned thirty and one years in Jerusalem. And he did that which was right in the sight of the Lord, and walked in all the way of David his father, and turned not aside to the right hand or to the left.

And it came to pass in the eighteenth year of King Josiah, that the king sent Shaphan the scribe to the house of the Lord, saying, "Go up to Hilkiah the high priest, that he may sum the silver which is brought into the house of the Lord, which the keepers of the door have gathered of the people: and let them deliver it into the hand of the doers of the work, that have the oversight of the house of the Lord: and let them give it to the doers of the work which is in the house of the Lord, to repair the breaches of the house, unto carpenters, and builders, and masons, and to buy timber and hewn stone to repair the house." Howbeit there was no reckoning made with them of the money that was delivered into their hand, because they dealt faithfully.

[2 *Kings* xxii. 1–7

The Publication of Deuteronomy

And Hilkiah the high priest said unto Shaphan the scribe, "I have found the Book of the Law in the house of the Lord." And Hilkiah gave the book to Shaphan, and he read it. And Shaphan the scribe came to the king, and brought the king word again, and said, "Thy servants have gathered the money that was found in the house, and have delivered it into the hand of them that do the work, that have the oversight of the house of the Lord." And Shaphan the scribe shewed the king, saying, "Hilkiah the priest hath delivered me a book." And Shaphan read it before the king. And it came to pass, when the king had heard the words of the Book of the Law, that he rent his clothes.

And the king commanded Hilkiah the priest, and Ahikam the son of Shaphan, and Achbor the son of Michaiah, and Shaphan the scribe, and Asahiah a servant of the king's, saying, "Go ye, enquire of the Lord for me, and for the people, and for all Judah, concerning the words of this book that is found: for great is the wrath of the Lord that is kindled against us, because our fathers have not hearkened unto the words of this book, to do according unto all that which is written concerning us." So Hilkiah the priest, and Ahikam, and Achbor, and Shaphan, and Asahiah, went unto Huldah the prophetess, the wife of Shallum, keeper of the wardrobe; (now she dwelt in Jerusalem in the college;) and they communed with her.

And she said unto them, "Thus saith the Lord God of Israel, tell the man that sent you to me, 'Behold, I will bring evil upon this place, and upon the inhabitants thereof, even all the words of the book which the king of Judah hath read: because they have forsaken Me, and have burned incense unto other gods, that they might provoke Me to anger with all the works of their hands; therefore My wrath shall be kindled against this place, and shall not be quenched.' But to the king of Judah which sent you to enquire of the Lord, thus shall ye say to him, 'Thus saith the Lord God of Israel, As touching the words which thou hast heard; because thine heart was tender, and thou hast humbled thyself before the Lord, when thou heardest what I spake against this place, and against the inhabitants thereof, that they should become a desolation and a curse, and hast rent thy clothes, and wept before Me; I also have heard thee, saith the Lord. Behold therefore, I will gather thee unto thy fathers, and thou shalt be gathered into thy grave in peace; and thine eyes shall not see all the evil which I will bring upon this place.'" And they brought the king word again.

[2 *Kings* xxii. 8–20

(For information about this Book of the Law, see pp. 57–66.)

The Reformation of King Josiah

And the king sent, and they gathered unto him all the elders of Judah and of Jerusalem. And the king went up into the house of the Lord, and all the men of Judah and all the inhabitants of Jerusalem with him, and the priests, and the prophets, and all the people, both small and great: and he read in their ears all the words of the Book of the Covenant which was found in the house of the Lord.

And the king stood by a pillar, and made a covenant before the Lord, to walk after the Lord and to keep His commandments and His testimonies and His statutes with all their heart and all their soul, to perform the words of this covenant that were written in this book. And all the people stood to the covenant. And the king commanded Hilkiah the high priest, and the priests of the second order, and the keepers of the door, to bring forth out of the temple of the Lord all the vessels that were made for Baal, and for the grove, and for all the host of heaven: and he burned them without Jerusalem in the fields of Kidron, and carried the ashes of them unto Beth-el. And he put down the idolatrous priests, whom the kings of Judah had ordained to burn incense in the high places in the cities of Judah, and in the places round about Jerusalem; them also that burned incense unto Baal, to the sun, and to the moon, and to the planets, and to all the host of heaven. And he brought out the grove from the house of the Lord, without Jerusalem, unto the brook Kidron, and burned it at the brook Kidron, and stamped it small to powder, and cast the powder thereof upon the graves of the children of the people. Moreover the altar that was at Beth-el, and the high place which Jeroboam the son of Nebat, who made Israel to sin, had made, both that altar and the high place he brake down, and burned the high place, and stamped it small to powder, and burned the grove.

[2 *Kings* xxiii. 1–6, 15

Death of Josiah

Now the rest of the acts of Josiah, and all that he did, are they not written in the Book of the Chronicles of the Kings of Judah? In his days Pharaoh-nechoh king of Egypt went up against the king of Assyria to the river Euphrates: and King Josiah went against him; and he slew him at Megiddo, when he had seen him. And his servants carried him in a chariot dead from Megiddo, and brought him to Jerusalem, and buried him in his own sepulchre. And the people of the land took Jehoahaz the son of Josiah, and anointed him, and made him king in his father's stead.

[2 *Kings* xxiii. 28–30

Somewhere about this point must have ended the parts of the narrative which were put into shape by the earliest of the Deuteronomic Historians. Not until they were actually in exile could the conclusion of the Book of Kings have been written.

VI

THE CONCLUSION OF THE BOOK OF KINGS

THE EXILE

IN the story of Jeremiah (see pp. 67–81) we have read how in 586 B.C. Jerusalem was captured and utterly destroyed by the Chaldeans. Nebuchadrezzar carried off into captivity in Babylon almost the entire population, accompanied by their blinded king, Zedekiah. In far-off Babylon, separated from home, country and temple, a section of the people of Judah grew so strong in faith that when, after fifty years, the Persian conqueror Cyrus entered Babylon in triumph, men were there ready to take advantage of his permission to return to the ruined city of Jerusalem.

THE HISTORY OF THE KINGDOM CONCLUDED

A historian of the Deuteronomic school, either one of those responsible for compiling the main part of the Book of Kings (see pp. 90–92), or another man of kindred ideals, some time during this period of fifty years of Exile, added a conclusion bringing the narrative down to the fall of Jerusalem.

This writing may have been begun early in the Exile while the events described were still fresh in the minds of those who had experienced them. But certain passages make it clear that the work was not completed until a later exilic date. For instance, the final passage of the book is:—

And it came to pass in the seven and thirtieth year of the captivity of Jehoiachin king of Judah, in the twelfth month, on the seven and twentieth day of the month, that Evil-merodach king of Babylon in the year that he began to reign did lift up the head of Jehoiachin king of Judah out of prison; and he spake kindly to him, and set his throne above the throne of the kings that were with him in Babylon; and changed his prison garments: and he did eat bread continually

THE CONCLUSION OF THE BOOK OF KINGS

before him all the days of his life. And his allowance was a continual allowance given him of the king, a daily rate for every day, all the days of his life. [2 *Kings* xxv. 27–30

We know from other historical sources that Amel-Marduk (Evil-merodach) succeeded Nebuchadrezzar in 562 B.C. and reigned two years. This fixes the conclusion after 560 B.C.

Throughout the book there are short passages here and there which must have been added some time after the Fall of Jerusalem. One such occurs in Solomon's Prayer at the dedication of the Temple:—

If Thy people go out to battle against their enemy, whithersoever Thou shalt send them, and shall pray unto the Lord toward the city which Thou hast chosen, and toward the house that I have built for Thy name: Then hear Thou in heaven their prayer and their supplication, and maintain their cause. If they sin against Thee, (for there is no man that sinneth not,) and Thou be angry with them, and deliver them to the enemy, so that they carry them away captives unto the land of the enemy, far or near; yet if they shall bethink themselves in the land whither they were carried captives, and repent, and make supplication unto Thee in the land of them that carried them captives, saying, "We have sinned, and have done perversely, we have committed wickedness;" and so return unto Thee with all their heart, and with all their soul, in the land of their enemies, which led them away captive, and pray unto Thee toward their land, which Thou gavest unto their fathers, the city which Thou hast chosen, and the house which I have built for Thy name: then hear Thou their prayer and their supplication in heaven Thy dwelling place, and maintain their cause, and forgive Thy people that have sinned against Thee, and all their transgressions wherein they have transgressed against Thee, and give them compassion before them who carried them captive, that they may have compassion on them.

[1 *Kings* viii. 44–50

The verses 46 to 50 must have been inserted by one who knew in himself the agony and full meaning of captivity and who had at the same time glimpsed the reality of the forgiveness of God. The desire of such a man must have been to make the whole book yet more definitely a great confession of sin, suitable for reading and meditation when the Jews gathered together in Babylon for worship.

THE FATE OF JERUSALEM

King Jehoiakim

And Pharaoh-nechoh made Eliakim the son of Josiah king in the room of Josiah his father, and turned his name to Jehoiakim, and took Jehoahaz away: and he came to Egypt, and died there. Jehoiakim was twenty and five years old when he began to reign; and he reigned eleven years in Jerusalem. In his days Nebuchadrezzar king of Babylon came up, and Jehoiakim became his servant three years: then he turned and rebelled against him. Now the rest of the acts of Jehoiakim, and all that he did, are they not written in the Book of the Chronicles of the Kings of Judah? So Jehoiakim slept with his fathers: and Jehoiachin his son reigned in his stead. And the king of Egypt came not again any more out of his land: for the king of Babylon had taken from the river of Egypt unto the river Euphrates all that pertained to the king of Egypt.

[2 *Kings* xxiii. 34, 36, xxiv. 1, 5–7

King Jehoiachin and the First Departure into Exile

Jehoiachin was eighteen years old when he began to reign, and he reigned in Jerusalem three months. At that time the servants of Nebuchadrezzar king of Babylon came up against Jerusalem, and the city was besieged. And Nebuchadrezzar king of Babylon came against the city, and his servants did besiege it. And Jehoiachin the king of Judah went out to the king of Babylon, he, and his mother, and his servants, and his princes, and his officers: and the king of Babylon took him in the eighth year of his reign. And he carried out thence all the treasures of the house of the Lord, and the treasures of the king's house, and cut in pieces all the vessels of gold which Solomon king of Israel had made in the temple of the Lord, as the Lord had said. And he carried away all Jerusalem, and all the princes, and all the mighty men of valour, even ten thousand captives, and all the craftsmen and smiths: none remained, save the poorest sort of the people of the land. And he carried away Jehoiachin to Babylon, and the king's mother, and the king's wives, and his officers, and the mighty of the land, those carried he into captivity from Jerusalem to Babylon. And all the men of might, even seven thousand, and craftsmen and smiths a thousand, all that were strong and apt for war, even them the king of Babylon brought captive to Babylon.

[2 *Kings* xxiv. 8, 10–16

King Zedekiah rebels against Babylon

And the king of Babylon made Mattaniah his father's brother king in his stead, and changed his name to Zedekiah. Zedekiah was twenty and one years old when he began to reign, and he reigned eleven years in Jerusalem. And he did that which was evil in the sight of the Lord, according to all that Jehoiakim had done. For through the

THE CONCLUSION OF THE BOOK OF KINGS

anger of the Lord it came to pass in Jerusalem and Judah, until He had cast them out from His presence, that Zedekiah rebelled against the king of Babylon.

[2 *Kings* xxiv. 17–20

The Fall of Jerusalem

And it came to pass in the ninth year of his reign, in the tenth month, in the tenth day of the month, that Nebuchadrezzar king of Babylon came, he, and all his host, against Jerusalem, and pitched against it; and they built forts against it round about. And the city was besieged unto the eleventh year of King Zedekiah. And on the ninth day of the fourth month the famine prevailed in the city, and there was no bread for the people of the land.

And the city was broken up, and all the men of war fled by night by the way of the gate between two walls, which is by the king's garden: (now the Chaldees were against the city round about:) and the king went the way toward the plain. And the army of the Chaldees pursued after the king, and overtook him in the plains of Jericho: and all his army were scattered from him. So they took the king, and brought him up to the king of Babylon to Riblah; and they gave judgment upon him. And they slew the sons of Zedekiah before his eyes, and put out the eyes of Zedekiah, and bound him with fetters of brass, and carried him to Babylon.

And in the fifth month, on the seventh day of the month, which is the nineteenth year of King Nebuchadrezzar king of Babylon, came Nebuzar-adan, captain of the guard, a servant of the king of Babylon, unto Jerusalem: and he burnt the house of the Lord, and the king's house, and all the houses of Jerusalem, and every great man's house burnt he with fire. And all the army of the Chaldees, that were with the captain of the guard, brake down the walls of Jerusalem round about. Now the rest of the people that were left in the city, and the fugitives that fell away to the king of Babylon, with the remnant of the multitude, did Nebuzar-adan the captain of the guard carry away. But the captain of the guard left of the poor of the land to be vinedressers and husbandmen: and as for the people that remained in the land of Judah, whom Nebuchadrezzar king of Babylon had left, even over them he made Gedaliah ruler.

[2 *Kings* xxv. 1–12, 22

The Fate of those left in Judah

And when all the captains of the armies, they and their men, heard that the king of Babylon had made Gedaliah governor, there came to Gedaliah to Mizpah, even Ishmael the son of Nethaniah, and Johanan the son of Careah, and Seraiah the son of Tanhumeth the Netophathite, and Jaazaniah the son of a Maachathite, they and their men. And Gedaliah sware to them, and to their men, and said unto them, "Fear not to be the servants of the Chaldees: dwell in the land, and serve the king of Babylon; and it shall be well with you." But it came to pass in the seventh month, that Ishmael the son of Nethaniah, the son of Elishama, of the seed royal, came, and ten men with him, and smote Gedaliah, that he died, and the Jews and the Chaldees that were with him at Mizpah. And all the people, both small and great, and the captains of the armies, arose, and came to Egypt: for they were afraid of the Chaldees.

[2 *Kings* xxv. 23–26

(For further details see Jeremiah, pp. 78–81.)

VII

THE TRAGEDY OF PATRIOTISM

1. THE PSALM OF AN EXILE

IT is always difficult to know exactly when any particular psalm was written (see p. 20), but Psalm cxxxvii clearly belongs to this time of Exile. It is a song of wistful longing for Jerusalem, which, however, ends in a cry to God for vengeance on their oppressors. Not yet had men in their religious development reached such prayers as Christ's "Father, forgive them, for they know not what they do," or Stephen's "Lord, lay not this sin to their charge."

Longing for Zion

>By the rivers of Babylon,
>There we sat down, yea, we wept,
>When we remembered Zion.
>We hanged our harps
>Upon the willows in the midst thereof.
>For there they that carried us away captive required of us a song;
>And they that wasted us required of us mirth, saying,
>"Sing us one of the songs of Zion."
>
>How shall we sing the Lord's song
>In a strange land?
>If I forget thee, O Jerusalem,
>Let my right hand forget her cunning.
>If I do not remember thee,
>Let my tongue cleave to the roof of my mouth;
>If I prefer not Jerusalem above my chief joy.
>
>[*Psalm* cxxxvii. 1–6

A Cry for Vengeance

>Remember, O Lord, the children of Edom
>In the day of Jerusalem;
>Who said, "Rase it, rase it,
>Even to the foundations thereof."
>O daughter of Babylon, who art to be destroyed;

Happy shall he be that rewardeth thee
As thou hast served us.
Happy shall he be that taketh and dasheth thy little ones
Against the stones.

[*Psalm* cxxxvii. 7–9]

2. THE MALICIOUS SPIRIT OF EDOM

In the very short Book of Obadiah, which contains altogether only twenty-one verses, two or perhaps three distinct prophetic messages appear to have been collated by a later editor. We quote here verses 8–14 which depict the malicious hostility of Edom (or Idumea) to Israel as displayed at the time of the Fall of Jerusalem in 586 B.C. Compare the last part of the above psalm: see also Isaiah xxxiv.

The Edomites (or Idumeans) were considered to be descendants of Esau, the twin brother of Jacob, that hungry materialist who sold his birthright for a mess of pottage. Their territory lay to the South-East of Judah.

Judgment on Edom
  Shall I not in that day, saith the Lord, even destroy the wise men out of Edom, and understanding out of the mount of Esau? And thy mighty men, O Teman, shall be dismayed, to the end that every one of the mount of Esau may be cut off by slaughter.

[*Obadiah vv.* 8, 9]

Edom's Malice at the Fall of Jerusalem
  For thy violence against thy brother Jacob shame shall cover thee, and thou shalt be cut off for ever. In the day that thou stoodest on the other side, in the day that the strangers carried away captive his forces, and foreigners entered into his gates, and cast lots upon Jerusalem, even thou wast as one of them. But thou shouldest not have looked on the day of thy brother in the day that he became a stranger; neither shouldest thou have rejoiced over the children of Judah in the day of their destruction; neither shouldest thou have spoken proudly in the day of distress. Thou shouldest not have entered into the gate of My people in the day of their calamity; yea, thou shouldest not have looked on their affliction in the day of their calamity, nor have laid hands on their substance in the day of their calamity; neither shouldest thou have stood in the crossway, to cut off those of his that did escape; neither shouldest thou have delivered up those of his that did remain in the day of distress.

[*Obadiah vv.* 10–14]

THE TRAGEDY OF PATRIOTISM

3. A SONG OF SORROW FOR THE WOES OF JERUSALEM

The following passages from the Book of Lamentations, to which Jeremiah's name has been attached in the way described on p. 18, were evidently written with the horrors of the siege of Jerusalem vividly in mind. They speak for themselves, in part explaining the dreadful close of the psalm on p. 151.

The Suffering of Children

> The tongue of the sucking child cleaveth
> To the roof of his mouth for thirst:
> The young children ask bread,
> And no man breaketh it unto them.
>
> [*Lamentations* iv. 4

Famine

> They that be slain with the sword are better
> Than they that be slain with hunger:
> For these pine away, stricken through
> For want of the fruits of the field.
>
> The hands of the pitiful women
> Have sodden their own children:
> They were their meat
> In the destruction of the daughter of My people.
>
> [*Lamentations* iv. 9, 10

Flight

> Our persecutors are swifter
> Than the eagles of heaven:
> They pursued us upon the mountains,
> They laid wait for us in the wilderness.
>
> [*Lamentations* iv. 19

A Cry of Bitter Grief to Jehovah

> Behold, O Lord, and consider to whom Thou hast done this:
> Shall the women eat their fruit,
> And children swaddled with their hands?
> Shall the priest and the prophet be slain
> In the sanctuary of the Lord?
> The young and the old lie
> On the ground in the streets:
> My virgins and my young men
> Are fallen by the sword;
> Thou hast slain them in the day of Thine anger;
> Thou hast killed and not pitied.

Thou hast called as in a solemn day
My terrors round about,
So that in the day of the Lord's anger
None escaped or remained:
Those that I have swaddled and brought up
Hath mine enemy consumed.
> [*Lamentations* ii. 20–22 (*Marginal reading of* ii. 20)

VIII

THE PROPHET EZEKIEL

ANOTHER VIEW OF THE EXILE

To do justice to Babylon, however, the majority of the exiles appear to have settled happily in their new homes. Jeremiah, as we have seen in his letter to the first exiles (p. 77), in the name of Jehovah bade them build houses and plant gardens and "seek the peace of the city".

Here first the Jews developed their commercial gifts: here, as agriculturists, they played an important part in feeding the large population of Babylon: here, roused by the literary gifts of their captors, they continued to compile consecutive histories of their race, using the ancient scraps of written material and the wealth of oral tradition. To a section of the people all these opportunities meant growth in the knowledge of God. Many of their descendants ultimately returned to Jerusalem, and thus the inhabitants of the rebuilt Jerusalem were a church rather than a nation. Two prophets during the Exile did much to save this Remnant of the people.

EZEKIEL AND HIS CALL

The first of these, Ezekiel, the son of a priest of Jerusalem, had been carried into captivity in Babylon with the first exiles in 597 B.C.: five years later he received the Divine call to begin his prophetic work. He denounced the wickedness of Jerusalem and maintained that, because of her wickedness, Jerusalem was doomed. When the events of 586 B.C. proved the truth of his message, his wisdom was acclaimed by his fellow-countrymen. Then for fifteen years he set himself to encourage the exiles, to build them up in faith and in the knowledge of God, to prepare them for a far holier life in Jerusalem in days to come. In fact, the catastrophe of 586 B.C. divides the work and even the Book of Ezekiel into two distinct parts. Twenty-four chapters of the book are devoted to the prophet's work in the period before the final destruction of Jerusalem, twenty-four chapters to his work in the period just after that event.

Ezekiel's call is described by himself in the first chapters of his book: for interest it is worth while to compare this with Isaiah's account of his call in Isaiah vi. 1–8 (p. 38) and with Jeremiah's account of his in Jeremiah i. 1–10 (p. 71). Ezekiel had an unusually vivid imagination, "always grandiose and often beautiful", as has been well said; occasionally he lost himself in trances, while at other times he beheld visions almost too awful and mysterious for words to describe. Some of the old Jewish scholars, for instance, thought that his account of the vision which accompanied his call to the prophetic work was "too full of mystery to be read by any but a mature person". These peculiar qualities of Ezekiel caused his work to appeal to men not easily roused to enthusiasm by the literature of the Bible: for instance, the great German poet Schiller so appreciated Ezekiel that he wished he knew the Hebrew language so as to be able to read this work in the tongue in which it was written.

Here we quote part of his account of his call as it is given in the English Authorized Version. We note how carefully he dates each part of his book: he is a most precise writer.

Ezekiel's Vision of God

Now it came to pass in the thirtieth year, in the fourth month, in the fifth day of the month, as I was among the captives by the river of Chebar, that the heavens were opened, and I saw visions of God. In the fifth day of the month, which was the fifth year of King Jehoiachin's captivity, the word of the Lord came expressly unto Ezekiel the priest, the son of Buzi, in the land of the Chaldeans by the river Chebar; and the hand of the Lord was there upon him. And I looked, and, behold, a whirlwind came out of the north, a great cloud, and a fire infolding itself, and a brightness was about it, and out of the midst thereof as the colour of amber, out of the midst of the fire. Also out of the midst thereof came the likeness of four living creatures. And this was their appearance; they had the likeness of a man. And every one had four faces, and every one had four wings.

And their feet were straight feet; and the sole of their feet was like the sole of a calf's foot: and they sparkled like the colour of burnished brass. And they had the hands of a man under their wings on their four sides; and they four had their faces and their wings. Their wings were joined one to another; they turned not when they went; they went every one straight forward. As for the likeness of their faces, they four had the face of a man, and the face of a lion, on the right side: and they four had the face of an ox on the left side; they four also had the face of an eagle. Thus were their faces: and their wings were stretched upward; two wings of every one were joined one to another, and two covered their bodies. And they went every one straight forward: whither the spirit was to go, they went; and they turned not when they went. As for the likeness of the living creatures, their appearance was like burning coals of fire, and like the appearance of lamps: it went up and down among the living creatures; and the fire was bright, and out of the fire went forth lightning. And the living creatures ran and returned as the appearance of a flash of lightning.

And above the firmament that was over their heads was the likeness of a throne, as the appearance of a sapphire stone: and upon the likeness of the throne was the likeness as the appearance of a man above upon it. And I saw as the colour of amber, as the appearance of fire round about within it, from the appearance of his loins even upward, and from the appearance of his loins even downward, I saw as it were the appearance of fire, and it had brightness round about. As the appearance of the bow that is in the cloud in the day of rain, so was the appearance of the brightness round about. This was the appearance of the likeness of the glory of the Lord. And when I saw it, I fell upon my face, and I heard a voice of One that spake.

[*Ezekiel* i. 1–14, 26–28

Ezekiel's Call and Commission

And He said unto me, "Son of man, stand upon thy feet, and I will speak unto thee." And the spirit entered into me when He spake unto me, and set me upon my feet, that I heard Him that spake unto me. And He said unto me, "Son of man, I send thee to the children of Israel, to a rebellious nation that hath rebelled against Me: they and their fathers have transgressed against Me, even unto this very day. For they are impudent children and stiffhearted. I do send thee unto them; and thou shalt say unto them, 'Thus saith the Lord God.' And they, whether they will hear, or whether they will forbear, (for they are a rebellious house,) yet shall know that there hath been a prophet among them. And thou, son of man, be not afraid of them, neither be afraid of their words, though briers and thorns be with thee, and thou dost dwell among scorpions: be not afraid of their words, nor be dismayed at their looks, though they be a rebellious house. And thou shalt speak My words unto them, whether they will hear, or whether they will forbear: for they are most rebellious. But thou, son of man, hear what I say unto thee, 'Be not thou rebellious like that rebellious house: open thy mouth, and eat that I give thee.'"

And when I looked, behold, an hand was sent unto me; and, lo, a roll of a book was therein; and He spread it before me; and it was written within and without: and there was written therein lamentations, and mourning, and woe. Moreover He said unto me, "Son of man, eat that thou findest; eat this roll, and go speak unto the house of Israel." So I opened my mouth, and He caused me to eat that roll. And it was in my mouth as honey for sweetness.

And He said unto me, "Son of man, go, get thee unto the house of Israel, and speak with My words unto them. For thou art not sent to a people of a strange speech and of an hard language, but to the house of Israel; not to many people of a strange speech and of an hard language, whose words thou canst not understand. Surely, had I sent thee to them, they would have hearkened unto thee. But the house of Israel will not hearken unto thee; for they will not hearken unto Me: for all the house of Israel are impudent and hard-hearted. Behold, I have made thy face strong against their faces, and thy forehead strong against their foreheads. As an adamant harder than flint have I made thy forehead: fear them not, neither be dismayed at their looks, though they be a rebellious house."

Then the spirit took me up, and I heard behind me a voice of a great rushing, saying, "Blessed be the glory of the Lord from His place." I heard also the noise of the wings of the living creatures that touched one another, and the noise of the wheels over against them, and a noise of a great rushing. So the spirit lifted me up, and took me away, and I went in bitterness, in the heat of my spirit; but the hand of the Lord was strong upon me. Then I came to them of the captivity at Tel-abib, that dwelt by the river of Chebar, and I sat where they sat, and remained there astonished among them seven days. And it came to pass at the end of seven days, that the word of the Lord came unto me, saying, "Son of man, I have made thee a watchman unto the house of Israel: therefore hear the word at My mouth, and give them warning from Me."

[*Ezekiel* ii. 1–10, iii. 1–9, 12–17

With this may be compared the Vision of the Cherubim in Ezekiel x.

EZEKIEL'S DRAMATIC APPEAL

Ezekiel's feeling of personal responsibility, joined to his practical wisdom, led him to impart teaching to the people under concrete forms: only so could their limited minds grasp great truths. By story and illustration he expressed the highest he knew, as Jesus used parable and miracle to reveal the Father in Heaven. Ezekiel himself says (Ezek. xx. 49), "Ah Lord God! they say of me, 'Doth he not speak parables?'"

At times the prophet acted in some dramatic way intended to rouse a curiosity eager enough to grasp his message, just as the prophet Jeremiah emphasized his words by such symbolic actions as the breaking of the potter's earthen vessel (Jer. xix. 1–13). For instance, one day in the sight of a staring crowd Ezekiel carried all his household goods to a spot inside the city wall, and then in hot haste he dug a hole in the soft clay through which, at night, he carried off his belongings. He explained to the puzzled spectators that even so would their wicked friends in Jerusalem be glad to escape from the doomed city. In fact he acted his prophecy of exile (see Ezek. xii. 1–15).

We give here two other Signs of Ezekiel, whereby he ensured that his message should be heard and understood by simple-minded men and women.

Ezekiel's Sign of the Tile

Thou also, son of man, take thee a tile, and lay it before thee, and portray upon it the city, even Jerusalem: and lay siege against it, and build a fort against it, and cast a mound against it; set the camp also against it, and set battering rams against it round about. Moreover take thou unto thee an iron pan, and set it for a wall of iron between thee and the city: and set thy face against it, and it shall be besieged, and thou shalt lay siege against it. This shall be a sign to the house of Israel.

[*Ezekiel* iv. 1–3

Ezekiel's Sign of Sighing

And the word of the Lord came unto me, saying, "Son of man, set thy face toward Jerusalem, and drop thy word toward the holy places, and prophesy against the land of Israel, and say to the land of Israel, 'Thus saith the Lord: Behold, I am against thee, and will draw forth My sword out of his sheath, and will cut off from thee the righteous and the wicked.' Sigh therefore, thou son of man, with the breaking of thy loins; and with bitterness sigh before their eyes. And it shall be, when they say unto thee, 'Wherefore sighest thou?' that thou shalt answer, 'For the tidings; because it cometh: and every heart shall melt, and all hands shall be feeble, and every spirit shall faint, and all knees shall be weak as water: behold, it cometh, and shall be brought to pass, saith the Lord God.'"

[*Ezekiel* xxi. 1–3, 6, 7

EZEKIEL AND PERSONAL RESPONSIBILITY

Like Jeremiah, Ezekiel realized the importance of the individual as such: in particular, he believed in the responsibility of each individual for his own actions, both good and bad. A man is not condemned because he is descended from guilty ancestors, neither will his parents' goodness acquit a child who does evil. At the same time Ezekiel held that a man may be redeemed from his own guilty past.

A Man to be judged by his Own Actions

The word of the Lord came unto me again, saying, "What mean ye, that ye use this proverb concerning the land of Israel, saying, 'The fathers have eaten sour grapes, and the children's teeth are set on edge'? As I live, saith the Lord God, ye shall not have occasion any more to use this proverb in Israel. Behold, all souls are Mine; as the soul of the father, so also the soul of the son is Mine: the soul that sinneth, it shall die. But if a man be just, and do that which is lawful and right, and hath not oppressed any, but hath restored to the debtor his pledge, hath spoiled none by violence, hath given his bread to the hungry, and hath covered the naked with a garment; he that hath not given forth upon usury, neither hath taken any increase, that hath withdrawn his hand from iniquity, hath executed true judgment between man and man, hath walked in My statutes, and hath kept My judgments, to deal truly; he is just, he shall surely live, saith the Lord God.

"If he beget a son that is a robber, a shedder of blood, and that doeth the like to any one of these things, shall he then live? He shall not live: he hath done all these abominations; he shall surely die; his blood shall be upon him. Now, lo, if he beget a son, that seeth all his father's sins which he hath done, and considereth, and doeth not such like, that hath given his bread to the hungry, and hath covered the naked with a garment, that hath taken off his hand from the poor, that hath not received usury nor increase, hath executed My judgments, hath walked in My statutes; he shall not die for the iniquity of his father, he shall surely live.

"Yet say ye, 'Why? doth not the son bear the iniquity of the father?' When the son hath done that which is lawful and right, and hath kept all My statutes, and hath done them, he shall surely live. The soul that sinneth, it shall die. The son shall not bear the iniquity of the father, neither shall the father bear the iniquity of the son: the righteousness of the righteous shall be upon him, and the wickedness of the wicked shall be upon him.

[*From Ezekiel* xviii. 1–20

THE PROPHET EZEKIEL

A Man to be redeemed from a Guilty Past

"But if the wicked will turn from all his sins that he hath committed, and keep all My statutes, and do that which is lawful and right, he shall surely live, he shall not die. All his transgressions that he hath committed, they shall not be mentioned unto him: in his righteousness that he hath done he shall live. Have I any pleasure at all that the wicked should die, and not that he should return from his ways, and live?"

[*Ezekiel* xviii. 21–23

THE DEATH OF EZEKIEL'S WIFE

Ezekiel's dramatic appeal reached its climax on the day when Nebuchadrezzar began the siege of Jerusalem, for on the same day the prophet's wife was suddenly taken from him, and he felt himself called by God to abstain from mourning. Ezekiel had to turn his whole experience of bereavement into a Sign to the people. This passage is the most tender in the Book of Ezekiel.

Ezekiel himself a Sign to the People

Also the word of the Lord came unto me, saying, "Son of man, behold, I take away from thee the desire of thine eyes with a stroke: yet neither shalt thou mourn nor weep, neither shall thy tears run down. Forbear to cry, make no mourning for the dead, bind the tire of thine head upon thee, and put on thy shoes upon thy feet, and cover not thy lips, and eat not the bread of men." So I spake unto the people in the morning: and at even my wife died; and I did in the morning as I was commanded. And the people said unto me, "Wilt thou not tell us what these things are to us, that thou doest so?" Then I answered them, "The word of the Lord came unto me, saying, Speak unto the house of Israel, 'Thus saith the Lord God; Behold, I will profane My sanctuary, the excellency of your strength, the desire of your eyes, and that which your soul pitieth; and your sons and your daughters whom ye have left shall fall by the sword. And ye shall do as I have done: ye shall not cover your lips, nor eat the bread of men. And your tires shall be upon your heads, and your shoes upon your feet: ye shall not mourn nor weep; but ye shall pine away for your iniquities, and mourn one toward another. Thus Ezekiel is unto you a sign: according to all that he hath done shall ye do: and when this cometh, ye shall know that I am the Lord God.'"

[*Ezekiel* xxiv. 15–24

THE HEART OF THE BIBLE

EZEKIEL'S PROPHETIC WORK AFTER THE FALL OF JERUSALEM

When Ezekiel himself in his own personal experience and the people as a whole in their national experience had passed through the valley of the shadow of death, the prophet set himself to prepare his people for a worthy future. To this task the second half of the Book of Ezekiel is devoted. First of all he dismisses the ancient foes of Israel, uttering oracles against such peoples as Edom, Moab, Egypt and Tyre. We quote here part of his oracle against Tyre. Ezekiel's writing is usually sheer prose, stuff which by no stressing of the beats could possibly be read as free verse, but when he speaks of the greatness and splendour of Tyre he rises to a poetic level.

The Glory of Tyre

The word of the Lord came again unto me, saying, "Now, thou son of man, take up a lamentation for Tyrus; and say unto Tyrus, 'O thou that art situate at the entry of the sea, which art a merchant of the people for many isles, thus saith the Lord God; O Tyrus, thou hast said, "I am of perfect beauty." Thy borders are in the midst of the seas, thy builders have perfected thy beauty. They have made all thy ship boards of fir trees of Senir: they have taken cedars from Lebanon to make masts for thee. Of the oaks of Bashan have they made thine oars; the company of the Ashurites have made thy benches of ivory, brought out of the isles of Chittim. Fine linen with broidered work from Egypt was that which thou spreadest forth to be thy sail; blue and purple from the isles of Elishah was that which covered thee. The inhabitants of Zidon and Arvad were thy mariners: thy wise men, O Tyrus, that were in thee, were thy pilots. Tarshish was thy merchant by reason of the multitude of all kind of riches; with silver, iron, tin, and lead, they traded in thy fairs. Javan, Tubal, and Meshech, they were thy merchants: they traded the persons of men and vessels of brass in thy market. They of the house of Togarmah traded in thy fairs with horses and horsemen and mules. Syria was thy merchant by reason of the multitude of the wares of thy making: they occupied in thy fairs with emeralds, purple, and broidered work, and fine linen, and coral, and agate. Judah, and the land of Israel, they were thy merchants: they traded in thy market wheat of Minnith, and Pannag, and honey, and oil, and balm. The ships of Tarshish did sing of thee in thy market: and thou wast replenished, and made very glorious in the midst of the seas.

[*From Ezekiel* xxvii. 1-25

The Woes of Tyre

"'Thy rowers have brought thee into great waters: the east wind hath broken thee in the midst of the seas. Thy riches, and thy fairs, thy merchandise, thy mariners, and thy pilots, thy calkers, and the occupiers of thy merchandise, and all thy men of war, that are in thee, and in all thy company which is in the midst of thee, shall fall into the midst of the seas in the day of thy ruin. The suburbs shall shake at the sound of the cry of thy pilots. And all that handle the oar, the mariners, and all the pilots of the sea, shall come down from their ships, they shall stand upon the land; and shall cause their voice to be heard against thee, and shall cry bitterly, and shall cast up dust upon their heads, they shall wallow themselves in the ashes: and they shall make themselves utterly bald for thee, and gird them with sackcloth, and they shall weep for thee with bitterness of heart and bitter wailing. And in their wailing they shall take up a lamentation for thee, and lament over thee, saying, "What city is like Tyrus, like the destroyed in the midst of the sea?" In the time when thou shalt be broken by the seas in the depths of the waters thy merchandise and all thy company in the midst of thee shall fall. All the inhabitants of the isles shall be astonished at thee, and their kings shall be sore afraid, they shall be troubled in their countenance. The merchants among the people shall hiss at thee; thou shalt be a terror, and never shalt be any more.'"

[*From Ezekiel* xxvii. 26–36

EZEKIEL AND THE SHEPHERDS

Having in some such fashion cleared his mind of the former opponents of Israel, Ezekiel set about the reconstruction of the nation. He was the first of the prophets to realize what all great teachers now admit, that it is only by the care of individuals, by pastoral work, that a good society can be built up. This led him to the importance of good governors for a people. The prophet painted God as the Good Shepherd, caring for His flock in their exile, preparing later to lead them home to quiet pastures. He addressed searching rebukes to those leaders of the people who failed to realize their responsibility for their flock. Ezekiel felt his first duty to be to those souls under his immediate care.

A Leader's Responsibility

Again the word of the Lord came unto me saying, "Son of man, speak to the children of thy people, and say unto them, 'When I bring the sword upon a land, it the people of the land take a man of their coasts, and set him for their watchman: if when he seeth the sword come upon the land, he blow the trumpet, and warn the people; then whosoever heareth the sound of the trumpet, and taketh not warning; if the sword come, and take him away, his blood shall be upon his own head. He heard the sound of the trumpet, and took not warning; his blood shall be upon him. But he that taketh warning shall deliver his soul. But if the watchman see the sword come, and blow not the trumpet, and the people be not warned; if the sword come, and take any person from among them, he is taken away in his iniquity; but his blood will I require at the watchman's hand.' "

[*Ezekiel* xxxiii. 1–6]

A Rebuke to Selfish Leaders

And the word of the Lord came unto me, saying, "Son of man, prophesy against the shepherds of Israel, prophesy, and say unto them, 'Thus saith the Lord God unto the shepherds; Woe be to the shepherds of Israel that do feed themselves! Should not the shepherds feed the flocks? Ye eat the fat, and ye clothe you with the wool, ye kill them that are fed: but ye feed not the flock. The diseased have ye not strengthened, neither have ye healed that which was sick, neither have ye bound up that which was broken, neither have ye brought again that which was driven away, neither have ye sought that which was lost; but with force and with cruelty have ye ruled them. And they were scattered, because there is no shepherd: and they became meat to all the beasts of the field, when they were scattered. My sheep wandered through all the mountains, and upon every high hill: yea, my flock was scattered upon all the face of the earth, and none did search or seek after them. Therefore, O ye shepherds, hear the word of the Lord; Behold, I am against the shepherds; and I will require My flock at their hand, and cause them to cease from feeding the flock; neither shall the shepherds feed themselves any more; for I will deliver My flock from their mouth, that they may not be meat for them.

[*Ezekiel* xxxiv. 1–6, 9, 10]

Comfort for the Exiles

" 'For thus saith the Lord God; Behold, I, even I, will both search My sheep, and seek them out. As a shepherd seeketh out his flock in the day that he is among his sheep that are scattered; so will I seek out My sheep, and will deliver them out of all places where they have been scattered in the cloudy and dark day. And I will bring them out from the people, and gather them from the countries, and will bring them to their own land, and feed them upon the mountains of Israel by the rivers, and in all the inhabited places of the country. I will feed My flock, and I will cause them to lie down, saith the Lord God. I will seek that which was lost, and bring again that which was driven away, and will bind up that which was broken, and will strengthen that which was sick. And I will make with them a covenant of peace, and will cause the evil beasts to cease out of the land: and they shall dwell safely in the wilderness, and sleep in the woods. And I will make them and the places round about My hill a blessing; and I will cause the shower to come down in his season; there shall be showers of blessing. And they shall no more be a prey to the heathen, neither shall the beast of the land devour them; but they shall dwell safely, and none shall make them afraid. And I will raise up for them a plant of renown, and they shall be no more consumed with hunger in the land, neither bear the shame of the heathen any more. Thus shall they know that I the Lord their God am with them, and that they, even the house of Israel, are My people, saith the Lord God. And ye My flock, the flock of My pasture, are men, and I am your God, saith the Lord God. I will take you from among the heathen, and gather you out of all countries, and will bring you into your own land. Then will I sprinkle clean water upon you, and ye shall be clean: from all your filthiness, and from all your idols, will I cleanse you. A new heart also will I give you, and a new spirit will I put within you: and I will take away the stony heart out of your flesh, and I will give you an heart of flesh. And I will put My spirit within you, and cause you to walk in My statutes, and ye shall keep My judgments, and do them. And ye shall dwell in the land that I gave to your fathers; and ye shall be My people, and I will be your God.'"

[*From Ezekiel* xxxiv. 11–31, xxxvi. 24–28

A VISION OF HOPE

Ezekiel conveyed consolation to the exiles as he had conveyed rebukes, by signs and visions into which he sometimes condensed much meaning.

The Vision of the Valley of Dry Bones

The hand of the Lord was upon me, and carried me out in the spirit of the Lord, and set me down in the midst of the valley which was full of bones, and caused me to pass by them round about: and, behold, there were very many in the open valley; and, lo, they were very dry. And He said unto me, "Son of man, can these bones live?" And I answered, "O Lord God, Thou knowest." Again He said unto me, "Prophesy upon these bones, and say unto them, 'O ye dry bones, hear the word of the Lord. Thus saith the Lord God unto these bones; Behold, I will cause breath to enter into you, and ye shall live: and I will lay sinews upon you, and will bring up flesh upon you, and cover you with skin, and put breath in you, and ye shall live; and ye shall know that I am the Lord.'" So I prophesied as I was commanded: and as I prophesied, there was a noise, and behold a shaking, and the bones came together, bone to his bone. And when I beheld, lo, the sinews and the flesh came up upon them, and the skin covered them above: but there was no breath in them. Then said He unto me, "Prophesy unto the wind, prophesy, son of man, and say to the wind, 'Thus saith the Lord God; Come from the four winds, O breath, and breathe upon these slain, that they may live.'" So I prophesied as He commanded me, and the breath came into them, and they lived, and stood up upon their feet, an exceeding great army.

[*Ezekiel* xxxvii. 1–10

Meaning of the Vision

Then He said unto me, "Son of man, these bones are the whole house of Israel: behold, they say, 'Our bones are dried, and our hope is lost: we are cut off for our parts.' Therefore prophesy and say unto them, 'Thus saith the Lord God; Behold, O My people, I will open your graves, and cause you to come up out of your graves, and bring you into the land of Israel. And ye shall know that I am the Lord, when I have opened your graves, O My people, and brought you up out of your graves, and shall put My spirit in you, and ye shall live, and I shall place you in your own land: then shall ye know that I the Lord have spoken it, and performed it, saith the Lord.'"

[*Ezekiel* xxxvii. 11–14

EZEKIEL'S VISION OF THE NEW JERUSALEM

The last part of his book (Ezek. xl–xlviii) the prophet devoted to a vision of the new City and Temple which, he hoped, would replace the old City and Temple destroyed by the Chaldeans in 586 B.C. Here Ezekiel showed some knowledge of design and architecture, but above all a passionate love for organizing details of worship, a great zeal for what we should call ritual. In fact it is the detail in these chapters that makes them somewhat wearisome to the ordinary reader.

But to the prophet himself these chapters were the climax of his work: in them he expressed the highest and best of which he had dreamed, carried out into the actual everyday facts of life and worship. Indeed the immense influence of this part of his book on the subsequent development of Jewish religion justifies Ezekiel in his opinion, for this influence was so marked that it is a matter of common agreement that he be called the "Father of Judaism".

Here Ezekiel drew a sharp contrast between sacred and secular, between the holy and the profane. By the isolation of its site, the new Temple was to be guarded from all pollution by ordinary folk in the ordinary moments of their lives. Not even all Levites might be priests. Those Levites who had in the old days, before the reformation of Josiah, served as priests of Jehovah in the high places throughout the land, were now set aside to be "keepers of the charge of the house, for all the service thereof, and for all that shall be done therein". Only the descendants of the family of the Levite Zadok were to enter as priests into the sanctuary of Jehovah, to come near to His table, to minister unto Him, to keep His charge.

Ezekiel carried this division between the holy and the profane into the relationship between Jehovah and His people, with the danger of losing sight of the individual's right to communion with Jehovah. Jehovah, taught Ezekiel, must be pacified by sin offerings for the offences and uncleanness of the people: the priest with his blood offering must act as go-between or mediator between Jehovah and His people.

It is easy to realize how different all these ideals were from those found in the Deuteronomic Code. They resulted in a church rather than a nation, and they move far on towards the ideals which belonged to the people amongst whom Jesus of Nazareth was born five and a half centuries after Ezekiel had completed his work. Yet the last words of the Book of Ezekiel give the kernel of these chapters: "And the name of the city from that day shall be, The Lord is there."

Ezekiel's Vision of the City

In the five and twentieth year of our captivity, in the beginning of the year, in the tenth day of the month, in the fourteenth year after that the city was smitten, in the selfsame day the hand of the Lord was upon me, and brought me thither. In the visions of God brought He me into the land of Israel, and set me upon a very high mountain, by which was as the frame of a city on the south. And He brought me thither, and, behold, there was a man, whose appearance was like the appearance of brass, with a line of flax in his hand, and a measuring reed; and he stood in the gate. And the man said unto me, "Son of man, behold with thine eyes, and hear with thine ears, and set thine heart upon all that I shall shew thee; for to the intent that I might shew them unto thee art thou brought hither: declare all that thou seest to the house of Israel."

[*Ezekiel* xl. 1–4]

The Return of the Glory of Jehovah into the Temple

Afterward He brought me to the gate, even the gate that looketh toward the east: and, behold, the glory of the God of Israel came from the way of the east: and His voice was like a noise of many waters: and the earth shined with His glory. And it was according to the appearance of the vision which I saw, even according to the vision that I saw when I came to destroy the city: and the visions were like the vision that I saw by the river Chebar; and I fell upon my face. And the glory of the Lord came into the house by the way of the gate whose prospect is toward the east. So the spirit took me up, and brought me into the inner court; and, behold, the glory of the Lord filled the house.

[*Ezekiel* xliii. 1–5]

The Law of Holiness

And I heard Him speaking unto me out of the house; and the man stood by me. And He said unto me, "Son of man, the place of My throne, and the place of the soles of My feet, where I will dwell in the midst of the children of Israel for ever, and My holy name, shall the house of Israel no more defile, neither they, nor their kings. In their setting of their threshold by My thresholds, and their post by My posts, and the wall between Me and them, they have even defiled My holy name by their abominations that they have committed: wherefore I have consumed them in Mine anger. Thou son of man, shew the house to the house of Israel, that they may be ashamed of their iniquities: and let them measure the pattern. And if they be ashamed of all that they have done, shew them the form of the house, and the fashion thereof, and the goings out thereof, and the comings in thereof, and all the forms thereof, and all the ordinances thereof, and all the forms thereof, and all the laws thereof: and write it in their sight, that they may keep the whole form thereof, and all the ordinances thereof, and do them. This is the law of the house; 'Upon the top of the mountain the whole limit thereof round about shall be most holy.' Behold, this is the law of the house."

[*Ezekiel* xliii. 6–12]

The Sin Offering

And He said unto me, "Son of man, thus saith the Lord God; these are the ordinances of the altar in the day when they shall make it, to offer burnt offerings thereon, and to sprinkle blood thereon. And thou shalt give to the priests the Levites that be of the seed of Zadok, which approach unto Me, to minister unto Me, saith the Lord God, a young bullock for a sin offering. And thou shalt take of the blood thereof, and put it on the four horns of it, and on the four corners of the settle, and upon the border round about: thus shalt thou cleanse and purge it."

[*Ezekiel* xliii. 18–20]

No Strangers

Then brought He me the way of the north gate before the house: and I looked, and, behold, the glory of the Lord filled the house of the Lord: and I fell upon my face. And the Lord said unto me, "Son of man, mark well, and behold with thine eyes, and hear with thine ears all that I say unto thee concerning all the ordinances of the house of the Lord, and all the laws thereof; and mark well the entering in of the house, with every going forth of the sanctuary. And thou shalt say to the rebellious, even to the house of Israel, 'Thus saith the Lord God; O ye house of Israel, let it suffice you of all your abominations, in that ye have brought into My sanctuary strangers, uncircumcised in heart, and uncircumcised in flesh, to be in My sanctuary, to pollute it, even My house, when ye offer My bread, the fat and the blood, and they have broken My covenant because of all your abominations. And ye have not kept the charge of Mine holy things: but ye have set keepers of My charge in My sanctuary for yourselves.'"

[*Ezekiel* xliv. 4–8]

Zadokites the Only Priests

Thus saith the Lord God; "No stranger, uncircumcised in heart, nor uncircumcised in flesh, shall enter into My sanctuary, of any stranger that is among the children of Israel. And the Levites that are gone away far from Me, when Israel went astray, which went astray away from Me after their idols; they shall even bear their iniquity. And they shall not come near unto Me, to do the office of a priest unto Me, nor to come near to any of My holy things, in the most holy place: but they shall bear their shame, and their abominations which they have committed. But I will make them keepers of the charge of the house, for all the service thereof, and for all that shall be done therein. But the priests the Levites, the sons of Zadok, that kept the charge of My sanctuary when the children of Israel went astray from Me, they shall come near to Me to minister unto Me, and they shall stand before Me to offer unto Me the fat and the blood," saith the Lord God: "they shall enter into My sanctuary, and they shall come near to My table, to minister unto Me, and they shall keep My charge."

[*Ezekiel* xliv. 9, 10, 14–16]

The Purity of the Priests

"And it shall come to pass, that when they enter in at the gates of the inner court, they shall be clothed with linen garments; and no wool shall come upon them, whiles they minister in the gates of the inner court, and within. They shall have linen bonnets upon their heads, and shall have linen breeches upon their loins; they shall not gird themselves with any thing that causeth sweat. Neither shall they shave their heads, nor suffer their locks to grow long; they shall only poll their heads. Neither shall any priest drink wine, when they enter into the inner court."

[*Ezekiel* xliv. 17, 18, 20, 21

The Priests' Duty

"And they shall teach My people the difference between the holy and profane, and cause them to discern between the unclean and the clean."

[*Ezekiel* xliv. 23

In this mass of rather dry details descriptive of the new Jerusalem that is to be after the Exile, Ezekiel inserts a beautiful vision of a life-giving river that is to issue from Jerusalem. The rivers of Babylon had become real to the exiles: "by the rivers of Babylon, there we sat down" (see Psalm cxxxvii). Jerusalem had been dependent on springs for its water supply, while the waters of the Dead Sea are so salt that no fish can live therein. But we note that Ezekiel appreciates the value of salt to human life: his practical mind decides that it would be wise to leave the marshes as they were so that salt might be gathered there as before.

The Vision of the River

Afterward he brought me again unto the door of the house; and, behold, waters issued out from under the threshold of the house eastward: for the forefront of the house stood toward the east, and the waters came down from under from the right side of the house, at the south side of the altar. Then brought he me out of the way of the gate northward, and led me about the way without unto the utter gate by the way that looketh eastward; and, behold, there ran out waters on the right side. And when the man that had the line in his hand went forth eastward, he measured a thousand cubits, and he brought me through the waters; the waters were to the ankles. Again he measured a thousand, and brought me through the waters; the waters were to the knees. Again he measured a thousand, and brought me through; the waters were to the loins. Afterward he measured a thousand; and it was a river that I could not pass over: for the waters were risen, waters to swim in, a river that could not be passed over. And he said unto me, "Son of man, hast thou seen this?" Then he brought me, and caused me to return to the brink of the river.

THE PROPHET EZEKIEL

Now when I had returned, behold, at the bank of the river were very many trees on the one side and on the other. Then said he unto me, "These waters issue out toward the east country, and go down into the desert, and go into the sea: which being brought forth into the sea, the waters shall be healed. And it shall come to pass, that every thing that liveth, which moveth, whithersoever the rivers shall come, shall live: and there shall be a very great multitude of fish, because these waters shall come thither: for they shall be healed; and every thing shall live whither the river cometh. And it shall come to pass, that the fishers shall stand upon it from En-gedi even unto En-eglaim; they shall be a place to spread forth nets; their fish shall be according to their kinds, as the fish of the great sea, exceeding many. But the miry places thereof and the marishes thereof shall not be healed; they shall be given to salt. And by the river upon the bank thereof, on this side and on that side, shall grow all trees for meat, whose leaf shall not fade, neither shall the fruit thereof be consumed: it shall bring forth new fruit according to his months, because their waters issued out of the sanctuary: and the fruit thereof shall be for meat, and the leaf thereof for medicine."

[*Ezekiel* xlvii. 1-12

The Final Word

And the name of the city from that day shall be, "The Lord is there."

[*Ezekiel* xlviii. 35

IX

AN EXILIC CODE OF LAW

THE HOLINESS CODE

WE have already met with two different codes of law, codes in which many ancient laws and certain new laws were woven together into a coherent whole: the first was the Book of the Covenant (p. 47), the second the Deuteronomic Code (p. 58). In Leviticus xvii–xxvi we have a third self-contained code of law in which very old laws have again been combined with some new ones, devised to meet the changing condition of the people. This code, attributed to Moses as the others were, is usually called the "Holiness Code", being referred to as H: its keynote is—

Speak unto all the congregation of the children of Israel, and say unto them, "Ye shall be holy, for I the Lord your God am holy."
[*Leviticus* xix. 2

EZEKIEL AND THE AUTHOR OF THE HOLINESS CODE

At this stage we must note the resemblance to Ezekiel. At first scholars thought that Ezekiel himself might be the author, but they have now decided that the author of the Holiness Code and Ezekiel both belonged to a group of friends living in exile in Babylon; that out of the common thinking and common talk of this group the two men developed similar ideas concerning certain matters. This Holiness Code may have been drawn up in the earlier years of the Exile, but it seems more probable that it was framed about 570 B.C., soon after Ezekiel had concluded his work by declaring his vision of the New Jerusalem.

Both men have endured the sorrow of the sin of the people and its issue in the fall of Jerusalem and the Exile. Both men think no longer of any large country belonging to the people, a country so large that its inhabitants could not easily bring their animals to the Temple for slaughter: in the new Jerusalem the Temple is to be easily reached by all, and all secular slaughter is prohibited. Both believe that God forgives repentant sinners. Both think of these forgiven exiles as in future kept holy and clean by unremitting attention to details of life and worship. Both men, though they know it not, are taking the first steps towards turning the observance of the law into a burden hardly to be borne.

THOU SHALT LOVE THY NEIGHBOUR AS THYSELF

In later times Jesus Christ commended the lawyer's summing up of the law: "Thou shalt love the Lord thy God with all thy heart, and with all thy soul, and with all thy strength, and with all thy mind; and thy neighbour as thyself." The first part of this summary is taken from the introduction to the Deuteronomic Code (Deut. vi. 5, p. 59): the second comes from this Holiness Code. The passage in which it occurs shows this code at its best, attempting to combine moral holiness with the ceremonial holiness it elsewhere describes in such detail.

Moral Laws

And when ye reap the harvest of your land, thou shalt not wholly reap the corners of thy field, neither shalt thou gather the gleanings of thy harvest. And thou shalt not glean thy vineyard, neither shalt thou gather every grape of thy vineyard; thou shalt leave them for the poor and stranger: I am the Lord your God.

Ye shall not steal, neither deal falsely, neither lie one to another.

And ye shall not swear by My name falsely, neither shalt thou profane the name of thy God: I am the Lord.

Thou shalt not defraud thy neighbour, neither rob him: the wages of him that is hired shall not abide with thee all night until the morning.

Thou shalt not curse the deaf, nor put a stumbling-block before the blind, but shalt fear thy God: I am the Lord.

Ye shall do no unrighteousness in judgment: thou shalt not respect the person of the poor, nor honour the person of the mighty: but in righteousness shalt thou judge thy neighbour.

Thou shalt not go up and down as a talebearer among thy people:

neither shalt thou stand against the blood of thy neighbour: I am the Lord.

Thou shalt not hate thy brother in thine heart: thou shalt in any wise rebuke thy neighbour, and not suffer sin upon him. Thou shalt not avenge, nor bear any grudge against the children of thy people, but thou shalt love thy neighbour as thyself: I am the Lord.

Ye shall keep My sabbaths, and reverence My sanctuary: I am the Lord.

Regard not them that have familiar spirits, neither seek after wizards, to be defiled by them: I am the Lord your God.

Thou shalt rise up before the hoary head, and honour the face of the old man, and fear thy God: I am the Lord.

Ye shall do no unrighteousness in judgment, in meteyard, in weight, or in measure. Just balances, just weights, a just ephah, and a just hin, shall ye have: I am the Lord your God, which brought you out of the land of Egypt.

[*From Leviticus* xix. 9–36

Disobedience to the Law caused the Exile

But if ye will not hearken unto Me, and will not do all these commandments; and if ye shall despise My statutes, or if your soul abhor My judgments, so that ye will not do all My commandments, but that ye break My covenant: I also will do this unto you: I will even appoint over you terror, consumption, and the burning ague, that shall consume the eyes, and cause sorrow of heart: and ye shall sow your seed in vain, for your enemies shall eat it. And I will set My face against you, and ye shall be slain before your enemies: they that hate you shall reign over you; and ye shall flee when none pursueth you.

And if ye will not yet for all this hearken unto Me, then I will punish you seven times more for your sins. And I will break the pride of your power; and I will make your heaven as iron, and your earth as brass: and your strength shall be spent in vain: for your land shall not yield her increase, neither shall the trees of the land yield their fruits.

And if ye walk contrary unto Me, and will not hearken unto Me; I will bring seven times more plagues upon you according to your sins. I will also send wild beasts among you, which shall rob you of your children, and destroy your cattle, and make you few in number; and your high ways shall be desolate.

And if ye will not for all this hearken unto Me, but walk contrary unto Me; then I will walk contrary unto you also in fury; and I, even I, will chastise you seven times for your sins. And I will bring the land into desolation: and your enemies which dwell therein shall be astonished at it. And I will scatter you among the heathen, and will draw out a sword after you: and your land shall be desolate, and your cities waste.

Then shall the land enjoy her sabbaths, as long as it lieth desolate, and ye be in your enemies' land; even then shall the land rest, and enjoy her sabbaths. As long as it lieth desolate it shall rest; because it did not rest in your sabbaths, when ye dwelt upon it.

And upon them that are left alive of you I will send a faintness into their hearts in the lands of their enemies; and the sound of a shaken leaf shall chase them; and they shall flee, as fleeing from a sword; and they shall fall when none pursueth. And they shall fall one upon another, as it were before a sword, when none pursueth: and ye shall have no power to stand before your enemies. And ye shall perish among the heathen, and the land of your enemies shall eat you up. And they that are left of you shall pine away in their iniquity in your enemies' lands; and also in the iniquities of their fathers shall they pine away with them.

[*From Leviticus* xxvi. 14–39

Hope for the Penitent

If they shall confess their iniquity, and the iniquity of their fathers, with their trespass which they trespassed against Me, and that also they have walked contrary unto Me; and that I also have walked contrary unto them, and have brought them into the land of their enemies; if then their uncircumcised hearts be humbled, and they then accept of the punishment of their iniquity: then will I remember My covenant with Jacob, and also My covenant with Isaac, and also My covenant with Abraham will I remember; and I will remember the land. And yet for all that, when they be in the land of their enemies, I will not cast them away, neither will I abhor them, to destroy them utterly, and to break My covenant with them: for I am the Lord their God. But I will for their sakes remember the covenant of their ancestors, whom I brought forth out of the land of Egypt in the sight of the heathen, that I might be their God: I am the Lord.

[*Leviticus* xxvi. 40–42, 44, 45

X

A HISTORY OF THE ESTABLISHMENT OF THE KINGDOM

1. INTRODUCTION

A CLAMANT NEED FOR HISTORICAL LITERATURE

WE have seen that the exiles, after all, settled in Babylon in comparative comfort; their minds, now set free from immediate pressure of national cares, were ready for literary adventures, stimulated in that direction also by the literary tastes and interests of their captors. But more vital needs urged these Hebrews to write. The history of the past must be studied more thoroughly that from it the people might better learn the ways of Jehovah. The writers of the Deuteronomic school considered that they must gather up yet more carefully all the precious relics of bygone days, in order to put them into a form suitable for use in the homes and assemblies of the people, for instruction, warning and comfort.

About this time, then, just as they had already put the Book of Kings into what is practically its form in the Bible, they set to work to write in the same fashion the history of the establishment of the kingdom. This history is found in the Books of Judges, 1 Samuel and 2 Samuel, which took substantially their present form in this Exilic period at the hands of the Deuteronomic Historians. Naturally these writers could not here insist on worship in the Temple, for there was as yet no temple in Jerusalem, and for the greater part of the narrative no Jerusalem. But they continued to emphasize the idea that when the Hebrews followed after other gods than Jehovah, they were sorely troubled by disasters; whereas, when they followed after Jehovah with their whole heart, they prospered.

But the Deuteronomists did not stop here. For the earliest

THE ESTABLISHMENT OF THE KINGDOM

periods of Hebrew history down to the times of Moses, they made a summary which can now be found in the first three chapters of the Book of Deuteronomy, put into the mouth of Moses as an introduction to the law-code given there. They also wrote much of what is now the Book of Joshua, telling of the first successes against the Canaanites just after the death of Moses: this part of their work has, however, been interwoven in the Old Testament with the writings of later historians, and we must consider it amongst the literature which came into being after the Exile.

A HISTORY OF THE ESTABLISHMENT OF THE KINGDOM

The Books of Judges and Samuel cover the period which begins with the days of settlement in Canaan, when, in scattered districts separated by many different heathen foes, the tribes made their homes and slowly grew towards the unity of a nation, and which ends with the establishment of David as king over the whole country, the defeat of all their heathen foes, and the achievement of national unity. The subject of these books forms, then, a simple thread of historical narrative, but the construction of the books is far more complex than is that of the Book of Kings. We must try to understand this now, lest later we be baffled, as many others have been, by difficulties due to these books containing different accounts of the same events.

We do not have separately in the Old Testament the very first attempts of the Hebrew people to construct historical narratives. Later editors, such as the Exilic writers whom we are now considering, have incorporated these earliest documents in their own work; it is clear that to separate them out from the books of the Bible can be no easy task. In fact, it is only the labour of great scholars working for centuries on the *Hebrew* text of the Old Testament that has enabled us to comprehend something of this earliest historical work. Here we state briefly what is known about it: later, in the selected passages, we shall notice examples of different accounts of the same event by different authors.

THE J NARRATIVE

On pp. 21–27 we have already considered the narratives from the hand of the courtier of King David, who was so moved by enthusiasm that he recorded in writing the exploits of David. Considerably later, some time about the time of Elijah, probably about 850 B.C., an unknown writer in the Southern kingdom set himself to write up from the very beginning of Hebrew history all he knew for himself, and all he had heard handed down from others in oral story or verse, together with any fragments of written material already in existence. He actually began with an account of the Creation of Man, proceeding from that to stories of Abraham, Isaac, Jacob, the Descent into Egypt, the Deliverance from Egypt under Moses, the Conquest of Canaan, the Philistine Peril, and David's final triumph over the Philistines: for this last section he made use of the narratives of David, parts of which we have already read.

All these popular tales this writer wove into one great comprehensive whole, thinking of history in a large way as the working out of the purpose of God. His details of old stories could not, of course, be always strictly accurate, but the wonderful literary art with which this author tells the story and the noble witness he always bears to the pure religion of Jehovah make his work of the utmost value to all who have known it. His narrative is always referred to as the J Narrative, because he uses for God the Hebrew word "Jehovah" or "Yahweh".

There are other indications of the presence of J in Old Testament narrative. It is characteristic of J to speak of God as if He were a man: in other words his representations of God are anthropomorphic. Jehovah "came down" to inspect the Tower of Babel (Gen. xi. 5); later at the Red Sea He "took off" the chariot wheels of the Egyptians (Exod. xiv. 25). It is definitely characteristic of J's language to call the Mount

THE ESTABLISHMENT OF THE KINGDOM

of the Law "Sinai", the inhabitants of Palestine "Canaanites", and the son of Isaac, after the birth of Benjamin, not "Jacob", but "Israel".

THE E NARRATIVE

In the Northern kingdom about a hundred years later a writer greatly influenced by the work of the prophet Elijah wrote very much the same story told from the Northern point of view. If we consider how differently an English and a Scots writer would tell, for instance, the story of Mary, Queen of Scots, we can realize part of the reason for the variance between the J and E narratives. But there is another important factor. This author lived through stormy days of kingly rule in the North, with the calamity of Ahab's secession from Jehovah burnt into his mind by what he knew of Elijah. Probably as the result of this experience he conceived of the kingship as in itself an evil thing, much as many modern countries have come to regard it during these last years of European history.

Whether this be the explanation or not, it is certain that this author resented Israel having any king save Jehovah. He does not begin his narrative until the time of Abraham: his masterpiece is the Joseph story: he ends his narrative with the suicide of King Saul in the day of his defeat. If we contrast this climax with the J climax of a victorious King David, we feel strongly the man's intrinsic hatred of kings and their rule. His work is called the E Narrative because throughout the earlier parts of it the writer uses for God the Hebrew word "Elohim" instead of Jehovah.

The author of E has more exalted ideas of God than the author of J shows. No longer is God represented as Himself coming down or taking off chariot wheels as a man might do: E tells of God sending angels to do His bidding and of God appearing to men by night in dreams. It is characteristic of the language of E, for example, to refer to Mount Sinai as "Horeb", to the Canaanites as "Amorites", to Isaac's son always as "Jacob" and never as "Israel".

THE JE COMPILATION

After the fall of Samaria in 722 B.C., Judah became the possessor of the E narrative as well as of the J narrative. Both were very popular among the people, but still more popular became a single history made to combine them both, usually referred to as JE. The compiler did not attempt to make J and E tally. Sometimes he set down the two distinct narratives side by side: sometimes he took a narrative as a whole from one source and embodied in it a little material from the other source: sometimes he took almost equal amounts of material from the two sources and skilfully wove them into a single story: occasionally he added a few sentences of his own. But on the whole he treated the narratives with the utmost reverence, touching them as little as possible. The result was that before the Exile began, Judah had three narratives of the beginnings of Hebrew history, to which we have referred as J, E, and JE.

THE ATTITUDE OF THE EXILIC HISTORIANS

It was this compilation JE of which most use was made by the Deuteronomists in writing the history of the Establishment of the Kingdom. But of certain things in it they disapproved, and being writers of history with a moral, they omitted what did not fit in with their moral purposes. However, a later editor, in the centuries following the Exile, replaced most of what had been omitted. The Deuteronomists' own contribution is referred to as D.

In the Books of Judges and Samuel, then, we have J, E and D, with occasional rare additions by early or later editors. Little wonder is it that some readers of these books have found, to their distress, difficulties and discrepancies. Our grandparents believed that every word in the Bible had been, as it were, dictated by God and so must be in every little detail accurate. They were overwhelmed if they recognized in the old stories these discrepancies or the apparent approval by Jehovah of actions, which we, taught by Christ, now condemn.

We, who know how by means far more wonderful than mere "verbal inspiration" God gave to us the Bible, find these anomalies but the natural result of the whole complex growth of our religion. In vision and understanding of God men grew according to the great natural law, "First the blade, then the ear, after that the full corn in the ear."

2. STORIES OF JUDGES IN ISRAEL

THE SETTLEMENT IN CANAAN

In the next contribution to Exilic literature which we are to study, then, we must retrace our steps from the captivity in Babylon right back to the period before there were any kings in Israel; when the tribes with haunting recollections of life in Egypt and more vivid memories of existence as nomads in the wilderness, invaded Canaan, gradually secured more and more of a foothold there, and slowly moved towards such a measure of national unity as made possible the anointing of a king over the whole nation. It is generally believed that this period covers roughly the two centuries before the time of Saul, whose own date is approximately 1025 B.C.

During this period the various tribes were settled in different parts of the country, particularly in the hilly districts. But between them were the strongholds of the Canaanites, and all around them were their other foes, Midianites, Philistines and Ammonites. The Israelites and their foes lived side by side in the land: very slow indeed was the driving out of the enemy: neither in geographical position nor in spirit were the Israelites *one* nation. Jehovah was their King-God. From time to time arose in one or other part of the country a deliverer of the tribe in that district from the attacks of some enemy; and as the result of a military success, the deliverer, whether man or woman, acquired political power and ruled over the tribe until death intervened. These deliverers and rulers were called "Judges"; for the Hebrew word has a wider meaning than our English translation "judge".

Our main source of information about this period is the Book of Judges and the first few chapters of the Book of Samuel, which tell of Samuel himself, the last of the judges in Israel. In Judges i. 1–ii. 5 may be read from an old source the account of the precarious existence of the tribes in these early days, untouched by any Deuteronomic moralizing. For instance, we read—

And the Lord was with Judah; and he drave out the inhabitants of the mountain; but could not drive out the inhabitants of the valley, because they had chariots of iron.

Neither did Ephraim drive out the Canaanites that dwelt in Gezer; but the Canaanites dwelt in Gezer among them.

Judges i. 19, 29

The Deuteronomic editor did not like this: it is one of those early passages omitted by the Deuteronomists, but preserved in the old separate source which remained popular among the people. Later in the centuries after the Exile some editor of the Deuteronomic Book of Judges inserted this passage as the beginning of the book.

A DEUTERONOMIST'S VIEW OF THE SETTLEMENT

The Deuteronomist began the Book of Judges by referring to the work of Joshua and adding, "The children of Israel went every man unto his inheritance to possess the land" (ii. 6), a more suitable version, since, following Jehovah, the Israelites were sure of all success: this man thought that suffering always implies that the sufferer has been in the wrong. He passed on to expound his views of the whole period. Since Judah was to him the most important tribe of all, he gave as the first Judge Othniel of the tribe of Judah, a man of no fame in tradition compared with Deborah, Gideon, or Samson.

Judges raised up

And the children of Israel did evil in the sight of the Lord, and served Baalim: and they forsook the Lord God of their fathers, which brought them out of the land of Egypt, and followed other gods, of the gods of the people that were round about them, and bowed themselves unto them, and provoked the Lord to anger. And they

THE ESTABLISHMENT OF THE KINGDOM

forsook the Lord, and served Baal and Ashtaroth. And the anger of the Lord was hot against Israel, and he delivered them into the hands of spoilers that spoiled them, and he sold them into the hands of their enemies round about, so that they could not any longer stand before their enemies. Whithersoever they went out, the hand of the Lord was against them for evil, as the Lord had said, and as the Lord had sworn unto them: and they were greatly distressed. Nevertheless the Lord raised up judges, which delivered them out of the hand of those that spoiled them. And when the Lord raised them up judges, then the Lord was with the judge, and delivered them out of the hand of their enemies all the days of the judge: for it repented the Lord because of their groanings by reason of them that oppressed them and vexed them. And it came to pass, when the judge was dead, that they returned, and corrupted themselves more than their fathers, in following other gods to serve them, and to bow down unto them; they ceased not from their own doings, nor from their stubborn way.

[*Judges* ii. 11–16, 18, 19

Othniel of Judah as the First Judge

The anger of the Lord was hot against Israel, and He sold them into the hand of Chushan-rishathaim king of Mesopotamia: and the children of Israel served Chushan-rishathaim eight years. And when the children of Israel cried unto the Lord, the Lord raised up a deliverer to the children of Israel, who delivered them, even Othniel the son of Kenaz, Caleb's younger brother. And the Spirit of the Lord came upon him, and he judged Israel, and went out to war: and the Lord delivered Chushan-rishathaim king of Mesopotamia into his hand; and his hand prevailed against Chushan-rishathaim. And the land had rest forty years. And Othniel the son of Kenaz died.

[*Judges* iii. 8–11

THE DEUTERONOMIC EDITOR AND THE OLD STORIES

We should note at the close of the passage just quoted the phrase "forty years". The phrases "twenty years", "forty years", or "eighty years" are sure signs of the Deuteronomic editor at his work. He forced the chronology of this period into these phrases much as a boy who knows the answer he wants for a sum succeeds in obtaining it somehow, whether his facts warrant him or not! Scholars have worked out the time allowed for this pre-monarchic period in Canaan by the Deuteronomist, and have found that the years add up to about four hundred, instead of the two centuries by which we know other sources roughly measure the length of the period.

But apart from such a minor point as time to men who were in no way interested in historical dates, after giving the sop of Othniel to the tribe of Judah, the Deuteronomist allows the great old stories of Ehud, Deborah and Barak, Gideon, Jephthah and Samson to make their dramatic appeal to the hearts and conscience of the exiles. These narratives handed down orally and then in writing from generation to generation are full of sheer human interest and shed much light on the social conditions of the time. Here they were left unaltered except that the editor set each in a framework, giving to each what he considered a suitable introduction and ending. For instance, here is the beginning and ending of the story of Ehud.

A Framework for the Story of a Judge
And the children of Israel did evil again in the sight of the Lord: and the Lord strengthened Eglon the king of Moab against Israel, because they had done evil in the sight of the Lord. And he gathered unto him the children of Ammon and Amalek, and went and smote Israel, and possessed the city of palm trees. So the children of Israel served Eglon the king of Moab eighteen years. But when the children of Israel cried unto the Lord, the Lord raised them up a deliverer, Ehud the son of Gera, a Benjamite, a man left-handed. . . . So Moab was subdued that day under the hand of Israel. And the land had rest fourscore years.

[*Judges* iii. 12–15, 30

As, then, we pass on to read parts of these old stories, we shall not be surprised at discrepancies or at primitive and crude ideas about Jehovah: these things are but natural in a record made from at least two previous sources dating back some centuries before the time of the Exile, the time when, most probably, a Deuteronomic editor compiled this part of the Book of Judges.

Deborah and Gideon

The stories of Deborah and Gideon may be read together for the sake of the contrast which they afford. The foe in one case was a highly organized military force, in the other a horde of wanderers from the Eastern desert. The deliverer in the one case was a woman of resolution and courage, a mother in Israel;

THE ESTABLISHMENT OF THE KINGDOM

in the other, a man slow and hesitating in his movements, yet driven at last to action by his patriotism, his family feelings and his faith in God. In each case we are told that the victory was complete.

Israel oppressed by a Canaanite King

And the children of Israel again did evil in the sight of the Lord, when Ehud was dead. And the Lord sold them into the hand of Jabin king of Canaan, that reigned in Hazor; the captain of whose host was Sisera, which dwelt in Harosheth of the Gentiles. And the children of Israel cried unto the Lord: for he had nine hundred chariots of iron; and twenty years he mightily oppressed the children of Israel.

[*Judges* iv. 1–3]

Deborah a Judge in Israel

And Deborah, a prophetess, the wife of Lapidoth, she judged Israel at that time. And she dwelt under the palm tree of Deborah between Ramah and Bethel in mount Ephraim: and the children of Israel came up to her for judgment. And she sent and called Barak the son of Abinoam out of Kedesh-naphtali, and said unto him, "Hath not the Lord God of Israel commanded, saying, 'Go and draw toward Mount Tabor, and take with thee ten thousand men of the children of Naphtali and of the children of Zebulun? And I will draw unto thee to the river Kishon Sisera, the captain of Jabin's army, with his chariots and his multitude; and I will deliver him into thine hand.'" And Barak said unto her, "If thou wilt go with me, then I will go: but if thou wilt not go with me, then I will not go." And she said, "I will surely go with thee: notwithstanding the journey that thou takest shall not be for thine honour; for the Lord shall sell Sisera into the hand of a woman." And Deborah arose, and went with Barak to Kedesh.

[*Judges* iv. 4–9]

Barak and Deborah defeat Sisera

And Barak called Zebulun and Naphtali to Kedesh; and he went up with ten thousand men at his feet: and Deborah went up with him. Now Heber the Kenite, which was of the children of Hobab the father in law of Moses, had severed himself from the Kenites, and pitched his tent unto the plain of Zaanaim, which is by Kedesh. And they shewed Sisera that Barak the son of Abinoam was gone up to mount Tabor. And Sisera gathered together all his chariots, even nine hundred chariots of iron, and all the people that were with him, from Harosheth of the Gentiles unto the river of Kishon. And Deborah said unto Barak, "Up; for this is the day in which the Lord hath delivered Sisera into thine hand: is not the Lord gone out before thee?" So Barak went down from mount Tabor, and ten thousand men after him. And the Lord discomfited Sisera, and all his chariots, and all his host, with the edge of the sword before Barak; so that Sisera lighted down off his chariot, and fled away on his feet. But Barak pursued after the chariots, and after the host, unto Harosheth of the Gentiles: and all the host of Sisera fell upon the edge of the sword; and there was not a man left. Howbeit Sisera fled away on his feet to the tent of Jael the wife of Heber the Kenite: for there was peace between Jabin the king of Hazor and the house of Heber the Kenite.

[*Judges* iv. 10–17

In the Book of Judges are two accounts of Sisera's death at the hand of Jael. In the prose account given next, she kills him while he sleeps, and we shudder at the woman's treachery. But in the poetical account she kills him as he is about to drink in her tent, striking him down while he stands beside her, a less treacherous and bolder action. This poetical account, the "Song of Deborah" (Judges v. 1–31, see p. 13), is one of the oldest fragments of Biblical literature and, as scholars tell us, is more likely to be accurate than the prose account, since poetry can be handed down more accurately than prose. Thus it has been said that Jael's honour has been vindicated by modern scholarship!

Death of Sisera

And Jael went out to meet Sisera, and said unto him, "Turn in, my lord, turn in to me; fear not." And when he had turned in unto her into the tent, she covered him with a mantle. And he said unto her, "Give me, I pray thee, a little water to drink; for I am thirsty." And she opened a bottle of milk, and gave him drink, and covered him. Again he said unto her, "Stand in the door of the tent, and it shall be, when any man doth come and inquire of thee, and say, 'Is there any man here?' that thou shalt say, 'No.'" Then Jael Heber's wife took a peg of the tent, and took an hammer in her hand, and went softly unto him, and smote the peg into his temples, and fastened it into the ground: for he was fast asleep and weary. So he died. And, behold, as Barak pursued Sisera, Jael came out to meet him, and said unto him, "Come, and I will shew thee the man whom thou seekest." And when he came into her tent, behold, Sisera lay dead, and the peg was in his temples. So God subdued on that day Jabin the king of Canaan before the children of Israel. And the hand of the children of Israel prospered, and prevailed against Jabin the king of Canaan, until they had destroyed Jabin king of Canaan. And the land had rest forty years.

[*Judges* iv. 18–24, v. 31

THE ESTABLISHMENT OF THE KINGDOM

The Land overrun by Midianites from the Desert

And the children of Israel did evil in the sight of the Lord: and the Lord delivered them into the hand of Midian seven years. And the hand of Midian prevailed against Israel: and because of the Midianites the children of Israel made them the dens which are in the mountains, and caves, and strong holds. And so it was, when Israel had sown, that the Midianites came up, and the Amalekites, and the children of the east, even they came up against them; and they encamped against them, and destroyed the increase of the earth, till thou come unto Gaza, and left no sustenance for Israel, neither sheep, nor ox, nor ass. For they came up with their cattle and their tents, and they came as grasshoppers for multitude; for both they and their camels were without number: and they entered into the land to destroy it. And Israel was greatly impoverished because of the Midianites; and the children of Israel cried unto the Lord.

[*Judges* vi. 1–6

Gideon's Call

And there came an angel of the Lord, and sat under an oak which was in Ophrah, that pertained unto Joash the Abi-ezrite: and his son Gideon threshed wheat by the winepress, to hide it from the Midianites. And the angel of the Lord appeared unto him, and said unto him, "The Lord is with thee, thou mighty man of valour." And Gideon said unto him, "Oh my Lord, if the Lord be with us, why then is all this befallen us? And where be all His miracles which our fathers told us of, saying, 'Did not the Lord bring us up from Egypt?' But now the Lord hath forsaken us, and delivered us into the hands of the Midianites." And the Lord looked upon him, and said, "Go in this thy might, and thou shalt save Israel from the hand of the Midianites: have not I sent thee?" And he said unto him, "Oh my Lord, wherewith shall I save Israel? Behold, my family is poor in Manasseh, and I am the least in my father's house." And the Lord said unto him, "Surely I will be with thee, and thou shalt smite the Midianites as one man." And he said unto him, "If now I have found grace in thy sight, then shew me a sign that thou talkest with me. Depart not hence, I pray thee, until I come unto thee, and bring forth my present, and set it before thee." And he said, "I will tarry until thou come again."

And Gideon went in, and made ready a kid, and unleavened cakes of an ephah of flour: the flesh he put in a basket, and he put the broth in a pot, and brought it out unto him under the oak, and presented it. And the angel of God said unto him, "Take the flesh and the unleavened cakes, and lay them upon this rock, and pour out the broth." And he did so. Then the angel of the Lord put forth the end of the staff that was in his hand, and touched the flesh and the unleavened cakes; and there rose up fire out of the rock, and consumed the flesh and the unleavened cakes. Then the angel of the Lord departed out of his sight. And when Gideon perceived that he was an angel of the Lord, Gideon said, "Alas, O Lord God, for because I have seen an angel of the Lord face to face!" And the Lord said unto him, "Peace be unto thee; fear not: thou shalt not die." Then Gideon built an altar there unto the Lord, and called it Jehovah-shalom: unto this day it is yet in Ophrah of the Abi-ezrites.

[*Judges* vi. 11-24

Gideon's Hand against Baal

And it came to pass the same night, that the Lord said unto him, "Take thy father's young bullock, even the second bullock of seven years old, and throw down the altar of Baal that thy father hath, and cut down the grove that is by it: and build an altar unto the Lord thy God upon the top of this rock, in the ordered place, and take the second bullock, and offer a burnt sacrifice with the wood of the grove which thou shalt cut down." Then Gideon took ten men of his servants, and did as the Lord had said unto him: and so it was, because he feared his father's household, and the men of the city, that he could not do it by day, that he did it by night.

And when the men of the city arose early in the morning, behold, the altar of Baal was cast down, and the grove was cut down that was by it, and the second bullock was offered upon the altar that was built. And they said one to another, "Who hath done this thing?" And when they inquired and asked, they said, "Gideon the son of Joash hath done this thing." Then the men of the city said unto Joash, "Bring out thy son, that he may die: because he hath cast down the altar of Baal, and because he hath cut down the grove that was by it." And Joash said unto all that stood against him, "Will ye plead for Baal? Will ye save him? He that will plead for him, let him be put to death whilst it is yet morning: if he be a god, let him plead for himself, because one hath cast down his altar." Therefore on that day he called him Jerubbaal, saying, "Let Baal plead against him, because he hath thrown down his altar."

[*Judges* vi. 25-32

Gideon prepares against the Midianites

Then all the Midianites and the Amalekites and the children of the east were gathered together, and went over, and pitched in the valley of Jezreel. But the Spirit of the Lord came upon Gideon, and he blew a trumpet; and Abi-ezer was gathered after him. And he sent messengers throughout all Manasseh; who also was gathered after him: and he sent messengers unto Asher, and unto Zebulun, and unto Naphtali; and they came up to meet them.

And Gideon said unto God, "If Thou wilt save Israel by mine hand, as Thou hast said, behold, I will put a fleece of wool in the floor; and if the dew be on the fleece only, and it be dry upon all the earth beside, then shall I know that Thou wilt save Israel by mine hand, as Thou hast said." And it was so: for he rose up early on the morrow, and thrust the fleece together, and wringed the dew out of the fleece, a bowl full of water. And Gideon said unto God, "Let not Thine anger be hot against me, and I will speak but this once: let me prove, I pray Thee, but this once with the fleece; let it now be dry only upon the fleece, and upon all the ground let there be dew." And God did so that night: for it was dry upon the fleece only, and there was dew on all the ground.

Then Jerubbaal, who is Gideon, and all the people that were with him, rose up early, and pitched beside the well of Harod: so that the host of the Midianites were on the north side of them, by the hill of Moreh, in the valley. And the Lord said unto Gideon, "The people that are with thee are too many for Me to give the Midianites into their hands, lest Israel vaunt themselves against Me, saying, 'Mine own hand hath saved me.' Now therefore go to, proclaim in the ears of the people, saying, 'Whosoever is fearful and afraid, let him return and depart early from Mount Gilead.'" And there returned of the people twenty and two thousand; and there remained ten thousand. And the Lord said unto Gideon, "The people are yet too many; bring them down unto the water, and I will try them for thee there: and it shall be, that of whom I say unto thee, 'This shall go with thee,' the same shall go with thee; and of whomsoever I say unto thee, 'This shall not go with thee,' the same shall not go." So he brought down the people unto the water: and the Lord said unto Gideon, "Every one that lappeth of the water with his tongue, as a dog lappeth, him shalt thou set by himself; likewise every one that boweth down upon his knees to drink." And the number of them that lapped, putting their hand to their mouth, were three hundred men: but all the rest of the people bowed down upon their knees to drink water. And the Lord said unto Gideon, "By the three hundred men that lapped will I save you, and deliver the Midianites into thine hand: and let all the other people go every man unto his place." So the people took victuals in their hand, and their trumpets: and he sent all the rest of Israel every man unto his tent, and retained those three hundred men: and the host of Midian was beneath him in the valley.

[*Judges* vi. 33–40, vii. 1–8]

Gideon's Victory

And it came to pass the same night, that the Lord said unto him, "Arise, get thee down unto the host; for I have delivered it into thine hand. But if thou fear to go down, go thou with Phurah thy servant down to the host: and thou shalt hear what they say; and afterward shall thine hands be strengthened to go down unto the host." Then went he down with Phurah his servant unto the outside of the armed men that were in the host. And the Midianites and the Amalekites and all the children of the east lay along in the valley like grasshoppers for multitude; and their camels were without number, as the sand by the sea side for multitude. And when Gideon was come, behold, there was a man that told a dream unto his fellow, and said, "Behold, I dreamed a dream, and, lo, a cake of barley bread tumbled into the host of Midian, and came unto a tent, and smote it that it fell, and overturned it, that the tent lay along." And his fellow answered and said, "This is nothing else save the sword of Gideon the son of Joash, a man of Israel: for into his hand hath God delivered Midian, and all the host."

And it was so, when Gideon heard the telling of the dream, and the interpretation thereof, that he worshipped, and returned into the host of Israel, and said, "Arise; for the Lord hath delivered into your hand the host of Midian." And he divided the three hundred men into three companies, and he put a trumpet in every man's hand, with empty pitchers, and lamps within the pitchers. And he said unto them, "Look on me, and do likewise: and, behold, when I come to the outside of the camp, it shall be that, as I do, so shall ye do. When I blow with a trumpet, I and all that are with me, then blow ye the trumpets also on every side of all the camp, and say, 'The sword of the Lord, and of Gideon.' "

So Gideon, and the hundred men that were with him, came unto the outside of the camp in the beginning of the middle watch; and they had but newly set the watch: and they blew the trumpets, and brake the pitchers that were in their hands. And the three companies blew the trumpets, and brake the pitchers, and held the lamps in their left hands, and the trumpets in their right hands to blow withal: and they cried, "The sword of the Lord, and of Gideon." And they stood every man in his place round about the camp: and all the host ran, and cried, and fled. And the three hundred blew the trumpets, and the Lord set every man's sword against his fellow, even throughout all the host: and the host fled. Thus was Midian subdued before the children of Israel, so that they lifted up their heads no more. And the country was in quietness forty years in the days of Gideon.

[*Judges* vii. 9–22, viii. 28

JEPHTHAH'S DAUGHTER

In this case it is the Judge's daughter, not the Judge himself, whose memory abides in Israel and beyond Israel. This maid shines as a star in her patriotism and love. A nameless heroine, she has found a place in Tennyson's *Dream of Fair Women*.

Jephthah the Outlaw asked to help against the Ammonites

Now Jephthah the Gileadite was a mighty man of valour: and Gilead begat Jephthah. And Gilead's wife bare him sons; and his wife's sons grew up, and they thrust out Jephthah, and said unto him, "Thou shalt not inherit in our father's house; for thou art the son of a strange woman." Then Jephthah fled from his brethren, and dwelt in the land of Tob: and there were gathered vain men to Jephthah, and went out with him. And it came to pass in process of time, that the children of Ammon made war against Israel. And it was so, that when the children of Ammon made war against Israel, the elders of Gilead went to fetch Jephthah out of the land of Tob: and they said unto Jephthah, "Come, and be our captain, that we may fight with the children of Ammon." And Jephthah said unto the elders of Gilead, "Did not ye hate me, and expel me out of my father's house? Why are ye come unto me now when ye are in distress?" And the elders of Gilead said unto Jephthah, "Therefore we turn again to thee now, that thou mayest go with us, and fight against the children of Ammon, and be our head over all the inhabitants of Gilead." And Jephthah said unto the elders of Gilead, "If ye bring me home again to fight against the children of Ammon, and the Lord deliver them before me, shall I be your head?" And the elders of Gilead said unto Jephthah, "The Lord be witness between us, if we do not so according to thy words." Then Jephthah went with the elders of Gilead, and the people made him head and captain over them: and Jephthah uttered all his words before the Lord in Mizpeh.

[*Judges* xi. 1–11]

Jephthah first tried to settle affairs by diplomacy, but failed: war followed. To ensure success, at the solemn moment of final preparation for battle, Jephthah, in sad ignorance of the true character of Jehovah, vowed a life in recompense for the help of God. After a military victory, the life to be sacrificed proved to be that of a girl, Jephthah's only child.

Jephthah's Vow and Victory

Then the Spirit of the Lord came upon Jephthah, and he passed over Gilead, and Manasseh, and passed over Mizpeh of Gilead, and from Mizpeh of Gilead he passed over unto the children of Ammon. And Jephthah vowed a vow unto the Lord, and said, "If Thou shalt without fail deliver the children of Ammon into mine hands, then it shall be, that whatsoever cometh forth of the doors of my house to meet me, when I return in peace from the children of Ammon, shall surely be the Lord's, and I will offer it up for a burnt offering."

So Jephthah passed over unto the children of Ammon to fight against them; and the Lord delivered them into his hands. And he smote them from Aroer, even till thou come to Minnith, even twenty cities, and unto the plain of the vineyards, with a very great slaughter. Thus the children of Ammon were subdued before the children of Israel.

[*Judges* xi. 29–33]

Jephthah's Daughter

And Jephthah came to Mizpeh unto his house, and, behold, his daughter came out to meet him with timbrels and with dances: and she was his only child; beside her he had neither son nor daughter. And it came to pass, when he saw her, that he rent his clothes, and said, "Alas, my daughter! Thou hast brought me very low, and thou art one of them that trouble me: for I have opened my mouth unto the Lord, and I cannot go back."

And she said unto him, "My father, if thou hast opened thy mouth unto the Lord, do to me according to that which hath proceeded out of thy mouth; forasmuch as the Lord hath taken vengeance for thee of thine enemies, even of the children of Ammon." And she said unto her father, "Let this thing be done for me: let me alone two months, that I may go up and down upon the mountains, and bewail my virginity, I and my fellows." And he said, "Go." And he sent her away for two months: and she went with her companions, and bewailed her virginity upon the mountains.

And it came to pass at the end of two months, that she returned unto her father, who did with her according to his vow which he had vowed. And it was a custom in Israel, that the daughters of Israel went yearly to lament the daughter of Jephthah the Gileadite four days in a year.

[*Judges* xi. 34-40

A Tragedy of Strength

The following story of Samson was one of the most popular of the Hebrews' tales of their ancestors. At the beginning of their struggle with the Philistines, we have Samson, a single-handed Hercules, goading and irritating his foes by his contempt and by his too devastating practical jokes; a tragic figure at the last, with sightless eyes, bringing to death with himself a crowd of the most noble lords of the Philistines. Later in this long struggle with the Philistines, we have David who, like Samson, began single-handed against Goliath, but who, unlike that Hercules, ended as their king, leading a united nation to the complete defeat of these most doughty foes. The Philistines, like the Hebrews, were foreigners in Canaan, a strong and comparatively cultured people recently come from Crete. The land of Palestine takes its name from them.

We may note that the name "Samson" means "Sunny" or

THE ESTABLISHMENT OF THE KINGDOM

"Little Sun". Samson's fate, however, was tragic. The man to whom, as the Hebrews believed, Divine strength had been given through his hair, proved himself weak in the hands of women, unable to keep his silent counsel in face of their clever wiles. The hair was in those days regarded as in a special way the seat of divine energy in a man, because it showed the most rapid growth. Thus Samson's parents took for him, and he kept for himself, a vow to abstain from wine and to let his hair grow unshorn. The word "Nazirite" used in the story in reference to this vow means "one separated", that is, one separated unto God. The order of Nazirites appears to have been established as a protest against the excesses which were apt to creep into the worship of Jehovah on days of high feasting and sacrifice. The Canaanites' extremely sensual worship of their gods was likely to infect the worshippers of Jehovah.

In this story is the riddle which, scholars tell us, goes back to very early times indeed (see p. 15). The tale of Samson itself is of perennial interest, and while the story at times descends to the low and trivial, its ending rises to a high level of devotion and achievement. Of Samson's birth and the Philistine oppression we may read in Judges xiii, while in the following two chapters we see how Samson's fondness for Philistine women both gives him opportunities to display to the Philistines his amazing physical strength and leads to a revelation of the mighty man's surprising weakness in the hands of a weeping and imploring woman. "He judged Israel in the days of the Philistines twenty years" (Judges xv. 20). We give here only the last chapter of Samson's life.

Samson's last attachment was to Delilah, a companion figure to Circe, another great enchantress who turned her victim, not indeed into a pig, but into a blinded weak prisoner sick with remorse. This forms the theme of one of our well-known operas, Saint-Saëns' *Samson and Delilah*. And in the tragic figure of "Samson Agonistes" (Samson the Wrestler) the blind Milton saw something of himself, and was thereby inspired to a great poem. A reference to this poem will best increase our appreciation of the closing scene of Samson's life.

Samson enticed by Delilah

And it came to pass afterward, that he loved a woman in the valley of Sorek, whose name was Delilah. And the lords of the Philistines came up unto her, and said unto her, "Entice him, and see wherein his great strength lieth, and by what means we may prevail against him, that we may bind him to afflict him: and we will give thee every one of us eleven hundred pieces of silver."

And Delilah said to Samson, "Tell me, I pray thee, wherein thy great strength lieth, and wherewith thou mightest be bound to afflict thee." And Samson said unto her, "If they bind me with seven green withs that were never dried, then shall I be weak, and be as another man." Then the lords of the Philistines brought up to her seven green withs which had not been dried, and she bound him with them. Now there were men lying in wait, abiding with her in the chamber. And she said unto him, "The Philistines be upon thee, Samson." And he brake the withs, as a thread of tow is broken when it toucheth the fire. So his strength was not known.

And Delilah said unto Samson, "Behold, thou hast mocked me, and told me lies: now tell me, I pray thee, wherewith thou mightest be bound." And he said unto her, "If they bind me fast with new ropes that never were occupied, then shall I be weak, and be as another man." Delilah therefore took new ropes, and bound him therewith, and said unto him, "The Philistines be upon thee, Samson." And there were liers in wait abiding in the chamber. And he brake them from off his arms like a thread.

And Delilah said unto Samson, "Hitherto thou hast mocked me, and told me lies: tell me wherewith thou mightest be bound." And he said unto her, "If thou weavest the seven locks of my head with the web." And she fastened it with the pin, and said unto him, "The Philistines be upon thee, Samson." And he awaked out of his sleep, and went away with the pin of the beam, and with the web.

And she said unto him, "How canst thou say, 'I love thee,' when thine heart is not with me? Thou hast mocked me these three times, and hast not told me wherein thy great strength lieth." And it came to pass, when she pressed him daily with her words, and urged him, so that his soul was vexed unto death, that he told her all his heart, and said unto her, "There hath not come a razor upon mine head; for I have been a Nazarite unto God from my mother's womb: if I be shaven, then my strength will go from me, and I shall become weak, and be like any other man." And when Delilah saw that he had told her all his heart, she sent and called for the lords of the Philistines, saying, "Come up this once, for he hath shewed me all his heart." Then the lords of the Philistines came up unto her, and

THE ESTABLISHMENT OF THE KINGDOM

brought money in their hand. And she made him sleep upon her knees; and she called for a man, and she caused him to shave off the seven locks of his head; and she began to afflict him, and his strength went from him. And she said, "The Philistines be upon thee, Samson." And he awoke out of his sleep, and said, "I will go out as at other times before, and shake myself." And he wist not that the Lord was departed from him.

[*Judges* xvi. 4–20]

The Death of Samson

But the Philistines took him, and put out his eyes, and brought him down to Gaza, and bound him with fetters of brass; and he did grind in the prison house. Howbeit the hair of his head began to grow again after he was shaven.

Then the lords of the Philistines gathered them together for to offer a great sacrifice unto Dagon their god, and to rejoice: for they said, "Our god hath delivered Samson our enemy into our hand." And when the people saw him, they praised their god: for they said, "Our god hath delivered into our hands our enemy, and the destroyer of our country, which slew many of us." And it came to pass, when their hearts were merry, that they said, "Call for Samson, that he may make us sport." And they called for Samson out of the prison house; and he made them sport: and they set him between the pillars. And Samson said unto the lad that held him by the hand, "Suffer me that I may feel the pillars whereupon the house standeth, that I may lean upon them."

Now the house was full of men and women; and all the lords of the Philistines were there; and there were upon the roof about three thousand men and women, that beheld while Samson made sport. And Samson called unto the Lord, and said, "O Lord God, remember me, I pray Thee, and strengthen me, I pray Thee, only this once, O God, that I may be at once avenged of the Philistines for my two eyes." And Samson took hold of the two middle pillars upon which the house stood, and on which it was borne up, of the one with his right hand, and of the other with his left. And Samson said, "Let me die with the Philistines." And he bowed himself with all his might; and the house fell upon the lords, and upon all the people that were therein. So the dead which he slew at his death were more than they which he slew in his life. Then his brethren and all the house of his father came down, and took him, and brought him up, and buried him between Zorah and Eshtaol in the buryingplace of Manoah his father. And he judged Israel twenty years.

[*Judges* xvi. 21–31]

THE GROWTH OF THE BOOK OF JUDGES

The selections we have read give an outline of the Deuteronomic Book of Judges compiled probably in the earlier years of the

Exile for the religious edification of the exiles in Babylon. We have noted that this book was based on two or three early written sources, each of these in turn being based on still earlier oral and written tradition: in some of the stories, for instance in the story of Jael and Sisera, we find in the Old Testament two of these sources used side by side. We have noted also that the Deuteronomists made the best of the Hebrews' invasion of Canaan, hiding their difficulties in conquering the land, because of the firm belief of the Deuteronomists that worldly success must attend those whose God is Jehovah; that they forced the chronology of the period into an artificial framework by their use of the phrases "twenty years", "forty years", and "eighty years", thus roughly doubling the historic length of the period of the Judges up to the establishment of a monarchy in Israel; that they magnified these hero-judges into saviours of the *whole* of Israel, whereas in actual fact most of them delivered only one part of the land.

The Deuteronomists then omitted from the older narratives the account of the difficulties of the settlement: they also, it appears, omitted two other primitive stories found in the last chapters of the book (Judges xvii–xxi), as well as the story of Abimelech, Gideon's son in which occurs the very early "Fable of Jotham" which has been quoted on p. 16. None of these did they consider of religious significance to the exiles.

But if this new Exilic Book of Judges became popular with the people, the old narratives remained as popular as ever. Thus, about two hundred years after the Exile, when again a period of literary enterprise came upon the Jews, it was natural for an editor to restore to the Book of Judges those parts of the old narratives which the Deuteronomist had for his good reasons omitted. This later editor too appears to have liked the idea of each tribe having one judge to its credit, so that he probably is the man who inserted the brief accounts of five or six other leaders of men—Tola, Jair, Ibzan, Elon and Abdon (Judges x. 1–5, xii. 8–15), and perhaps Shamgar (iii. 31). He turned the book into "The Book of the Twelve Judges".

THE ESTABLISHMENT OF THE KINGDOM 197

Two Primitive Tales

Here we give two of these old narratives, deliberately omitted from the Deuteronomic Book of Judges because lacking in religious significance to the exiles, but reinserted by an appreciative editor some two hundred years or so later. The first is the story of Gideon's son Abimelech: the second an account of the migration of the tribe of Dan and the foundation of a Danite sanctuary in the far North of Canaan.

Abimelech made King in Shechem

And Abimelech the son of Jerubbaal went to Shechem unto his mother's brethren, and communed with them, and with all the family of the house of his mother's father, saying, "Speak, I pray you, in the ears of all the men of Shechem. 'Whether is better for you, either that all the sons of Jerubbaal, which are threescore and ten persons, reign over you, or that one reign over you? Remember also that I am your bone and your flesh.'" And his mother's brethren spake of him in the ears of all the men of Shechem all these words: and their hearts inclined to follow Abimelech; for they said, "He is our brother."

And they gave him threescore and ten pieces of silver out of the house of Baal-berith, wherewith Abimelech hired vain and light persons, which followed him. And he went unto his father's house at Ophrah, and slew his brethren the sons of Jerubbaal, being threescore and ten persons, upon one stone: notwithstanding yet Jotham the youngest son of Jerubbaal was left; for he hid himself. And all the men of Shechem gathered together, and all the house of Millo, and went, and made Abimelech king, by the plain of the pillar that was in Shechem.

[*Judges* ix. 1–6

The story of Abimelech appears to have been compiled from material from the two sources J and E. There follows (verses 7–21) "The Fable of Jotham" already given on p. 16, used as a text on which to hang curses on both Abimelech and the men of Shechem. The narrative develops into an account of the warfare between Abimelech and Shechem. Abimelech defeats Shechem, but escapes only to die at Thebez.

Abimelech defeats Shechem

When Abimelech had reigned three years over Israel, then God sent an evil spirit between Abimelech and the men of Shechem; and the men of Shechem dealt treacherously with Abimelech: that the cruelty done to the threescore and ten sons of Jerubbaal might come, and their blood be laid upon Abimelech their brother, which slew them; and upon the men of Shechem, which aided him in the killing of his brethren. And the men of Shechem set liers in wait for him in the top of the mountains, and they robbed all that came along that way by them: and it was told Abimelech.

And Gaal the son of Ebed came with his brethren, and went over to Shechem: and the men of Shechem put their confidence in him. And they went out into the fields, and gathered their vineyards, and trod the grapes, and made merry, and went into the house of their god, and did eat and drink, and cursed Abimelech. And Gaal the son of Ebed said, "Who is Abimelech, and who is Shechem, that we should serve him? Is not he the son of Jerubbaal? And would to God this people were under my hand! Then would I remove Abimelech."

And when Zebul the ruler of the city heard the words of Gaal the son of Ebed, his anger was kindled. And he sent messengers unto Abimelech privily, saying, "Behold, Gaal the son of Ebed and his brethren be come to Shechem; and, behold, they fortify the city against thee." And Abimelech rose up, and all the people that were with him, by night, and they laid wait against Shechem in four companies. And Gaal the son of Ebed went out, and stood in the entering of the gate of the city: and Abimelech rose up, and the people that were with him, from lying in wait.

And when Gaal saw the people, he said to Zebul, "Behold, there come people down from the top of the mountains." And Zebul said unto him, "Thou seest the shadow of the mountains as if they were men." And Gaal spake again and said, "See there come people down by the middle of the land, and another company come along by the plain." Then said Zebul unto him, "Where is now thy mouth, wherewith thou saidst, 'Who is Abimelech, that we should serve him?' Is not this the people that thou hast despised? Go out, I pray now, and fight with them." And Gaal went out before the men of Shechem, and fought with Abimelech. And Abimelech chased him, and he fled before him, and many were overthrown and wounded, even unto the entering of the gate.

And Abimelech dwelt at Arumah: and Zebul thrust out Gaal and his brethren, that they should not dwell in Shechem. And it came to pass on the morrow, that the people went out into the field; and they told Abimelech. And he took the people, and divided them into three companies, and laid wait in the field, and looked, and, behold, the people were come forth out of the city; and he rose up against them, and smote them. And Abimelech, and the company that was with him, rushed forward, and stood in the entering of the gate of the city: and the two other companies ran upon all the people that were in the fields, and slew them. And Abimelech fought against the city all that day; and he took the city, and slew the people that was therein, and beat down the city, and sowed it with salt.

THE ESTABLISHMENT OF THE KINGDOM 199

And when all the men of the tower of Shechem heard that, they entered into an hold of the house of the god Berith. And it was told Abimelech, that all the men of the tower of Shechem were gathered together. And Abimelech gat him up to Mount Zalmon, he and all the people that were with him; and Abimelech took an ax in his hand, and cut down a bough from the trees, and took it, and laid it on his shoulder, and said unto the people that were with him, "What ye have seen me do, make haste, and do as I have done." And all the people likewise cut down every man his bough, and followed Abimelech, and put them to the hold, and set the hold on fire upon them; so that all the men of the tower of Shechem died also, about a thousand men and women.

[*Judges* ix. 22-49]

The Death of Abimelech

Then went Abimelech to Thebez, and encamped against Thebez, and took it. But there was a strong tower within the city, and thither fled all the men and women, and all they of the city, and shut it to them, and gat them up to the top of the tower. And Abimelech came unto the tower, and fought against it, and went hard unto the door of the tower to burn it with fire. And a certain woman cast a piece of a millstone upon Abimelech's head, and all to brake his skull. Then he called hastily unto the young man his armourbearer, and said unto him, "Draw thy sword, and slay me, that men say not of me, 'A woman slew him.'" And his young man thrust him through, and he died.

[*Judges* ix. 50-54]

We next read the story of the Danites and their sanctuary.

Micah's Images

There was a man of Mount Ephraim, whose name was Micah. And he said unto his mother, "The eleven hundred shekels of silver that were taken from thee, about which thou cursedst, and spakest of it also in mine ears, behold, the silver is with me; I took it. Now therefore I will restore it unto thee." And he restored the eleven hundred shekels of silver to his mother. And his mother said, "Blessed of the Lord be my son. I had dedicated the silver unto the Lord from my hand for my son, to make a graven image and a molten image." And his mother took two hundred shekels of silver, and gave them to the founder, who made thereof a graven image and a molten image: and they were in the house of Micah. And the man Micah had an house of gods, and made an ephod, and teraphim, and consecrated one of his sons who became his priest. In those days there was no king in Israel, but every man did that which was right in his own eyes.

[*Judges* xvii. 1-6]

THE HEART OF THE BIBLE

Micah's Priest

And there was a young man of Beth-lehem-judah of the family of Judah, who was a Levite, and he sojourned there. And the man departed out of the city from Beth-lehem-judah to sojourn where he could find a place: and he came to Mount Ephraim to the house of Micah, as he journeyed. And Micah said unto him, "Whence comest thou?" And he said unto him, "I am a Levite of Beth-lehem-judah, and I go to sojourn where I may find a place."

And Micah said unto him, "Dwell with me, and be unto me a father and a priest, and I will give thee ten shekels of silver by the year, and a suit of apparel, and thy victuals." So the Levite went in. And the Levite was content to dwell with the man; and the young man was unto him as one of his sons. And Micah consecrated the Levite; and the young man became his priest, and was in the house of Micah. Then said Micah, "Now know I that the Lord will do me good, seeing I have a Levite to my priest."

[*Judges* xvii. 7–13]

Micah's House visited by Danite Spies

In those days there was no king in Israel: and in those days the tribe of the Danites sought them an inheritance to dwell in; for unto that day all their inheritance had not fallen unto them among the tribes of Israel. And the children of Dan sent of their family five men from their coasts, men of valour, from Zorah, and from Eshtaol, to spy out the land, and to search it; and they said unto them, "Go, search the land." When they came to Mount Ephraim, to the house of Micah, they lodged there.

When they were by the house of Micah, they knew the voice of the young man the Levite: and they turned in thither, and said unto him, "Who brought thee hither? What makest thou in this place? What hast thou here?" And he said unto them, "Thus and thus dealeth Micah with me, and hath hired me, and I am his priest." And they said unto him, "Ask counsel, we pray thee, of God, that we may know whether our way which we go shall be prosperous." And the priest said unto them, "Go in peace: before the Lord is your way wherein ye go."

[*Judges* xviii. 1–6]

The Spies' Report

Then the five men departed, and came to Laish, and saw the people that were therein, how they dwelt careless, after the manner of the Zidonians, quiet and secure; and there was no magistrate in the land, that might put them to shame in any thing; and they were far from the Zidonians, and had no business with any man. And they came unto their brethren to Zorah and Eshtaol: and their brethren said unto them, "What say ye?" And they said, "Arise, that we may go up against them: for we have seen the land, and, behold, it is very

THE ESTABLISHMENT OF THE KINGDOM

good: and are ye still? Be not slothful to go, and to enter to possess the land. When ye go, ye shall come unto a people secure, and to a large land: for God hath given it into your hands; a place where there is no want of any thing that is in the earth."

[*Judges* xviii. 7-10]

The Danites' Migration and Sanctuary

And there went from thence of the family of the Danites, out of Zorah and out of Eshtaol, six hundred men appointed with weapons of war. And they went up, and pitched in Kirjath-jearim, in Judah. And they passed thence unto Mount Ephraim, and came unto the house of Micah.

Then answered the five men that went to spy out the country of Laish, and said unto their brethren, "Do ye know that there is in these houses an ephod, and teraphim, and a graven image, and a molten image? Now therefore consider what ye have to do." And they turned thitherward, and came to the house of the young man the Levite, even unto the house of Micah, and saluted him. And the six hundred men appointed with their weapons of war, which were of the children of Dan, stood by the entering of the gate.

And the five men that went to spy out the land went up, and came in thither, and took the graven image, and the ephod, and the teraphim, and the molten image: and the priest stood in the entering of the gate with the six hundred men that were appointed with weapons of war. And these went into Micah's house, and fetched the carved image, the ephod, and the teraphim, and the molten image. Then said the priest unto them, "What do ye?" And they said unto him, "Hold thy peace, lay thine hand upon thy mouth, and go with us, and be to us a father and a priest: is it better for thee to be a priest unto the house of one man, or that thou be a priest unto a tribe and a family in Israel?" And the priest's heart was glad, and he took the ephod, and the teraphim, and the graven image, and went in the midst of the people. So they turned and departed, and put the little ones and the cattle and the carriage before them.

And when they were a good way from the house of Micah, the men that were in the houses near to Micah's house were gathered together, and overtook the children of Dan. And they cried unto the children of Dan. And they turned their faces, and said unto Micah, "What aileth thee, that thou comest with such a company?" And he said, "Ye have taken away my gods which I made, and the priest, and ye are gone away: and what have I more? And what is this that ye say unto me, What aileth thee?" And the children of Dan said unto him, "Let not thy voice be heard among us, lest angry fellows run upon thee, and thou lose thy life, with the lives of thy household." And the children of Dan went their way: and when Micah saw that they were too strong for him, he turned and went back unto his house.

And they took the things which Micah had made, and the priest which he had, and came unto Laish, unto a people that were at quiet and secure: and they smote them with the edge of the sword, and burnt the city with fire. And there was no deliverer, because it was far from Zidon, and they had no business with any man; and it was in the valley that lieth by Beth-rehob. And they built a city, and dwelt therein. And they called the name of the city Dan, after the name of Dan their father, who was born unto Israel: howbeit the name of the city was Laish at the first. And the children of Dan set up the graven image.

[*Judges* xviii. 11–30

These two narratives have not one trace of the Deuteronomist about them: they are simple stories of primitive times before there was any king in Israel. We owe to some editor writing probably two centuries after the Exile their reinsertion in the Book of Judges.

We have thus seen that the story of the growth of the Book of Judges is a complex one, and not one iota simpler is the story of the growth of the Book of Samuel. In it too we shall find contradictions and discrepancies, differing accounts of the same events set down side by side, with here and there the Deuteronomic Compiler introducing, as it were, his deep organ notes of religious exhortation and instruction.

Samuel, the Last of the Judges

The history of the Hebrew people has now reached a new stage of development; in the next few stories we are to see the birth of the *national* spirit. At last, under the leadership of a succession of great men—Samuel, Saul, David, Solomon—they stand forth as conquerors over all their surrounding enemies, in possession of their own country, united as a nation, *the* nation of Jehovah. In the first of these stories the centre of the religious life of the nation is where the ark abides: in the last is built in Jerusalem a Temple, to be the permanent home of the ark, the heart of the people, a place of worship for the whole nation. Here we shall see the most triumphant phase of the history of the Hebrews; we shall see how it was that they became so firmly attached to Canaan and to Jerusalem, the City of God.

THE ESTABLISHMENT OF THE KINGDOM

Yet these victories and successes, striking though they were, hid a worm of corruption in their midst—the evil spirit that is in men: not through these things could the world be saved. The nation had far to travel before the Saviour of the World could be born.

The beginning of this triumphant epoch in Hebrew history was in darkness, and the cause of the darkness was still the Philistine foe. Not yet was there sufficient strength among the people to meet adequately such a virile enemy. Eli, it is true, led a religious life, but he could not restrain his sons from a wickedness which brought destruction to themselves and others. Israel placed hope not in Jehovah and in His righteousness, but in the presence of the ark: a great superstition, not an act of vital faith in God. Death came to many and the ark for a time was lost. At last after many years the Hebrew people said to Samuel, "Cease not to cry unto the Lord our God for us that He will save us out of the hand of the Philistines": "so the Philistines were subdued."

The Grief of a Childless Woman

Now there was a certain man of Ramathaim-zophim, of Mount Ephraim, and his name was Elkanah. And he had two wives; the name of the one was Hannah, and the name of the other Peninnah: and Peninnah had children, but Hannah had no children. And this man went up out of his city yearly to worship and to sacrifice unto the Lord of hosts in Shiloh. And the two sons of Eli, Hophni and Phinehas, the priests of the Lord, were there.

Hannah rose up after they had eaten in Shiloh, and after they had drunk. Now Eli the priest sat upon a seat by a post of the temple of the Lord. And she was in bitterness of soul, and prayed unto the Lord, and wept sore. And she vowed a vow, and said, "O Lord of hosts, if Thou wilt indeed look on the affliction of Thine handmaid, and remember me, and not forget Thine handmaid, but wilt give unto Thine handmaid a man child, then I will give him unto the Lord all the days of his life, and there shall no razor come upon his head." And it came to pass, as she continued praying before the Lord, that Eli marked her mouth. Now Hannah, she spake in her heart; only her lips moved, but her voice was not heard: therefore Eli thought she had been drunken. And Eli said unto her, "How long wilt thou be drunken? Put away thy wine from thee." And Hannah answered and said, "No, my lord, I am a woman of a sorrowful spirit: I have drunk neither wine nor strong drink, but have poured out my soul before the Lord. Count not thine handmaid for a daughter of Belial: for out of the abundance of my complaint and grief have I spoken hitherto." Then Eli answered and said, "Go in peace: and the God of Israel grant thee thy petition that thou hast asked of Him." And she said, "Let thine handmaid find grace in thy sight." So the woman went her way, and did eat, and her countenance was no more sad.

[1 Samuel i. 1–3, 9–18

The Birth of Samuel

And they rose up in the morning early, and worshipped before the Lord, and returned, and came to their house to Ramah: and the Lord remembered Hannah. Wherefore it came to pass that she bare a son, and called his name Samuel, saying, "Because I have asked him of the Lord." And the man Elkanah, and all his house, went up to offer unto the Lord the yearly sacrifice, and his vow. But Hannah went not up; for she said unto her husband, "I will not go up until the child be weaned, and then I will bring him, that he may appear before the Lord, and there abide for ever." And Elkanah her husband said unto her, "Do what seemeth thee good; tarry until thou have weaned him; only the Lord establish His word." So the woman abode, and gave her son suck until she weaned him.

[1 Samuel i. 19–23

The Child Samuel dedicated to God

And when she had weaned him, she took him up with her, with three bullocks, and one ephah of flour, and a bottle of wine, and brought him unto the house of the Lord in Shiloh: and the child was young. And they slew a bullock, and brought the child to Eli. And she said, "Oh my lord, as thy soul liveth, my lord, I am the woman that stood by thee here, praying unto the Lord. For this child I prayed; and the Lord hath given me my petition which I asked of him: therefore also I have lent him to the Lord; as long as he liveth he shall be lent to the Lord." And he worshipped the Lord there. And Elkanah went to Ramah to his house. And the child did minister unto the Lord before Eli the priest.

Now the sons of Eli were sons of Belial; they knew not the Lord. But Samuel ministered before the Lord, being a child, girded with a linen ephod. Moreover his mother made him a little coat, and brought it to him from year to year, when she came up with her husband to offer the yearly sacrifice.

[1 Samuel i. 24–28, ii. 11, 12, 18, 19

The Wickedness of Eli's Sons

Now Eli was very old, and heard all that his sons did unto all Israel; and he said unto them, "Why do ye such things? I hear of your evil dealings by all this people. Nay, my sons; for it is no good report that I hear: ye make the Lord's people to transgress.

THE ESTABLISHMENT OF THE KINGDOM

If one man sin against another, the judge shall judge him: but if a man sin against the Lord, who shall intreat for him?" Notwithstanding they hearkened not unto the voice of their father, because the Lord would slay them. And the child Samuel grew on, and was in favour both with the Lord, and also with men.

[1 *Samuel* ii. 22–26

The Deuteronomic Compiler was so anxious that the people should not miss the significance of Eli's failure to rule over his own household that at this point (1 Sam. ii. 27–36) he inserted an account of a visit to Eli from a "man of God" to rebuke him. In the next chapter, in the midst of the old story of Samuel's call (iii. 11–14), he again takes the opportunity to give additional religious instruction on a father's responsibility for the wickedness of his children.

The Call of Samuel

And the child Samuel ministered unto the Lord before Eli. And the word of the Lord was precious in those days; there was no open vision. And it came to pass at that time, when Eli was laid down in his place, and his eyes began to wax dim, that he could not see; and ere the lamp of God went out in the temple of the Lord, where the ark of God was, and Samuel was laid down to sleep; that the Lord called Samuel: and he answered, "Here am I." And he ran unto Eli, and said, "Here am I; for thou calledst me." And he said, "I called not; lie down again." And he went and lay down. And the Lord called yet again, "Samuel." And Samuel arose and went to Eli, and said, "Here am I; for thou didst call me." And he answered, "I called not, my son; lie down again." Now Samuel did not yet know the Lord, neither was the word of the Lord yet revealed unto him.

And the Lord called Samuel again the third time. And he arose and went to Eli, and said, "Here am I; for thou didst call me." And Eli perceived that the Lord had called the child. Therefore Eli said unto Samuel, "Go, lie down: and it shall be, if He call thee, that thou shalt say, 'Speak, Lord; for Thy servant heareth.'" So Samuel went and lay down in his place. And the Lord came, and stood, and called as at other times, "Samuel, Samuel." Then Samuel answered, "Speak; for Thy servant heareth." And the Lord said to Samuel, "Behold, I will do a thing in Israel, at which both the ears of every one that heareth it shall tingle. In that day I will perform against Eli all things which I have spoken concerning his house: when I begin, I will also make an end. For I have told him that I will judge his house for ever for the iniquity which he knoweth; because his sons made themselves vile, and he restrained them not. And therefore I have sworn unto the house of Eli, that the iniquity of Eli's house shall not be purged with sacrifice nor offering for ever."

And Samuel lay until the morning, and opened the doors of the house of the Lord. And Samuel feared to shew Eli the vision. Then Eli called Samuel, and said, "Samuel, my son." And he answered, "Here am I." And he said, "What is the thing that the Lord hath said unto thee? I pray thee hide it not from me: God do so to thee, and more also, if thou hide any thing from me of all the things that He said unto thee." And Samuel told him every whit, and hid nothing from him. And he said, "It is the Lord: let Him do what seemeth Him good."

And Samuel grew, and the Lord was with him, and did let none of his words fall to the ground. And all Israel from Dan even to Beer-sheba knew that Samuel was established to be a prophet of the Lord. And the Lord appeared again in Shiloh: for the Lord revealed Himself to Samuel in Shiloh by the word of the Lord.

[1 *Samuel* iii. 1–21

The Philistines' Triumph

Now Israel went out against the Philistines to battle, and pitched beside Eben-ezer: and the Philistines pitched in Aphek. And the Philistines put themselves in array against Israel: and when they joined battle, Israel was smitten before the Philistines: and they slew of the army in the field about four thousand men.

And when the people were come into the camp, the elders of Israel said, "Wherefore hath the Lord smitten us to-day before the Philistines? Let us fetch the ark of the covenant of the Lord out of Shiloh unto us, that, when it cometh among us, it may save us out of the hand of our enemies." So the people sent to Shiloh, that they might bring from thence the ark of the covenant of the Lord of hosts, which dwelleth between the cherubim: and the two sons of Eli, Hophni and Phinehas, were there with the ark of the covenant of God. And when the ark of the covenant of the Lord came into the camp, all Israel shouted with a great shout, so that the earth rang again. And when the Philistines heard the noise of the shout, they said, "What meaneth the noise of this great shout in the camp of the Hebrews?" And they understood that the ark of the Lord was come into the camp.

And the Philistines were afraid, for they said, "God is come into the camp." And they said, "Woe unto us! There hath not been such a thing heretofore. Woe unto us! Who shall deliver us out of the hand of these mighty Gods? These are the Gods that smote the Egyptians with all the plagues in the wilderness. Be strong, and quit yourselves like men, O ye Philistines, that ye be not servants unto the Hebrews, as they have been to you: quit yourselves like men, and fight." And the Philistines fought, and Israel was smitten, and they fled every man into his tent: and there was a very great slaughter;

for there fell of Israel thirty thousand footmen. And the ark of God was taken; and the two sons of Eli, Hophni and Phinehas, were slain.

And there ran a man of Benjamin out of the army, and came to Shiloh the same day with his clothes rent, and with earth upon his head. And when he came, lo, Eli sat upon a seat by the wayside watching: for his heart trembled for the ark of God. And when the man came into the city, and told it, all the city cried out. And when Eli heard the noise of the crying, he said, "What meaneth the noise of this tumult?" And the man came in hastily, and told Eli. Now Eli was ninety and eight years old; and his eyes were dim, that he could not see. And the man said unto Eli, "I am he that came out of the army, and I fled to day out of the army." And he said, "What is there done, my son?" And the messenger answered and said, "Israel is fled before the Philistines, and there hath been also a great slaughter among the people, and thy two sons also, Hophni and Phinehas, are dead, and the ark of God is taken." And it came to pass, when he made mention of the ark of God, that he fell from off the seat backward by the side of the gate, and his neck brake, and he died: for he was an old man, and heavy. And he had judged Israel forty years.

[1 *Samuel* iv. 1–18

In 1 Samuel v and vi we may read a strange old story of mysterious and dire happenings which befell the Philistines in whose city the ark was at any time placed. These things befell also the men of Beth-shemesh, whither finally the Philistines returned the ark in a cart. It is possible that this story is based on the fact that the ark carried with it the infection of some plague. These men, with their childish ideas of God, thought that such trouble came because they offended against the majesty of Jehovah by touching the ark: we know better of the Father in Heaven. Very probably the ark was a centre of plague infection about which little was known in those days: see the description of the plague which attacked Sennacherib and his army (p. 141). Finally, it was sent to Kirjath-jearim, where a man was "sanctified to keep the ark of the Lord".

Samuel leads the People to Victory

And it came to pass, while the ark abode in Kirjath-jearim, that the time was long; for it was twenty years: and all the house of Israel lamented after the Lord. And Samuel spake unto all the house of Israel, saying, "If ye do return unto the Lord with all your hearts, then put away the strange gods and Ashtaroth from among you, and prepare your hearts unto the Lord, and serve Him only: and He will deliver you out of the hand of the Philistines." And when the Philistines heard that the children of Israel were gathered together to Mizpeh, the lords of the Philistines went up against Israel. And when the children of Israel heard it, they were afraid of the Philistines. And the children of Israel said to Samuel, "Cease not to cry unto the Lord our God for us, that He will save us out of the hand of the Philistines." And Samuel took a sucking lamb, and offered it for a burnt offering wholly unto the Lord: and Samuel cried unto the Lord for Israel; and the Lord heard him. And as Samuel was offering up the burnt offering, the Philistines drew near to battle against Israel: but the Lord thundered with a great thunder on that day upon the Philistines, and discomfited them; and they were smitten before Israel. And the men of Israel went out of Mizpeh, and pursued the Philistines, and smote them, until they came under Beth-car. Then Samuel took a stone, and set it between Mizpeh and Shen, and called the name of it Eben-ezer, saying, "Hitherto hath the Lord helped us." So the Philistines were subdued. And Samuel judged Israel all the days of his life. And he went from year to year in circuit to Beth-el, and Gilgal, and Mizpeh, and judged Israel in all those places. And his return was to Ramah; for there was his house; and there he judged Israel; and there he built an altar unto the Lord.

[*From* 1 *Samuel* vii

3. THE CHOICE OF SAUL AS KING. TWO NARRATIVES

EXAMPLES OF COMBINED NARRATIVES

We now come to a part of the narrative where the complete text in the Bible shows very evident contradictions. In some parts the desire for a king is regarded as the natural development of the national spirit, and Samuel, without any criticism, gives the people the needed help. In other parts the desire for a king is taken as a sign of wickedness in the nation: the people are warned that trouble will come of it.

A little later we meet with two entirely different accounts of the first introduction of David to Saul. In the one David comes as a shepherd musician to play to the sick and melancholy king. In the other, bringing food to his brothers on the eve of the battle with the Philistines. David, a stranger lad, offers himself as champion against Goliath, so attracting unto himself the notice of King Saul.

THE ESTABLISHMENT OF THE KINGDOM

Here we have tried, with the help of scholars who know well the original *Hebrew* Book of Samuel, to disentangle the two narratives where real difficulty would otherwise arise. We should recollect (see p. 178) that the author of the J Narrative was a very vivid story-teller, with a deep sense of the purpose of God working itself out in Hebrew history: that the author of the E Narrative hated the idea of Israel having any king but Jehovah; while the contributors of D cared most about the worship of God in the Temple in Jerusalem and were certain that all iniquity brought disaster and that all righteousness brought joy and victory.

(a) THE J NARRATIVE

Saul seeks his Father's Asses

Now there was a man of Benjamin, whose name was Kish. And he had a son, whose name was Saul, a choice young man, and a goodly: and there was not among the children of Israel a goodlier person than he: from his shoulders and upward he was higher than any of the people. And the asses of Kish Saul's father were lost. And Kish said to Saul his son, "Take now one of the servants with thee, and arise, go seek the asses." And he passed through Mount Ephraim, and passed through the land of Shalisha, but they found them not: then they passed through the land of Shalim, and there they were not: and he passed through the land of the Benjamites, but they found them not.

And when they were come to the land of Zuph, Saul said to his servant that was with him, "Come, and let us return; lest my father leave caring for the asses, and take thought for us." And he said unto him, "Behold now, there is in this city a man of God, and he is an honourable man; all that he saith cometh surely to pass: now let us go thither; peradventure he can shew us our way that we should go." Then said Saul to his servant, "But, behold, if we go, what shall we bring the man? The bread is spent in our vessels, and there is not a present to bring to the man of God: what have we?" And the servant answered Saul again, and said, "Behold, I have here at hand the fourth part of a shekel of silver: that will I give to the man of God, to tell us our way." Then said Saul to his servant, "Well said; come, let us go." So they went unto the city where the man of God was.

And as they went up the hill to the city, they found young maidens going out to draw water, and said unto them, "Is the seer here?" And they answered them, and said, "He is; behold, he is before you: make haste now, for he came to-day to the city; for there is a sacrifice of the people to-day in the high place: as soon as ye be come into the city, ye shall straightway find him, before he go up to the high place to eat: for the people will not eat until he come, because he doth bless the sacrifice; and afterwards they eat that be bidden. Now therefore get you up; for about this time ye shall find him." And they went up into the city: and when they were come into the city, behold, Samuel came out against them, to go up to the high place. Now the Lord had told Samuel in his ear a day before Saul came, saying, "To-morrow about this time I will send thee a man out of the land of Benjamin, and thou shalt anoint him to be captain over My people Israel, that he may save My people out of the hand of the Philistines: for I have looked upon My people, because their cry is come unto Me." And when Samuel saw Saul, the Lord said unto him, "Behold the man whom I spake to thee of! This same shall reign over My people."

[*From* 1 *Samuel* ix. 1–17

Saul meets Samuel

Then Saul drew near to Samuel in the gate, and said, "Tell me, I pray thee, where the seer's house is." And Samuel answered Saul, and said, "I am the seer: go up before me unto the high place; for ye shall eat with me to-day, and to-morrow I will let thee go, and will tell thee all that is in thine heart. And as for thine asses that were lost three days ago, set not thy mind on them; for they are found. And on whom is all the desire of Israel? Is it not on thee, and on all thy father's house?" And Saul answered and said, "Am not I a Benjamite, of the smallest of the tribes of Israel? And my family the least of all the families of the tribe of Benjamin? Wherefore then speakest thou so to me?"

And Samuel took Saul and his servant, and brought them into the parlour, and made them sit in the chiefest place among them that were bidden, which were about thirty persons. And Samuel said unto the cook, "Bring the portion which I gave thee, of which I said unto thee, 'Set it by thee.'" And the cook took up the shoulder, and that which was upon it, and set it before Saul. And Samuel said, "Behold that which is left! Set it before thee, and eat: for unto this time hath it been kept for thee since I said, 'I have invited the people.'" So Saul did eat with Samuel that day. And when they were come down from the high place into the city, Samuel communed with Saul upon the top of the house.

[1 *Samuel* ix. 18–25

Samuel anoints Saul

And they arose early: and it came to pass about the spring of the day, that Samuel called Saul to the top of the house, saying, "Up, that I may send thee away." And Saul arose, and they went out both of them, he and Samuel, abroad. And as they were going down to the end of the city, Samuel said to Saul, "Bid the servant pass on

THE ESTABLISHMENT OF THE KINGDOM

before us," (and he passed on,) "but stand thou still a while, that I may shew thee the word of God."

Then Samuel took a vial of oil and poured it upon his head, and kissed him, and said, "Is it not because the Lord hath anointed thee to be captain over His inheritance? When thou art departed from me to-day, then thou shalt find two men by Rachel's sepulchre in the border of Benjamin at Zelzah; and they will say unto thee, 'The asses which thou wentest to seek are found: and, lo, thy father hath left the care of the asses, and sorroweth for you, saying, What shall I do for my son?' Then shalt thou go on forward from thence, and thou shalt come to the plain of Tabor, and there shall meet thee three men going up to God to Beth-el, one carrying three kids, and another carrying three loaves of bread. And they will salute thee, and give thee two loaves of bread; which thou shalt receive of their hands. After that thou shalt come to the hill of God, where is the garrison of the Philistines: and it shall come to pass, when thou art come thither to the city, that thou shalt meet a company of prophets coming down from the high place with a psaltery, and a tabret, and a pipe, and a harp, before them; and they shall prophesy: and the Spirit of the Lord will come upon thee, and thou shalt prophesy with them, and shalt be turned into another man. And let it be, when these signs are come unto thee, that thou do as occasion serve thee; for God is with thee."

And it was so, that when he had turned his back to go from Samuel, God gave him another heart: and all those signs came to pass that day. And when they came thither to the hill, behold, a company of prophets met him; and the Spirit of God came upon him, and he prophesied among them. And when he had made an end of prophesying, he came to the high place.

And Saul's uncle said unto him and to his servant, "Whither went ye?" And he said, "To seek the asses: and when we saw that they were no where, we came to Samuel." And Saul's uncle said, "Tell me, I pray thee, what Samuel said unto you." And Saul said unto his uncle, "He told us plainly that the asses were found." But of the matter of the kingdom, whereof Samuel spake, he told him not.

[1 *Samuel* ix. 26, 27, x. 1–7, 9, 10, 13–16

Saul defeats the Ammonites

Then Nahash the Ammonite came up, and encamped against Jabesh-gilead: and all the men of Jabesh said unto Nahash, "Make a covenant with us, and we will serve thee." And Nahash the Ammonite answered them, "On this condition will I make a convenant with you, that I may thrust out all your right eyes, and lay it for a reproach upon all Israel." And the elders of Jabesh said unto him, "Give us seven days' respite, that we may send messengers unto all the coasts of Israel: and then, if there be no man to save us, we will come out to thee."

Then came the messengers to Gibeah of Saul, and told the tidings in the ears of the people: and all the people lifted up their voices, and wept. And, behold, Saul came after the herd out of the field; and Saul said, "What aileth the people that they weep?" And they told him the tidings of the men of Jabesh. And the Spirit of God came upon Saul when he heard those tidings, and his anger was kindled greatly. And he took a yoke of oxen, and hewed them in pieces, and sent them throughout all the coasts of Israel by the hands of messengers, saying, "Whosoever cometh not forth after Saul and after Samuel, so shall it be done unto his oxen." And the fear of the Lord fell on the people, and they came out with one consent.

And when he numbered them in Bezek, the children of Israel were three hundred thousand, and the men of Judah thirty thousand. And they said unto the messengers that came, "Thus shall ye say unto the men of Jabesh-gilead, 'To-morrow, by that time the sun be hot, ye shall have help.'" And the messengers came and shewed it to the men of Jabesh; and they were glad. Therefore the men of Jabesh said, "To-morrow we will come out unto you, and ye shall do with us all that seemeth good unto you." And it was so on the morrow, that Saul put the people in three companies; and they came into the midst of the host in the morning watch, and slew the Ammonites until the heat of the day: and it came to pass, that they which remained were scattered, so that two of them were not left together.

[1 *Samuel* xi. 1–11

The People make Saul King

And all the people went to Gilgal; and there they made Saul king before the Lord in Gilgal; and there they sacrificed sacrifices of peace offerings before the Lord; and there Saul and all the men of Israel rejoiced greatly.

[1 *Samuel* xi. 15

SCHOOLS OF PROPHETS

In this story we have met with a reference to prophets—men who spoke out to their fellows the word of God as they understood it. In these early days there existed schools or guilds of prophets (see p. 124), who roused themselves to ecstasy by music and dancing, and by their ecstasy convinced the people that they spoke the word of God. Samuel appears to have been the greatest prophet of his time.

The vital part which prophets played in the national life was to keep alive the belief in the Spirit of God. It is true that there were many false prophets: religious ecstasy is no proof

THE ESTABLISHMENT OF THE KINGDOM

that a man has seen this everyday world in the light of Jehovah, and has heard His message for it. In later days men set more store by the wisdom and insight of the prophet's message than by his ecstatic fervour: compare the case of Isaiah, for instance. But the times of this narrative were early times when such ecstasy was taken as the proof of the presence of the Spirit of God.

(b) THE E NARRATIVE

The People ask for a King

And it came to pass, when Samuel was old, that he made his sons judges over Israel. Now the name of his firstborn was Joel; and the name of his second, Abiah: they were judges in Beer-sheba. And his sons walked not in his ways, but turned aside after lucre, and took bribes, and perverted judgment. Then all the elders of Israel gathered themselves together, and came to Samuel unto Ramah, and said unto him, "Behold, thou art old, and thy sons walk not in thy ways: now make us a king to judge us like all the nations."

[1 *Samuel* viii. 1–5

Samuel opposes the People

But the thing displeased Samuel, when they said, "Give us a king to judge us." And Samuel prayed unto the Lord. And the Lord said unto Samuel, "Hearken unto the voice of the people in all that they say unto thee: for they have not rejected thee, but they have rejected Me, that I should not reign over them. According to all the works which they have done since the day that I brought them up out of Egypt even unto this day, wherewith they have forsaken Me, and served other gods, so do they also unto thee. Now therefore hearken unto their voice: howbeit yet protest solemnly unto them, and shew them the manner of the king that shall reign over them."

And Samuel told all the words of the Lord unto the people that asked of him a king. And he said, "This will be the manner of the king that shall reign over you: he will take your sons, and appoint them for himself, for his chariots, and to be his horsemen; and some shall run before his chariots. And he will appoint him captains over thousands, and captains over fifties; and will set them to ear his ground, and to reap his harvest, and to make his instruments of war, and instruments of his chariots. And he will take your daughters to be confectionaries, and to be cooks, and to be bakers. And he will take your fields, and your vineyards, and your oliveyards, even the best of them, and give them to his servants. And he will take the tenth of your seed, and of your vineyards, and give to his officers, and to his servants. And he will take your menservants, and your maidservants, and your goodliest young men, and your asses, and put them to his work. He will take the tenth of your sheep: and ye shall be his servants. And ye shall cry out in that day because of your king which ye shall have chosen you; and the Lord will not hear you in that day."

Nevertheless the people refused to obey the voice of Samuel; and they said, "Nay; but we will have a king over us; that we also may be like all the nations; and that our king may judge us, and go out before us, and fight our battles." And Samuel heard all the words of the people, and he rehearsed them in the ears of the Lord. And the Lord said to Samuel, "Hearken unto their voice, and make them a king." And Samuel said unto the men of Israel, "Go ye every man unto his city."

[1 *Samuel* viii. 6–22

Saul chosen King at Mizpeh

And Samuel called the people together unto the Lord to Mizpeh; and said unto the children of Israel, "Thus saith the Lord God of Israel, 'I brought up Israel out of Egypt, and delivered you out of the hand of the Egyptians, and out of the hand of all kingdoms, and of them that oppressed you': and ye have this day rejected your God, who Himself saved you out of all your adversities and your tribulations; and ye have said unto Him, 'Nay, but set a king over us.' Now therefore present yourselves before the Lord by your tribes, and by your thousands."

And when Samuel had caused all the tribes of Israel to come near, the tribe of Benjamin was taken. When he had caused the tribe of Benjamin to come near by their families, the family of Matri was taken, and Saul the son of Kish was taken: and when they sought him, he could not be found. Therefore they enquired of the Lord further, if the man should yet come thither. And the Lord answered, "Behold, he hath hid himself among the stuff." And they ran and fetched him thence: and when he stood among the people, he was higher than any of the people from his shoulders and upward. And Samuel said to all the people, "See ye him whom the Lord hath chosen, that there is none like him among all the people?" And all the people shouted, and said "God save the king."

[1 *Samuel* x. 17–24

Here we have not only these two different accounts of Saul becoming king, but a long address put into the mouth of Samuel on this occasion by a D contributor, just as long speeches were put into the mouth of Moses in Deuteronomy. The Deuteronomist wished to make clear the moral of the narrative. We note how in the middle of the address he forgot that Samuel was the supposed spokesman and makes him mention himself

THE ESTABLISHMENT OF THE KINGDOM

in the third person as one of those sent by Jehovah to deliver Israel.

Samuel's Address to the People

And Samuel said unto all Israel, "Behold, I have hearkened unto your voice in all that ye said unto me, and have made a king over you. And now, behold, the king walketh before you: and I am old and gray-headed; and, behold, my sons are with you: and I have walked before you from my childhood unto this day. Behold, here I am: witness against me before the Lord, and before His anointed: whose ox have I taken? Whose ass have I taken? Whom have I defrauded? Whom have I oppressed? Of whose hand have I received any bribe to blind mine eyes therewith?" And they said, "Thou hast not defrauded us, nor oppressed us, neither hast thou taken ought of any man's hand." And he said unto them, "The Lord is witness against you, and His anointed is witness this day, that ye have not found ought in my hand." And they answered, "He is witness."

And Samuel said unto the people, "It is the Lord that advanced Moses and Aaron, and that brought your fathers up out of the land of Egypt. Now therefore stand still, that I may reason with you before the Lord of all the righteous acts of the Lord, which He did to you and to your fathers. When Jacob was come into Egypt, and your fathers cried unto the Lord, then the Lord sent Moses and Aaron, which brought forth your fathers out of Egypt, and made them dwell in this place. And when they forgat the Lord their God, He sold them into the hand of Sisera, captain of the host of Hazor, and into the hand of the Philistines, and into the hand of the king of Moab, and they fought against them. And they cried unto the Lord, and said, 'We have sinned, because we have forsaken the Lord, and have served Baalim and Ashtaroth: but now deliver us out of the hand of our enemies, and we will serve Thee.' And the Lord sent Jerubbaal, and Bedan, and Jephthah, and Samuel, and delivered you out of the hand of your enemies on every side, and ye dwelled safe. And when ye saw that Nahash the king of the children of Ammon came against you, ye said unto me, 'Nay; but a king shall reign over us': when the Lord your God was your King. Now therefore behold the king whom ye have chosen, and whom ye have desired! Behold, the Lord hath set a king over you. If ye will fear the Lord, and serve Him, and obey His voice, and not rebel against the commandment of the Lord, then shall both ye and also the king that reigneth over you continue following the Lord your God: but if ye will not obey the voice of the Lord, but rebel against the commandment of the Lord, then shall the hand of the Lord be against you, as it was against your fathers.

"Now therefore stand and see this great thing, which the Lord will do before your eyes. Is it not wheat harvest to-day? I will call unto the Lord, and He shall send thunder and rain; that ye may perceive and see that your wickedness is great, which ye have done in the sight of the Lord, in asking you a king." So Samuel called unto the Lord; and the Lord sent thunder and rain that day: and all the people greatly feared the Lord and Samuel. And all the people said unto Samuel, "Pray for thy servants unto the Lord thy God, that we die not: for we have added unto all our sins this evil, to ask us a king."

And Samuel said unto the people, "Fear not: ye have done all this wickedness: yet turn not aside from following the Lord, but serve the Lord with all your heart; and turn ye not aside: for then should ye go after vain things, which cannot profit nor deliver; for they are vain. For the Lord will not forsake His people for His great name's sake: because it hath pleased the Lord to make you His people. Moreover as for me, God forbid that I should sin against the Lord in ceasing to pray for you: but I will teach you the good and the right way: only fear the Lord, and serve Him in truth with all your heart: for consider how great things He hath done for you. But if ye shall still do wickedly, ye shall be consumed, both ye and your king."

[*From* 1 *Samuel* xii. 1-25

Saul's Early Struggles with the Philistines

Saul chose him three thousand men of Israel; whereof two thousand were with Saul in Michmash and in Mount Beth-el, and a thousand were with Jonathan in Gibeah of Benjamin: and the rest of the people he sent every man to his tent. And Jonathan smote the garrison of the Philistines that was in Geba, and the Philistines heard of it. And Saul blew the trumpet throughout all the land, saying, "Let the Hebrews hear." And all Israel heard say that Saul had smitten a garrison of the Philistines, and that Israel also was had in abomination with the Philistines. And the people were called together after Saul to Gilgal.

And the Philistines gathered themselves together to fight with Israel, thirty thousand chariots, and six thousand horsemen, and people as the sand which is on the sea shore in multitude: and they came up, and pitched in Michmash, eastward from Beth-aven. When the men of Israel saw that they were in a strait, (for the people were distressed,) then the people did hide themselves in caves, and in thickets, and in rocks, and in high places, and in pits. And some of the Hebrews went over Jordan to the land of Gad and Gilead. And Saul numbered the people that were present with him, about six hundred men. And Saul, and Jonathan his son, and the people that were present with them, abode in Gibeah of Benjamin: but the Philistines encamped in Michmash.

Now there was no smith found throughout all the land of Israel: for the Philistines said, "Lest the Hebrews make them swords or spears": but all the Israelites went down to the Philistines, to sharpen every man his share, and his coulter, and his axe, and his mattock.

THE ESTABLISHMENT OF THE KINGDOM

Yet they had a file for the mattocks, and for the coulters, and for the forks, and for the axes, and to sharpen the goads. So it came to pass in the day of battle, that there was neither sword nor spear found in the hand of any of the people that were with Saul and Jonathan: but with Saul and with Jonathan his son was there found.

[1 *Samuel* xiii. 2–7, 15, 16, 19–22

Jonathan's Faith and Courage

Now it came to pass upon a day, that Jonathan the son of Saul said unto the young man that bare his armour, "Come, and let us go over to the Philistines' garrison, that is on the other side." But he told not his father.

And Jonathan said to the young man that bare his armour, "Come, and let us go over unto the garrison of these uncircumcised: it may be that the Lord will work for us: for there is no restraint to the Lord to save by many or by few." And his armourbearer said unto him, "Do all that is in thine heart: turn thee; behold, I am with thee according to thy heart." Then said Jonathan, "Behold, we will pass over unto these men, and we will discover ourselves unto them. If they say thus unto us, 'Tarry until we come to you'; then we will stand still in our place, and will not go up unto them. But if they say thus, 'Come up unto us'; then we will go up: for the Lord hath delivered them into our hand: and this shall be a sign unto us."

And both of them discovered themselves unto the garrison of the Philistines: and the Philistines said, "Behold, the Hebrews come forth out of the holes where they had hid themselves." And the men of the garrison answered Jonathan and his armourbearer, and said, "Come up to us, and we will shew you a thing." And Jonathan said unto his armourbearer, "Come up after me: for the Lord hath delivered them into the hand of Israel." And Jonathan climbed up upon his hands and upon his feet, and his armourbearer after him: and they fell before Jonathan; and his armourbearer slew after him. And that first slaughter, which Jonathan and his armourbearer made, was about twenty men, within as it were an half acre of land, which a yoke of oxen might plow. And there was trembling in the host, in the field, and among all the people: the garrison, and the spoilers, they also trembled, and the earth quaked: so it was a very great trembling.

And the watchmen of Saul in Gibeah of Benjamin looked; and, behold, the multitude melted away, and they went on beating down one another. Then said Saul unto the people that were with him, "Number now, and see who is gone from us." And when they had numbered, behold, Jonathan and his armourbearer were not there. And Saul said unto Ahiah, "Bring hither the ark of God." For the ark of God was at that time with the children of Israel.

And it came to pass, while Saul talked unto the priest, that the noise that was in the host of the Philistines went on and increased: and Saul said unto the priest, "Withdraw thine hand." And Saul and all the people that were with him assembled themselves, and they came to the battle: and, behold, every man's sword was against his fellow, and there was a very great discomfiture. Moreover the Hebrews that were with the Philistines before that time, which went up with them into the camp from the country round about, even they also turned to be with the Israelites that were with Saul and Jonathan. Likewise all the men of Israel which had hid themselves in Mount Ephraim, when they heard that the Philistines fled, even they also followed hard after them in the battle. So the Lord saved Israel that day: and the battle passed over unto Beth-aven.

[1 *Samuel* xiv. 1, 6–23

Jonathan, Saul's son, even in his first appearance shows a religious faith which suggests David. "There is no restraint with the Lord to save by many or by few" is parallel to that spirit in David which faced Goliath with a sling and a stone. Little wonder that the two men when they met became fast friends.

The remainder of 1 Samuel xiv tells a story of a curse vowed by Saul which had consequences somewhat similar to those of Jephthah's vow. Jonathan's life, however, was spared as the result of the people's intervention. The narrative still shows some strange and crude ideas about Jehovah. It concludes with a summary of Saul's prolonged fighting against "all his enemies on every side", Moab, Ammon, Edom, Zobah, Amalek; also "there was sore war against the Philistines all the days of Saul: and when Saul saw any strong man, or any valiant man, he took him unto him." The struggle for existence as a nation was becoming intense.

4. THE DECLINE AND FALL OF KING SAUL. TWO NARRATIVES

No king ever began his reign with higher expectations than did Saul, or with more solemn dedication. Hitherto no leader of Israel had been so uniformly successful in conquering his foes. But with great opportunities go great temptations, and after all its promise Saul's life proved to be tragic.

We have in the Bible again two different accounts of the

THE ESTABLISHMENT OF THE KINGDOM

setting of Saul's sun and the dawning of David's day: sometimes it is possible to disentangle the narratives, but sometimes, for instance in the story of David and Goliath, the different narratives have been so closely interwoven to form the whole that scholars of the Hebrew versions are puzzled and vary considerably in their conclusions. For ourselves, we need only remember, if perplexed by difficulties and discrepancies, that the Book of Samuel grew into its present form under the hands of a Deuteronomic editor who used two or more old written sources for his material.

It is clear which narrative was the one preferred by the Deuteronomist. This narrative which is given in 1 Samuel xv tells of Saul's great victory over the Amelekites and of how it provided occasion for his fall. He had the word of God utterly to exterminate the foe, this being Samuel's view of the will of God. Humanity and loving-kindness were not known in those days as attributes of Jehovah: the emphasis was put upon his hatred of sin. But Saul spared the best of the flocks and the herds and the life of King Agag. Was this because his morality was ahead of his times? It should be remembered that a sacrifice of the best of the flocks and herds meant also a feast of the best, and that a conquered king in Saul's presence added to Saul's glory. Samuel came to the disobedient king to proclaim another word of God. Here the note of the Deuteronomic editor is clearly heard, for into Samuel's mouth he puts words which sum up much of the moral teaching of such later prophets as Isaiah and Micah:

Hath the Lord as great delight in burnt offerings and sacrifices as in obeying the voice of the Lord? Behold, to obey is better than sacrifice, and to hearken than the fat of rams.

[1 *Samuel* xv. 22

The narrative continues:—

Samuel anoints David

And Samuel came no more to see Saul until the day of his death: nevertheless Samuel mourned for Saul: and the Lord repented that he had made Saul king over Israel. And the Lord said unto Samuel, "How long wilt thou mourn for Saul, seeing I have rejected him from reigning over Israel? Fill thine horn with oil, and go, I will send thee to Jesse the Beth-lehemite: for I have provided me a king among his sons." And Samuel said, "How can I go? If Saul hear it, he will kill me." And the Lord said, "Take an heifer with thee, and say, 'I am come to sacrifice to the Lord.' And call Jesse to the sacrifice, and I will shew thee what thou shalt do: and thou shalt anoint unto Me him whom I name unto thee." And Samuel did that which the Lord spake, and came to Beth-lehem. And the elders of the town trembled at his coming, and said, "Comest thou peaceably?" And he said, "Peaceably: I am come to sacrifice unto the Lord: sanctify yourselves, and come with me to the sacrifice." And he sanctified Jesse and his sons, and called them to the sacrifice.

And it came to pass, when they were come, that he looked on Eliab, and said, "Surely the Lord's anointed is before Him." But the Lord said unto Samuel, "Look not on his countenance, or on the height of his stature; because I have refused him: for the Lord seeth not as man seeth; for man looketh on the outward appearance, but the Lord looketh on the heart." Then Jesse called Abinadab, and made him pass before Samuel. And he said, "Neither hath the Lord chosen this." Then Jesse made Shammah to pass by. And he said, "Neither hath the Lord chosen this." Again, Jesse made seven of his sons to pass before Samuel. And Samuel said unto Jesse, "The Lord hath not chosen these." And Samuel said unto Jesse, "Are here all thy children?" And he said, "There remaineth yet the youngest, and, behold, he keepeth the sheep." And Samuel said unto Jesse, "Send and fetch him: for we will not sit down till he come hither." And he sent, and brought him in. Now he was ruddy, and withal of a beautiful countenance, and goodly to look to. And the Lord said, "Arise, anoint him: for this is he." Then Samuel took the horn of oil, and anointed him in the midst of his brethren: and the Spirit of the Lord came upon David from that day forward.

[1 *Samuel* xv. 35, xvi. 1–13

David and Goliath

Now the Philistines gathered together their armies to battle, and were gathered together at Shochoh. And Saul and the men of Israel were gathered together, and pitched by the valley of Elah, and set the battle in array against the Philistines. And the Philistines stood on a mountain on the one side, and Israel stood on a mountain on the other side: and there was a valley between them.

And there went out a champion out of the camp of the Philistines, named Goliath, of Gath, whose height was six cubits and a span. And he had an helmet of brass upon his head, and he was armed with a coat of mail; and the weight of the coat was five thousand shekels of brass. And he had greaves of brass upon his legs, and a target of brass between his shoulders. And the staff of his spear was like a weaver's beam; and his spear's head weighed six hundred shekels of

THE ESTABLISHMENT OF THE KINGDOM

iron: and one bearing a shield went before him. And he stood and cried unto the armies of Israel, and said unto them, "Why are ye come out to set your battle in array? Am not I a Philistine, and ye servants to Saul? Choose you a man for you, and let him come down to me. If he be able to fight with me, and to kill me, then will we be your servants: but if I prevail against him, and kill him, then shall ye be our servants, and serve us." And the Philistine said, "I defy the armies of Israel this day; give me a man, that we may fight together." When Saul and all Israel heard those words of the Philistine they were dismayed, and greatly afraid. And Jesse said unto David his son, "Take now for thy brethren an ephah of this parched corn, and these ten loaves, and run to the camp to thy brethren; and carry these ten cheeses unto the captain of their thousand, and look how thy brethren fare, and take their pledge." Now Saul, and they, and all the men of Israel, were in the valley of Elah, fighting with the Philistines.

And David rose up early in the morning, and left the sheep with a keeper, and took, and went, as Jesse had commanded him; and he came to the trench, as the host was going forth to the fight, and shouted for the battle. For Israel and the Philistines had put the battle in array, army against army. And David left his baggage in the hand of the keeper of the baggage, and ran into the army, and came and saluted his brethren. And as he talked with them, behold, there came up the champion, the Philistine of Gath, Goliath by name, out of the armies of the Philistines, and spake according to the same words: and David heard them. And all the men of Israel, when they saw the man, fled from him, and were sore afraid. And the men of Israel said, "Have ye seen this man that is come up? Surely to defy Israel is he come up: and it shall be, that the man who killeth him, the king will enrich him with great riches, and will give him his daughter, and make his father's house free in Israel." And David spake to the men that stood by him, saying, "What shall be done to the man that killeth this Philistine, and taketh away the reproach from Israel? Who is this uncircumcised Philistine, that he should defy the armies of the living God?" And the people answered him after this manner, saying, "So shall it be done to the man that killeth him."

And Eliab his eldest brother heard when he spake unto the men; and Eliab's anger was kindled against David, and he said, "Why camest thou down hither? With whom hast thou left those few sheep in the wilderness? I know thy pride, and the naughtiness of thine heart; thou art come down that thou mightest see the battle." And David said, "What have I now done? Is there not a cause?" And he turned from him toward another, and spake after the same manner: and the people answered him again after the former manner. And when the words were heard which David spake, they rehearsed them before Saul: and he sent for him.

And David said to Saul, "Let no man's heart fail because of him;

thy servant will go and fight with this Philistine." And Saul said to David, "Thou art not able to go against this Philistine to fight with him: for thou art but a youth, and he a man of war from his youth." And David said unto Saul, "Thy servant kept his father's sheep, and there came a lion, and a bear, and took a lamb out of the flock: and I went out after him, and smote him, and delivered it out of his mouth: and when he arose against me, I caught him by his beard, and smote him, and slew him. Thy servant slew both the lion and the bear: and this uncircumcised Philistine shall be as one of them, seeing he hath defied the armies of the living God." David said moreover, "The Lord that delivered me out of the paw of the lion, and out of the paw of the bear, He will deliver me out of the hand of this Philistine." And Saul said unto David, "Go, and the Lord be with thee."

And Saul armed David with his armour, and he put an helmet of brass upon his head; also he armed him with a coat of mail. And David girded his sword upon his armour, and he assayed to go; for he had not proved it. And David said unto Saul, "I cannot go with these; for I have not proved them." And David put them off him. And he took his staff in his hand, and chose him five smooth stones out of the brook, and put them in a shepherd's bag which he had, even in a scrip; and his sling was in his hand: and he drew near to the Philistine. And the Philistine came on and drew near unto David; and the man that bare the shield went before him.

And when the Philistine looked about, and saw David, he disdained him: for he was but a youth, and ruddy, and of a fair countenance. And the Philistine said unto David, "Am I a dog, that thou comest to me with staves?" And the Philistine cursed David by his gods. And the Philistine said to David, "Come to me, and I will give thy flesh unto the fowls of the air, and to the beasts of the field." Then said David to the Philistine, "Thou comest to me with a sword, and with a spear, and with a shield: but I come to thee in the name of the Lord of hosts, the God of the armies of Israel, whom thou hast defied. This day will the Lord deliver thee into mine hand; and I will smite thee, and take thine head from thee; and I will give the carcases of the host of the Philistines this day unto the fowls of the air, and to the wild beasts of the earth; that all the earth may know that there is a God in Israel. And all this assembly shall know that the Lord saveth not with sword and spear: for the battle is the Lord's, and He will give you into our hands."

And it came to pass, when the Philistine arose, and came and drew nigh to meet David, that David hasted, and ran toward the army to meet the Philistine. And David put his hand in his bag, and took thence a stone, and slang it, and smote the Philistine in his forehead, that the stone sunk into his forehead; and he fell upon his face to the earth. So David prevailed over the Philistine with a sling and with a stone, and smote the Philistine, and slew him; but there was no sword

THE ESTABLISHMENT OF THE KINGDOM

in the hand of David. Therefore David ran, and stood upon the Philistine, and took his sword, and drew it out of the sheath thereof, and slew him, and cut off his head therewith. And when the Philistines saw their champion was dead, they fled. And the men of Israel and of Judah arose, and shouted, and pursued the Philistines, until thou come to the valley, and to the gates of Ekron. And the wounded of the Philistines fell down by the way to Shaaraim, even unto Gath, and unto Ekron. And the children of Israel returned from chasing after the Philistines, and they spoiled their tents.

And when Saul saw David go forth against the Philistine, he said unto Abner, the captain of the host, "Abner, whose son is this youth?" And Abner said, "As thy soul liveth, O king, I cannot tell." And the king said, "Enquire thou whose son the stripling is." And as David returned from the slaughter of the Philistine, Abner took him, and brought him before Saul with the head of the Philistine in his hand. And Saul said to him, "Whose son art thou, thou young man?" And David answered, "I am the son of thy servant Jesse the Beth-lehemite."

[1 *Samuel* xvii. 1–11, 17–53, 55–58
Cf. 2 *Samuel* xxi. 19; 1 *Chronicles* xx. 5

David and Jonathan

And it came to pass, when he had made an end of speaking unto Saul, that the soul of Jonathan was knit with the soul of David, and Jonathan loved him as his own soul. And Saul took him that day, and would let him go no more home to his father's house. Then Jonathan and David made a covenant, because he loved him as his own soul. And Jonathan stripped himself of the robe that was upon him, and gave it to David, and his garments, even to his sword, and to his bow, and to his girdle.

[1 *Samuel* xviii. 1–4

Saul's Jealousy

And Saul was afraid of David, because the Lord was with him, and was departed from Saul. Therefore Saul removed him from him, and made him his captain over a thousand; and he went out and came in before the people. And David behaved himself wisely in all his ways; and the Lord was with him. Wherefore when Saul saw that he behaved himself very wisely, he was afraid of him. But all Israel and Judah loved David, because he went out and came in before them.

And Saul spake to Jonathan his son, and to all his servants, that they should kill David. But Jonathan Saul's son delighted much in David: and Jonathan told David, saying, "Saul my father seeketh to kill thee: now therefore, I pray thee, take heed to thyself until the morning, and abide in a secret place, and hide thyself: and I will go out and stand beside my father in the field where thou art, and I will commune with my father of thee; and what I see, that I will tell thee."

And Jonathan spake good of David unto Saul his father, and said unto him, "Let not the king sin against his servant, against David;

because he hath not sinned against thee, and because his works have been to thee-ward very good: for he did put his life in his hand, and slew the Philistine, and the Lord wrought a great salvation for all Israel: thou sawest it, and didst rejoice: wherefore then wilt thou sin against innocent blood, to slay David without a cause?" And Saul hearkened unto the voice of Jonathan: and Saul sware, "As the Lord liveth, he shall not be slain." And Jonathan called David, and Jonathan shewed him all those things. And Jonathan brought David to Saul, and he was in his presence, as in times past.

And there was war again: and David went out, and fought with the Philistines, and slew them with a great slaughter; and they fled from him. And the evil spirit from the Lord was upon Saul, as he sat in his house with his javelin in his hand: and David played with his hand. And Saul sought to smite David even to the wall with the javelin; but he slipped away out of Saul's presence, and he smote the javelin into the wall: and David fled, and escaped that night, and came to Samuel to Ramah, and told him all that Saul had done to him. And he and Samuel went and dwelt in Naioth.

[1 *Samuel* xviii. 12–16, xix. 1–10, 18

A SECOND NARRATIVE

We should note that in the earlier narrative Saul first meets David when David volunteers to fight single-handed against Goliath. But there is another account of the introduction of David to Saul. The evil that is in a man—in Saul's case vanity and self-indulgence—was slowly destroying a great king; as he grew older, he fell a prey to a form of religious melancholia. The writers of old were not troubled about the ethical nature of God: to them He was a god who sent alike good and evil. An "evil spirit from the Lord" troubled Saul. Then to his human need of help came the beauty, music, and faith of David.

David, like Jonathan, reckoned the unseen Jehovah as a living moving force in life, stronger than any giant. But David came from the open hillside, from stars and sun and sheep, while Jonathan came from the army of his father-king. Throughout this narrative there pulse the heart-beats of their great friendship, "passing the love of women", as David said. This friendship was founded on an individual living faith in Jehovah, proved by personal courage and loyalty.

Browning has treated David's first relationship with Saul in his poem *Saul*: the reading of this enhances one's appreciation of the Biblical narrative.

David comes to play for Saul
The Spirit of the Lord departed from Saul, and an evil spirit from the Lord troubled him. And Saul's servants said unto him, "Behold now, an evil spirit from God troubleth thee. Let our lord now command thy servants, which are before thee, to seek out a man, who is a cunning player on an harp: and it shall come to pass, when the evil spirit from God is upon thee, that he shall play with his hand, and thou shalt be well." And Saul said unto his servants, "Provide me now a man that can play well, and bring him to me." Then answered one of the servants, and said, "Behold, I have seen a son of Jesse the Beth-lehemite, that is cunning in playing, and a mighty valiant man, and a man of war, and prudent in matters, and a comely person, and the Lord is with him."
Wherefore Saul sent messengers unto Jesse, and said, "Send me David thy son, which is with the sheep." And Jesse took an ass laden with bread, and a bottle of wine, and a kid, and sent them by David his son unto Saul. And David came to Saul, and stood before him: and he loved him greatly; and he became his armourbearer. And Saul sent to Jesse, saying, "Let David, I pray thee, stand before me; for he hath found favour in my sight." And it came to pass, when the evil spirit from God was upon Saul, that David took an harp, and played with his hand: so Saul was refreshed, and was well, and the evil spirit departed from him.

[1 *Samuel* xvi. 14–23]

Saul's Jealousy
David went out whithersoever Saul sent him, and behaved himself wisely: and Saul set him over the men of war, and he was accepted in the sight of all the people, and also in the sight of Saul's servants.
And it came to pass as they came, when David was returned from the slaughter of the Philistine, that the women came out of all cities of Israel, singing and dancing, to meet King Saul, with tabrets, with joy, and with instruments of musick. And the women answered one another as they played, and said,

"Saul hath slain his thousands,
And David his ten thousands."

And Saul was very wroth, and the saying displeased him; and he said, "They have ascribed unto David ten thousands, and to me they have ascribed but thousands: and what can he have more but the kingdom?" And Saul eyed David from that day and forward.

And it came to pass on the morrow, that the evil spirit from God came upon Saul, and he prophesied in the midst of the house: and David played with his hand, as at other times: and there was a javelin in Saul's hand. And Saul cast the javelin; for he said, "I will smite David even to the wall with it." And David avoided out of his presence twice.

[1 *Samuel* xviii. 5–11]

David and Jonathan

David came and said before Jonathan, "What have I done? What is mine iniquity? What is my sin before thy father, that he seeketh my life?" And he said unto him, "God forbid; thou shalt not die: behold, my father will do nothing either great or small, but that he will shew it me: and why should my father hide this thing from me? It is not so." And David sware moreover, and said, "Thy father certainly knoweth that I have found grace in thine eyes; and he saith, 'Let not Jonathan know this, lest he be grieved': but truly as the Lord liveth, and as thy soul liveth, there is but a step between me and death."

Then Jonathan said to David, "To-morrow is the new moon: and thou shalt be missed, because thy seat will be empty. And when thou hast stayed three days, then thou shalt go down quickly, and come to the place where thou didst hide thyself when the business was in hand, and shalt remain by the stone Ezel. And I will shoot three arrows on the side thereof, as though I shot at a mark. And, behold, I will send a lad, saying, 'Go, find out the arrows.' If I expressly say unto the lad, 'Behold, the arrows are on this side of thee, take them'; then come thou: for there is peace to thee, and no hurt; as the Lord liveth. But if I say thus unto the young man, 'Behold, the arrows are beyond thee'; go thy way: for the Lord hath sent thee away. And as touching the matter which thou and I have spoken of, behold the Lord be between thee and me for ever."

So David hid himself in the field: and when the new moon was come, the king sat him down to eat meat. And the king sat upon his seat, as at other times, even upon a seat by the wall: and Jonathan arose, and Abner sat by Saul's side, and David's place was empty. Nevertheless Saul spake not any thing that day: for he thought, "Something hath befallen him, he is not clean; surely he is not clean." And it came to pass on the morrow, which was the second day of the month, that David's place was empty: and Saul said unto Jonathan his son, "Wherefore cometh not the son of Jesse to meat, neither yesterday, nor to-day?" And Jonathan answered Saul, "David earnestly asked leave of me to go to Beth-lehem: and he said, 'Let me go, I pray thee; for our family hath a sacrifice in the city; and my brother, he hath commanded me to be there: and now, if I have found favour in thine eyes, let me get away, I pray thee, and see my brethren.' Therefore he cometh not unto the king's table."

THE ESTABLISHMENT OF THE KINGDOM

Then Saul's anger was kindled against Jonathan, and he said unto him, "Thou son of the perverse rebellious woman, do not I know that thou hast chosen the son of Jesse to thine own confusion? For as long as the son of Jesse liveth upon the ground, thou shalt not be established, nor thy kingdom. Wherefore now send and fetch him unto me, for he shall surely die." And Jonathan answered Saul his father, and said unto him, "Wherefore shall he be slain? What hath he done?" And Saul cast a javelin at him to smite him: whereby Jonathan knew that it was determined of his father to slay David. So Jonathan arose from the table in fierce anger, and did eat no meat the second day of the month: for he was grieved for David, because his father had done him shame.

And it came to pass in the morning, that Jonathan went out into the field at the time appointed with David, and a little lad with him. And he said unto his lad, "Run, find out now the arrows which I shoot." And as the lad ran, he shot an arrow beyond him. And when the lad was come to the place of the arrow which Jonathan had shot, Jonathan cried after the lad, and said, "Is not the arrow beyond thee?" And Jonathan cried after the lad, "Make speed, haste, stay not." And Jonathan's lad gathered up the arrows, and came to his master. But the lad knew not any thing: only Jonathan and David knew the matter. And Jonathan said to David, "Go in peace, forasmuch as we have sworn both of us in the name of the Lord, saying, 'The Lord be between me and thee, and between my seed and thy seed for ever.'" And he arose and departed: and Jonathan went into the city.

[1 *Samuel* xx. 1–3, 18–39, 42

5. DAVID THE OUTLAW AND DAVID THE KING

The latter parts of this Deuteronomic History of the Establishment of the Kingdom are much easier to follow, as they do not present anything like the same difficulties and discrepancies. The last chapters of it appear indeed to have been taken direct from that Court History of David from which we read selections on pp. 21–27. It remains to fill in the gap between the beginning of this cleavage between Saul and David and David's firm hold as king over the whole nation, which is assumed in the Court History to which we have just referred.

We have seen that Saul's vanity was hurt and his jealousy aroused by the exploits and popularity of David. The stricken man was no longer captain of his soul; he could not restrain the evidences of his hatred. Thus darkness deepens in the story, for not even Jonathan's intervention availed for long to curb his father's ill-will. David was driven into exile, as also were his friends. When David generously used an occasion when he could have slain Saul merely to prove his goodwill to the king, Saul believed for the moment: David wisely realized that it was only for a time, and therefore retreated to the shelter of the Philistines' territory (see note on p. 234) until news of the final tragedy arrived—the death of both Saul and Jonathan in battle with the Philistines.

We may note how David grows and develops during this period of exile. He draws to himself a body of strong young men, in fact, a band of outlaws. They raid some of the surrounding foes, and David makes friends in the Southern parts of Judah by his restraint and goodwill. But he is an outlaw, a different person from the youthful shepherd watching his flock by night among the lonely hills.

David's Life as an Outlaw

Then came David to Nob to Ahimelech the priest: and Ahimelech was afraid at the meeting of David, and said unto him, "Why art thou alone, and no man with thee?" And David said unto Ahimelech the priest, "The king hath commanded me a business, and hath said unto me, 'Let no man know any thing of the business whereabout I send thee, and what I have commanded thee': and I have appointed my servants to such and such a place. Now therefore what is under thine hand? Give me five loaves of bread in mine hand, or what there is present." And the priest answered David, and said, "There is no common bread under mine hand, but there is hallowed bread." So the priest gave him hallowed bread: for there was no bread there but the shewbread, that was taken from before the Lord, to put hot bread in the day when it was taken away.

David escaped to the cave Adullam: and when his brethren and all his father's house heard it, they went down thither to him. And every one that was in distress, and every one that was in debt, and every one that was discontented, gathered themselves unto him; and he became a captain over them: and there were with him about four hundred men.

And David went thence to Mizpeh of Moab: and he said unto the king of Moab, "Let my father and my mother, I pray thee, come forth, and be with you, till I know what God will do for me." And he brought them before the king of Moab: and they dwelt with him all the while that David was in the hold.

THE ESTABLISHMENT OF THE KINGDOM 229

Then they told David, saying, "Behold, the Philistines fight against Keilah, and they rob the threshing-floors." Therefore David enquired of the Lord, saying, "Shall I go and smite these Philistines?" And the Lord said unto David, "Go, and smite the Philistines, and save Keilah." And David's men said unto him, "Behold, we be afraid here in Judah: how much more then if we come to Keilah against the armies of the Philistines?" Then David enquired of the Lord yet again. And the Lord answered him and said, "Arise, go down to Keilah; for I will deliver the Philistines into thine hand." So David and his men went to Keilah, and fought with the Philistines, and brought away their cattle, and smote them with a great slaughter. So David saved the inhabitants of Keilah.

And it was told Saul that David was come to Keilah. And Saul said, "God hath delivered him into mine hand; for he is shut in, by entering into a town that hath gates and bars." And Saul called all the people together to war, to go down to Keilah, to besiege David and his men. And David knew that Saul secretly practised mischief against him. Then said David, "O Lord God of Israel, Thy servant hath certainly heard that Saul seeketh to come to Keilah, to destroy the city for my sake. Will the men of Keilah deliver me up into his hand? Will Saul come down, as thy servant hath heard? O Lord God of Israel, I beseech Thee, tell Thy servant." And the Lord said, "He will come down." Then said David, "Will the men of Keilah deliver me and my men into the hand of Saul?" And the Lord said, "They will deliver thee up." Then David and his men, which were about six hundred, arose and departed out of Keilah, and went whithersoever they could go. And it was told Saul that David was escaped from Keilah; and he forbare to go forth.

And David abode in the wilderness in strong holds, and remained in a mountain in the wilderness of Ziph. And Saul sought him every day, but God delivered him not into his hand. And David saw that Saul was come out to seek his life: and David was in the wilderness of Ziph in a wood. And Jonathan Saul's son arose, and went to David into the wood, and strengthened his hand in God. And he said unto him, "Fear not: for the hand of Saul my father shall not find thee; and thou shalt be king over Israel, and I shall be next unto thee; and that also Saul my father knoweth." And they two made a covenant before the Lord: and David abode in the wood, and Jonathan went to his house.

Then came up the Ziphites to Saul to Gibeah, saying, "Doth not David hide himself with us in strong holds in the wood, in the hill of Hachilah, which is on the south of Jeshimon? Now therefore, O king, come down according to all the desire of thy soul to come down; and our part shall be to deliver him into the king's hand." And Saul said, "Blessed be ye of the Lord; for ye have compassion on me. Go, I pray you, prepare yet, and know and see his place where his haunt is, and who hath seen him there: for it is told me that he dealeth very subtilly. See therefore, and take knowledge of all the lurking places where he hideth himself, and come ye again to me with the certainty, and I will go with you: and it shall come to pass, if he be in the land, that I will search him out throughout all the thousands of Judah."

And they arose, and went to Ziph before Saul: but David and his men were in the wilderness of Maon, in the plain on the south of Jeshimon. Saul also and his men went to seek him. And they told David: wherefore he came down into a rock, and abode in the wilderness of Maon. And when Saul heard that, he pursued after David in the wilderness of Maon. And Saul went on this side of the mountain, and David and his men on that side of the mountain: and David made haste to get away for fear of Saul; for Saul and his men compassed David and his men round about to take them. But there came a messenger unto Saul, saying, "Haste thee, and come; for the Philistines have invaded the land." Wherefore Saul returned from pursuing after David, and went against the Philistines. And David went up from thence, and dwelt in strong holds at En-gedi.

[1 *Samuel* xxi. 1–6, xxii. 1–4, xxiii. 1–29

The Story of Abigail

And Samuel died; and all the Israelites were gathered together, and lamented him, and buried him in his house at Ramah. And David arose, and went down to the wilderness of Paran. And there was a man in Maon, whose possessions were in Carmel; and the man was very great, and he had three thousand sheep, and a thousand goats: and he was shearing his sheep in Carmel. Now the name of the man was Nabal; and the name of his wife Abigail: and she was a woman of good understanding, and of a beautiful countenance: but the man was churlish and evil in his doings; and he was of the house of Caleb. And David heard in the wilderness that Nabal did shear his sheep.

And David sent out ten young men, and David said unto the young men, "Get you up to Carmel, and go to Nabal, and greet him in my name: and thus shall ye say to him that liveth in prosperity, 'Peace be both to thee, and peace be to thine house, and peace be unto all that thou hast. And now I have heard that thou hast shearers: now thy shepherds which were with us, we hurt them not, neither was there ought missing unto them, all the while they were in Carmel. Ask thy young men, and they will shew thee. Wherefore let the young men find favour in thine eyes: for we come in a good day: give, I pray thee, whatsoever cometh to thine hand unto thy servants, and to thy son David.' "

And when David's young men came, they spake to Nabal according to all those words in the name of David, and ceased. And Nabal answered David's servants, and said, "Who is David? And who is the son of Jesse? There be many servants now a days that break away every man from his master. Shall I then take my bread, and my water, and my flesh that I have killed for my shearers, and give it unto men, whom I know not whence they be?" So David's young men turned their way, and went again, and came and told him all those sayings. And David said unto his men, "Gird ye on every man his sword." And they girded on every man his sword; and David also girded on his sword: and there went up after David about four hundred men; and two hundred abode by the stuff.

But one of the young men told Abigail, Nabal's wife, saying, "Behold, David sent messengers out of the wilderness to salute our master; and he railed on them. But the men were very good unto us, and we were not hurt, neither missed we any thing, as long as we were conversant with them, when we were in the fields: they were a wall unto us both by night and day, all the while we were with them keeping the sheep. Now therefore know and consider what thou wilt do; for evil is determined against our master, and against all his household: for he is such a son of Belial, that a man cannot speak to him."

Then Abigail made haste, and took two hundred loaves, and two bottles of wine, and five sheep ready dressed, and five measures of parched corn, and an hundred clusters of raisins, and two hundred cakes of figs, and laid them on asses. And she said unto her servants, "Go on before me; behold, I come after you." But she told not her husband Nabal. And it was so, as she rode on the ass, that she came down by the covert of the hill, and, behold, David and his men came down against her; and she met them. Now David had said, "Surely in vain have I kept all that this fellow hath in the wilderness, so that nothing was missed of all that pertained unto him: and he hath requited me evil for good. So and more also do God unto the enemies of David, if I leave of all that pertain to him by the morning light any man."

And when Abigail saw David, she hasted, and lighted off the ass, and fell before David on her face, and bowed herself to the ground, and fell at his feet, and said, "Upon me, my lord, upon me let this iniquity be: and let thine handmaid, I pray thee, speak in thine audience, and hear the words of thine handmaid. Let not my lord, I pray thee, regard this man of Belial, even Nabal[1]: for as his name is, so is he; Nabal is his name, and folly is with him: but I thine handmaid saw not the young men of my lord, whom thou didst send. Now therefore, my lord, as the Lord liveth, and as thy soul liveth, seeing the Lord hath withholden thee from coming to shed blood, and from avenging thyself with thine own hand, now let thine enemies, and they that seek evil to my lord, be as Nabal. And now this blessing which thine handmaid hath brought unto my lord, let it even be given unto the young men that follow my lord. I pray thee, forgive the trespass of thine handmaid: for the Lord will certainly make my lord a sure house; because my lord fighteth the battles of the Lord, and

---

[1] "Nabal" means "Fool".

evil hath not been found in thee all thy days. Yet a man is risen to pursue thee, and to seek thy soul: but the soul of my lord shall be bound in the bundle of life with the Lord thy God; and the souls of thine enemies, them shall He sling out, as out of the middle of a sling. And it shall come to pass, when the Lord shall have done to my lord according to all the good that He hath spoken concerning thee, and shall have appointed thee ruler over Israel; that this shall be no grief unto thee, nor offence of heart unto my lord, either that thou hast shed blood causeless, or that my lord hath avenged himself: but when the Lord shall have dealt well with my lord, then remember thine handmaid."

And David said to Abigail, "Blessed be the Lord God of Israel, which sent thee this day to meet me: and blessed be thy advice, and blessed be thou, which hast kept me this day from coming to shed blood, and from avenging myself with mine own hand. For in very deed, as the Lord God of Israel liveth, which hath kept me back from hurting thee, except thou hadst hasted and come to meet me, surely there had not been left unto Nabal by the morning light any man." So David received of her hand that which she had brought him, and said unto her, "Go up in peace to thine house; see, I have hearkened to thy voice, and have accepted thy person."

And Abigail came to Nabal; and, behold, he held a feast in his house, like the feast of a king; and Nabal's heart was merry within him, for he was very drunken: wherefore she told him nothing, less or more, until the morning light. But it came to pass in the morning, when the wine was gone out of Nabal, and his wife had told him these things, that his heart died within him, and he became as a stone. And it came to pass about ten days after, that the Lord smote Nabal, that he died. And when David heard that Nabal was dead, he said, "Blessed be the Lord, that hath pleaded the cause of my reproach from the hand of Nabal, and hath kept His servant from evil: for the Lord hath returned the wickedness of Nabal upon his own head." And David sent and communed with Abigail, to take her to him to wife. And when the servants of David were come to Abigail to Carmel, they spake unto her, saying, "David sent us unto thee, to take thee to him to wife." And she arose, and bowed herself on her face to the earth, and said, "Behold, let thine handmaid be a servant to wash the feet of the servants of my lord." And Abigail hasted, and arose, and rode upon an ass, with five damsels of hers that went after her; and she went after the messengers of David, and became his wife. David also took Ahinoam of Jezreel; and they were also both of them his wives. [1 *Samuel* xxv. 1-43

In the Old Testament are two different stories of David sparing the life of Saul. We may read one here: the other is to be found in 1 Samuel xxiv.

THE ESTABLISHMENT OF THE KINGDOM

David spares the Life of Saul

And the Ziphites came unto Saul to Gibeah, saying, "Doth not David hide himself in the hill of Hachilah, which is before Jeshimon?" Then Saul arose, and went down to the wilderness of Ziph, having three thousand chosen men of Israel with him, to seek David in the wilderness of Ziph. And Saul pitched in the hill of Hachilah, which is before Jeshimon, by the way. But David abode in the wilderness, and he saw that Saul came after him into the wilderness. David therefore sent out spies, and understood that Saul was come in very deed.

And David arose, and came to the place where Saul had pitched: and David beheld the place where Saul lay, and Abner the son of Ner, the captain of his host: and Saul lay in the trench, and the people pitched round about him. Then answered David and said to Ahimelech, and to Abishai, saying, "Who will go down with me to Saul to the camp?" And Abishai said, "I will go down with thee." So David and Abishai came to the people by night: and, behold, Saul lay sleeping within the trench, and his spear stuck in the ground at his bolster: but Abner and the people lay round about him. Then said Abishai to David, "God hath delivered thine enemy into thine hand this day: now therefore let me smite him, I pray thee, with the spear even to the earth at once, and I will not smite him the second time." And David said to Abishai, "Destroy him not: for who can stretch forth his hand against the Lord's anointed, and be guiltless?"

David said furthermore, "As the Lord liveth, the Lord shall smite him; or his day shall come to die; or he shall descend into battle, and perish. The Lord forbid that I should stretch forth mine hand against the Lord's anointed: but, I pray thee, take thou now the spear that is at his bolster, and the cruse of water, and let us go." So David took the spear and the cruse of water from Saul's bolster; and they gat them away, and no man saw it, nor knew it, neither awaked: for they were all asleep; because a deep sleep from the Lord was fallen upon them.

Then David went over to the other side, and stood on the top of an hill afar off; a great space being between them: and David cried to the people, and to Abner the son of Ner, saying, "Answerest thou not, Abner?" Then Abner answered and said, "Who art thou that criest to the king?" And David said to Abner, "Art not thou a valiant man? And who is like to thee in Israel? Wherefore then hast thou not kept thy lord the king? There came one of the people in to destroy the king thy lord. This thing is not good that thou hast done. As the Lord liveth, ye are worthy to die, because ye have not kept your master, the Lord's anointed. And now see where the king's spear is, and the cruse of water that was at his bolster."

And Saul knew David's voice, and said, "Is this thy voice, my son David?" And David said, "It is my voice, my lord, O king." And he said, "Wherefore doth my lord thus pursue after his servant? For what have I done? Or what evil is in mine hand? Now therefore, I pray thee, let my lord the king hear the words of his servant. If the Lord have stirred thee up against me, let Him accept an offering: but if they be the children of men, cursed be they before the Lord; for they have driven me out this day from abiding in the inheritance of the Lord, saying, 'Go, serve other gods.' Now therefore, let not my blood fall to the earth before the face of the Lord: for the king of Israel is come out to seek a flea, as when one doth hunt a partridge in the mountains."

Then said Saul, "I have sinned: return, my son David: for I will no more do thee harm, because my soul was precious in thine eyes this day: behold, I have played the fool, and have erred exceedingly." And David answered and said, "Behold the king's spear! Let one of the young men come over and fetch it. The Lord render to every man his righteousness and his faithfulness: for the Lord delivered thee into my hand to-day, but I would not stretch forth mine hand against the Lord's anointed. And, behold, as thy life was much set by this day in mine eyes, so let my life be much set by in the eyes of the Lord, and let Him deliver me out of all tribulation." Then Saul said to David, "Blessed be thou, my son David: thou shalt both do great things, and also shalt still prevail." So David went on his way, and Saul returned to his place.

[1 *Samuel* xxvi. 1–25

David's position was now critical. No longer was there any safety for him in Israel. He was reduced to the expedient of putting himself under the Philistine king, Achish of Gath, fighting his battles and trusting that somehow his mother wit would save him from the necessity of choosing between fighting his own people and returning to peril in his own country. Truth to tell, when such a war came the Philistine lords thought it unwise to subject David to the temptation involved in going to war against the Hebrews, and protested so forcibly to King Achish that he was compelled to send David back to Philistine territory. In this war Saul and Jonathan were slain, and thereby David's position completely altered.

David takes Refuge with the Philistines

And David said in his heart, "I shall now perish one day by the hand of Saul: there is nothing better for me than that I should speedily escape into the land of the Philistines; and Saul shall despair of me, to seek me any more in any coast of Israel: so shall I escape out of his hand." And David arose, and he passed over with the six hundred men that were with him unto Achish, the son of Maoch, king of Gath. And David dwelt with Achish at Gath, he and his men, every man with his household, even David with his two wives, Ahinoam the Jezreelitess, and Abigail the Carmelitess, Nabal's wife. And it was told Saul that David was fled to Gath: and he sought no more again for him.

And David said unto Achish, "If I have now found grace in thine eyes, let them give me a place in some town in the country, that I may dwell there: for why should thy servant dwell in the royal city with thee?" Then Achish gave him Ziklag that day: wherefore Ziklag pertaineth unto the kings of Judah unto this day. And the time that David dwelt in the country of the Philistines was a full year and four months.

[1 *Samuel* xxvii. 1–7

Death of King Saul

Now the Philistines fought against Israel: and the men of Israel fled from before the Philistines, and fell down slain in Mount Gilboa. And the Philistines followed hard upon Saul and upon his sons; and the Philistines slew Jonathan, and Abinadab, and Melchi-shua, Saul's sons. And the battle went sore against Saul, and the archers hit him; and he was sore wounded of the archers. Then said Saul unto his armourbearer, "Draw thy sword, and thrust me through therewith; lest these uncircumcised come and thrust me through, and abuse me." But his armourbearer would not; for he was sore afraid. Therefore Saul took a sword and fell upon it. And when his armourbearer saw that Saul was dead, he fell likewise upon his sword, and died with him. So Saul died, and his three sons, and his armourbearer, and all his men, that same day together.

[1 *Samuel* xxxi. 1–6

In the first chapter of 2 Samuel we may read of how this news was brought to David, two narratives again being interwoven. David's lamentation over the death of Saul and Jonathan is the poem, called the "Song of the Bow", which has already been quoted on p. 17 as an example of the earliest Hebrew poetry. There is little reason to doubt that the poem comes direct to us from the inspired heart of this outlaw so soon to be a great king.

KING DAVID

David the outlaw had made many friends in the South of Judah; he had led raids against the foes of the people, and he had shared the spoils with those that stayed at home. When Saul died, Judah rallied round David and anointed him king.

For about seven years he reigned in Judah, dwelling at Hebron, the captain of his army being Joab, a man of wisdom and might, who played an important part in the affairs of King David.

But while Judah in the South rallied round David, all the Northern districts gathered round Saul's son, Ish-bosheth, and declared him king in Mahanaim: the captain of his army was Abner. For a few years these two kings reigned over the Hebrews. We must note that now the name "Israel" comes to be applied only to the tribes in the North, and does not include Judah in the South. These years saw not a little civil war. Ish-bosheth was a weak king, owing his position to Abner; in an unlucky moment for himself he offended the pride of his captain, with the result that Abner went to Hebron to make plans for handing over the Northern kingdom to David. But, while in Hebron, he was murdered, without the cognisance of David. His death delayed the union of the two kingdoms, but soon Ish-bosheth was assassinated by two of his officers, and David was then proclaimed king of the whole country. The line of Saul vanished: the line of David was to continue for many long years.

Once king of the whole country, David, with Joab's able help, worked hard to consolidate the kingdom. In turn he conquered Syria or Aram in the North-East, Ammon and Moab to the East, and Edom to the South. The Philistines also were so thoroughly defeated that never again did they become a national peril to the Hebrews. But the most important feat which David accomplished was to take the fortress of Zion or Jerusalem from the Jebusites, a fortress so strong that its inhabitants believed that even the blind and the lame could defend it against all comers. Yet David made this sensational conquest and established the great natural fortress as the capital of his kingdom. If we recollect the part that Jerusalem has played in history from the time of David right down to recent times, we may apprehend something of the importance of this victory. But David made Jerusalem not only the secular capital of his kingdom, but also its chief place for worship.

THE ESTABLISHMENT OF THE KINGDOM 237

To Jerusalem the Ark was brought with the utmost rejoicing. It added to the importance of this success that Jerusalem had belonged neither to Judah nor to Israel, and so could be now regarded as belonging to both.

This growth of David's power as king is depicted in the earlier chapters of 2 Samuel (ii–viii). From these we make brief selections: the only point worthy of note is the echo of the Deuteronomist in the story of David's desire to build a house for Jehovah. When we remember the emphasis placed by the Deuteronomists on worship being centralized at Jerusalem, we can easily understand how much this old story appealed to them and the reasons which led them to place additional stress upon it in compiling this book.

Summary of David's Reign

David was thirty years old when he began to reign, and he reigned forty years. In Hebron he reigned over Judah seven years and six months: and in Jerusalem he reigned thirty and three years over all Israel and Judah. And the king and his men went to Jerusalem unto the Jebusites, the inhabitants of the land: which spake unto David, saying, "Except thou take away the blind and the lame, thou shalt not come in hither": thinking, "David cannot come in hither." Nevertheless David took the strong hold of Zion: the same is the city of David. So David dwelt in the fort, and called it the city of David. And David went on, and grew great, and the Lord God of hosts was with him.

And Hiram king of Tyre sent messengers to David, and cedar trees, and carpenters, and masons: and they built David an house. And David perceived that the Lord had established him king over Israel, and that he had exalted his kingdom for His people Israel's sake. And David took him more concubines and wives out of Jerusalem, after he was come from Hebron: and there were yet sons and daughters born to David. David did dedicate unto the Lord the silver and gold of all nations which he subdued; of Syria, and of Moab, and of the children of Ammon, and of the Philistines, and of Amalek. And the Lord preserved David whithersoever he went. And David reigned over all Israel; and David executed judgment and justice unto all his people. And Joab the son of Zeruiah was over the host.

[2 *Samuel* v. 4–13, viii. 11, 12, 14–16

David brings the Ark to Jerusalem

David went and brought up the ark of God from the house of Obed-edom into the city of David with gladness. And it was so, that when they that bare the ark of the Lord had gone six paces, he sacrificed oxen and fatlings. And David danced before the Lord with all his might; and David was girded with a linen ephod. So David and all the house of Israel brought up the ark of the Lord with shouting, and with the sound of the trumpet. And they brought in the ark of the Lord, and set it in his place, in the midst of the tabernacle that David had pitched for it: and David offered burnt offerings and peace offerings before the Lord. And as soon as David had made an end of offering burnt offerings and peace offerings, he blessed the people in the name of the Lord of hosts. And he dealt among all the people, even among the whole multitude of Israel, as well to the women as men, to every one a cake of bread, and a good piece of flesh, and a flagon of wine. So all the people departed every one to his house.

[2 *Samuel* vi. 12–19

David desires to build a House for Jehovah

And it came to pass, when the king sat in his house, and the Lord had given him rest round about from all his enemies; that the king said unto Nathan the prophet, "See now, I dwell in an house of cedar, but the ark of God dwelleth within curtains." And Nathan said to the king, "Go, do all that is in thine heart; for the Lord is with thee." And it came to pass that night, that the word of the Lord came unto Nathan, saying, "Go and tell my servant David, Thus saith the Lord, Shalt thou build Me an house for Me to dwell in? Whereas I have not dwelt in any house since the time that I brought up the children of Israel out of Egypt, even to this day, but have walked in a tent and in a tabernacle. In all the places wherein I have walked with all the children of Israel spake I a word with any of the tribes of Israel, whom I commanded to feed My people Israel, saying, 'Why build ye not Me an house of cedar?' Now therefore so shalt thou say unto my servant David, Thus saith the Lord of hosts, I took thee from the sheepcote, from following the sheep, to be ruler over My people, over Israel: and I was with thee whithersoever thou wentest, and have cut off all thine enemies out of thy sight, and have made thee a great name, like unto the name of the great men that are in the earth. Moreover I will appoint a place for My people Israel, and will plant them, that they may dwell in a place of their own, and move no more; neither shall the children of wickedness afflict them any more, as beforetime, and as since the time that I commanded judges to be over My people Israel, and have caused thee to rest from all thine enemies. Also the Lord telleth thee that He will make thee an house. And when thou shalt sleep with thy fathers, I will set up thy seed after thee, and I will establish his kingdom. He shall build an house for My name, and I will stablish the throne of his kingdom for ever. I will be his father, and he shall be My son. If he commit iniquity, I will chasten him with the rod of men, and with the stripes of the children of men: but My mercy shall not depart away from him, as

THE ESTABLISHMENT OF THE KINGDOM 239

I took it from Saul, whom I put away before thee. And thine house and thy kingdom shall be established for ever before thee: thy throne shall be established for ever." According to all these words, and according to all this vision, so did Nathan speak unto David.

[2 *Samuel* vii. 1–17

DAVID'S SIN AND ITS CONSEQUENCES

David thus proved himself a strong and wise king. But again the evil that is in a man's heart was the undoing of a promising life. In his personal life David sinned greatly and for the rest of his life he suffered much from the natural consequences of his sin working themselves out in his family. Yet, while Saul lost his soul and sank ever into deeper error, David, by his repentance and humble acceptance of the sorrow which came to him, lives still in our minds as a great and good king. The hoped-for Messiah, the ideal king that was to be, was later referred to as the "Son of David". Jesus of Nazareth accepted the title.

The narrative of these later events in David's life given in the latter chapters of the Second Book of Samuel has been taken by the Deuteronomist Compiler evidently direct from the early Court History of David from which selections are to be found on pp. 21–27 in connection with a study of the earliest narratives to be found in the Bible. To these pages the reader should now turn again in order to trace out the remainder of David's reign with its mixture of success and failure. Even under David the union of North and South under one king proved to be more nominal than real.

This completes the main part of the History of the Establishment of the Kingdom as compiled by Deuteronomic writers during the Exile. It is easy to understand how rich in encouragement to the exiles the private and public reading of such a narrative must have been. We return now to another great prophet whose messages brought light and comfort to the Jews during the last years of the Exile in Babylon.

XI

THE GREAT UNKNOWN PROPHET OF THE EXILE

A GREAT PROPHET-POET

STRANGE to say, of one of the greatest of the Hebrew prophets we know not even the name. This unknown prophet had a literary style of unique beauty and power combined with such an understanding of God and His ways that he was the first to express some of the deepest and widest truths about religion. His anonymous writings are given an important position in the Old Testament, being set beside the writings of the great pre-Exilic prophet Isaiah, in chapters xl-lv of the book bearing his name.

His writings, however, give us no clue to the name or personality of the man. We merely know that he was a wonderful poet and a religious genius; that he wrote during the latter years of the Exile; and that he succeeded in inspiring some of the exiles with his ideas.

1. COMFORT FOR THE PEOPLE

The first selection here given expresses this unknown prophet's primary work, the consoling of those exiles who were dispirited by God's apparent neglect, and the inspiring of those exiles who were attached to the luxuries of Babylon. This man could see afar a possible opportunity for a return to Jerusalem to rebuild there the city of God and its Temple, and was therefore anxious that a company of men and women should be ready to take immediate advantage of the opportunity when it came.

In magnificent yet tender language the prophet seeks to comfort the hearts of the people, by impressing on them God's care for them, God's supreme place in the whole universe, and the strength that comes to those who wait upon this mighty God. Here first we find in Hebrew literature the clear

GREAT UNKNOWN PROPHET OF THE EXILE

realization that Jehovah is not only the God of the people Israel, but the God of the whole earth, the Creator of the universe: here we escape into a large idea of the nature of Jehovah.

Words of Comfort

> Comfort ye, comfort ye My people,
> Saith your God.
> Speak ye comfortably to Jerusalem,
> And cry unto her,
> That her warfare is accomplished,
> That her iniquity is pardoned:
> For she hath received of the Lord's hand
> Double for all her sins.
>
> The voice of him that crieth in the wilderness,
> "Prepare ye the way of the Lord,
> Make straight in the desert
> A highway for our God.
> Every valley shall be exalted,
> And every mountain and hill shall be made low:
> And the crooked shall be made straight,
> And the rough places plain:
> And the glory of the Lord shall be revealed,
> And all flesh shall see it together:
> For the mouth of the Lord hath spoken it."
>
> O Zion, that bringest good tidings,
> Get thee up into the high mountains;
> O Jerusalem, that bringest good tidings,
> Lift up thy voice with strength;
> Lift it up,
> Be not afraid;
> Say unto the cities of Judah,
> "Behold your God!"
>
> Behold, the Lord God will come with strong hand,
> And His arm shall rule for Him:
> Behold His reward is with Him
> And His work before Him.
> He shall feed His flock like a shepherd:
> He shall gather the lambs with His arm,
> And carry them in His bosom,
> And shall gently lead those that are with young.
>
> [*Isaiah* xl. 1–5, 9–11

THE HEART OF THE BIBLE

The Greatness of Jehovah

The voice said, "Cry."
And he said, "What shall I cry?
All flesh is grass,
And all the goodliness thereof is as the flower of the field:
The grass withereth, the flower fadeth:
Because the spirit of the Lord bloweth upon it:
Surely the people is grass.
The grass withereth, the flower fadeth:
But the word of our God shall stand for ever."

Who hath measured the waters in the hollow of His hand,
And meted out heaven with the span,
And comprehended the dust of the earth in a measure,
And weighed the mountains in scales,
And the hills in a balance?

Who hath directed the spirit of the Lord,
Or being His counsellor hath taught Him?
With whom took He counsel, and who instructed Him,
And taught Him in the path of judgment,
And shewed to Him the way of understanding?

Behold, the nations are as a drop of a bucket,
And are counted as the small dust of the balance:
Behold, He taketh up the isles as a very little thing.
All nations before Him are as nothing;
They are counted to Him less than nothing, and vanity.

To whom then will ye liken God?
Or what likeness will ye compare unto Him?
Have ye not known? Have ye not heard?
Hath it not been told you from the beginning?
Have ye not understood from the foundations of the earth?
It is He that sitteth upon the circle of the earth,
And the inhabitants thereof are as grasshoppers;
That stretcheth out the heavens as a curtain,
And spreadeth them out as a tent to dwell in:
That bringeth the princes to nothing;
He maketh the judges of the earth as vanity.

"To whom then will ye liken Me,
Or shall I be equal?" saith the Holy One.
Lift up your eyes on high,
And behold who hath created these things,
That bringeth out their host by number:
He calleth them all by names
By the greatness of His might, for that He is strong in power;
Not one faileth.

[*Isaiah* xl. 6–8, *and from* 12–26]

Strength for the Weak
>Why sayest thou, O Jacob,
>And speakest, O Israel,
>"My way is hid from the Lord,
>And my judgment is passed over from my God"?
>Hast thou not known?
>Hast thou not heard,
>That the everlasting God,
>The Lord, the Creator of the ends of the earth,
>Fainteth not, neither is weary?
>There is no searching of His understanding.
>
>He giveth power to the faint;
>And to them that have no might He increaseth strength.
>Even the youths shall faint and be weary,
>And the young men shall utterly fall:
>But they that wait upon the Lord shall renew their strength;
>They shall mount up with wings as eagles;
>They shall run, and not be weary;
>And they shall walk, and not faint.
>
>[*Isaiah* xl. 27-31]

2. TO CYRUS THE CONQUEROR

The unknown prophet of the Exile thus believed that God rules not only in Israel, but also in other lands and over other peoples. Looking out on the chaos and strife of the nations, he saw that the chance of a Babylonian defeat and a consequent Jewish liberation lay in the possible victory of the Persian conqueror Cyrus, whose power was then being felt from afar.

As Cyrus marched on in triumph, surer and surer did the prophet become that Cyrus himself was, unconsciously, God's instrument for releasing the exiles. To this Cyrus he uttered the message of Jehovah, thus again extending the Jews' somewhat narrow ideas about God. Some exiles probably disapproved of Cyrus being called "The anointed of the Lord", but the prophet reminded them that Jehovah is He Who hath created earth, man, the heavens and all their host.

Cyrus called by Jehovah
>Thus saith the Lord to His anointed, to Cyrus, whose right hand I have holden, to subdue nations before him; and I will loose the loins of kings, to open before him the two leaved gates; and the gates

shall not be shut; "I will go before thee, and make the crooked places straight: I will break in pieces the gates of brass, and cut in sunder the bars of iron: and I will give thee the treasures of darkness and hidden riches of secret places, that thou mayest know that I, the Lord, which call thee by thy name, am the God of Israel. For Jacob My servant's sake, and Israel Mine elect, I have even called thee by thy name: I have surnamed thee, though thou hast not known Me. I am the Lord, and there is none else, there is no God beside Me: I girded thee, though thou hast not known Me: that they may know from the rising of the sun, and from the west, that there is none beside Me. I am the Lord, and there is none else."
[*Isaiah* xlv. 1–6]

Cyrus to free the Captives
Thus saith the Lord, the Holy One of Israel, and his Maker, "Ask Me of things to come concerning My sons, and concerning the work of My hands command ye Me. I have made the earth, and created man upon it: I, even My hands, have stretched out the heavens, and all their host have I commanded. I have raised him up in righteousness, and I will direct all his ways: he shall build My city, and he shall let go My captives, not for price nor reward," saith the Lord of hosts.
[*Isaiah* xlv. 11–13]

3. THE SUFFERING SERVANT OF JEHOVAH

We have noted over and over again how firmly the Deuteronomists held to the idea that prosperity always follows right-doing and suffering the doing of evil. Wherever they saw pain and distress they searched until they found, or invented, some personal or national sin which had caused the suffering. Thus his contemporaries believed that Jeremiah suffered because he was an evil-doer. The Unknown Prophet of the Exile reached a deeper understanding of another aspect of this problem of suffering, and therein lies his greatest contribution to the development of religion.

This man thinks intensely of the whole earth as the Lord's; he looks forward to a day when all the nations of the earth shall bow before Him, and thus comes to realize the great mission of the people Israel. They had been chosen by God, not for their own sakes, but that they, a nation, might be the servant of God to lead other nations to God. As the prophets were to Israel, so must Israel be to the whole world.

But Israel had suffered many things, had been greatly afflicted and is now in helpless captivity, not a servant, but a "suffering servant". The prophet muses with God upon these things until he reaches the new idea of Israel saving the world, not through her success, but through her suffering and self-sacrifice. The suffering is because of sin, it is true, some of it the sin of Israel, some of it the sin of the world beyond Israel. By enduring this suffering with meekness, patience and love, Israel should save mankind. It is amazing that this man of God should have reached so lofty a truth.

The people of whom he hoped this, although they had suffered enough and served enough to inspire the prophet's vision of truth, were not good enough to carry out their mission. All too soon it was the glory of the Jews and the glory of Jerusalem that they were seeking, not the glory of God and the good of mankind. But what Israel failed to do, what even the Remnant or pious kernel of Israel failed to do, Jesus of Nazareth himself accomplished in the fullness of time.

To what extent, in his youth, Jesus fed his soul on these old passages of Scripture, we cannot tell; but we know that, when he entered on his public ministry, they had become part and parcel of his thoughts about himself and his work. Israel had failed to realize the ideal of the suffering servant of Jehovah; even the Remnant of Israel had failed; but Jesus Christ fulfilled the ideal so perfectly that now not one of us can read the following passages without feeling that they find their real interpretation in Jesus and in Jesus alone.

In the following selections, while the translation of the Authorized Version is generally adhered to, slight alterations have been made when the meaning is not clear.

Blessing for the Gentiles

> Behold My servant, whom I uphold;
> Mine elect, in whom My soul delighteth;
> I have put My spirit upon him:
> He shall bring forth justice for the nations.
> He shall not cry, nor lift up,
> Nor cause his voice to be heard in the street.

A bruised reed shall he not break,
And the smouldering wick shall he not quench:
He shall bring forth justice for truth.
He shall not fail nor be discouraged,
Till he have set justice in the earth:
And the isles shall wait for his law.
[*Isaiah* xlii. 1–4]

To the Servant of Jehovah comes Glory after Suffering
Behold, My servant shall deal prudently,
He shall be exalted and extolled, and be very high.
As many were astonied at thee:
(His visage was so marred more than any man,
And his form more than the sons of men:)
So shall he sprinkle many nations;
The kings shall shut their mouths at him:
For that which had not been told them they shall see;
And that which they had not heard shall they consider.
[*Isaiah* lii. 13–15]

The Heathen describe the Servant's Suffering
Who hath believed our report?
And to whom is the arm of the Lord revealed?
He shall grow up before Him as a tender plant,
And as a root out of dry ground:
He is despised and rejected of men:
A man of sorrows and acquainted with grief:
And we hid as it were our faces from him;
He was despised, and we esteemed him not.
[*Isaiah* liii. 1–3]

The Heathen confess the Servant's Suffering to be for them
Surely he hath borne our griefs,
And carried our sorrows:
Yet we did esteem him stricken,
Smitten of God, and afflicted.
But he was wounded for our transgressions,
He was bruised for our iniquities:
The chastisement of our peace was upon him,
And with his stripes we are healed.
All we like sheep have gone astray;
We have turned every one to his own way;
And the Lord hath laid on him
The iniquity of us all.
[*Isaiah* liii. 4–6]

The Servant's Patience

> He was oppressed, and he was afflicted,
> Yet he opened not his mouth:
> He is brought as a lamb to the slaughter,
> And as a sheep before her shearers is dumb,
> So he openeth not his mouth.
> He was taken from prison and from judgment:
> And who shall declare his generation?
> For he was cut off out of the land of the living:
> For the transgression of My people was he stricken.
> And he made his grave with the wicked,
> And with the rich in his death;
> He had done no violence,
> Neither was there any deceit in his mouth.
> [*Isaiah* liii. 7–9]

Jehovah's Purpose and Triumph

> Yet it pleased the Lord to bruise him;
> He hath put him to grief:
> When he shalt make his soul an offering for sin,
> The pleasure of the Lord shall prosper in his hand.
> He shall see of the travail of his soul, and shall be satisfied:
> By his knowledge shall My righteous servant justify many;
> For he shall bear their iniquities.
>
> Therefore will I divide him a portion with the great,
> And he shall divide his spoil with the strong;
> Because he hath poured out his soul unto death:
> And he was numbered with the transgressors;
> And he bare the sin of many,
> And made intercession for the transgressors.
> [*Isaiah* liii. 10–12]

4. THE RETURN TO JERUSALEM

The following passages need little explanation. The people feared and trembled at the difficulties of the return to Jerusalem, at the long journey through the desert, with danger from wild beasts and lack of food and water, at the desolate ruins amid which they must build their new homes. The prophet pours reassurance and hope into their ears.

THE HEART OF THE BIBLE

The Terrors of the Journey

Go ye forth of Babylon, flee ye from the Chaldeans,
With a voice of singing declare ye, tell this,
Utter it even to the end of the earth;
Say ye, "The Lord hath redeemed His servant Jacob."

And they thirsted not when He led them through the deserts:
He caused the waters to flow out of the rock for them:
He clave the rock also,
And the waters gushed out.

They shall feed in the ways,
And their pastures shall be in all high places.
They shall not hunger nor thirst;
Neither shall the heat nor sun smite them:
For He that hath mercy on them shall lead them,
Even by the springs of water shall He guide them.
And I will make all My mountains a way,
And My highways shall be exalted.

Sing, O heavens, and be joyful, O earth:
And break forth into singing, O mountains:
For the Lord hath comforted His people,
And will have mercy upon His afflicted.
[*Isaiah* xlviii. 20, 21, xlix. 9–11, 13

Jerusalem restored

How beautiful upon the mountains
Are the feet of him that bringeth good tidings,
That publisheth peace;
That bringeth good tidings of good,
That publisheth salvation;
That saith unto Zion, "Thy God reigneth!"

Thy watchmen shall lift up the voice;
With the voice together shall they sing:
For they shall see eye to eye,
When the Lord shall bring again Zion.
Break forth into joy,
Sing together, ye waste places of Jerusalem:
For the Lord hath comforted His people,
He hath redeemed Jerusalem.
The Lord hath made bare His holy arm
In the eyes of all the nations:
And all the ends of the earth
Shall see the salvation of our God.
[*Isaiah* lii. 1–70

The Promise of Joy and Peace

    For a small moment have I forsaken thee;
    But with great mercies will I gather thee.
    In a little wrath I hid My face from thee for a moment,
    But with everlasting kindness will I have mercy on thee,
    Saith the Lord thy Redeemer.

    For the mountains shall depart,
    And the hills be removed:
    But My kindness shall not depart from thee,
    Neither shall the covenant of My peace be removed,
    Saith the Lord that hath mercy on thee.

    O thou afflicted,
    Tossed with tempest, and not comforted,
    Behold, I will lay thy stones with fair colours,
    And lay thy foundations with sapphires.
    And I will make thy windows of agates,
    And thy gates of carbuncles,
    And all thy borders of pleasant stones.
    And all thy children shall be taught of the Lord,
    And great shall be the peace of thy children.

    Ho, every one that thirsteth, come ye to the waters,
    And he that hath no money; come ye, buy and eat;
    Yea, come, buy wine and milk
    Without money and without price.
    Wherefore do ye spend your money for that which is not
        bread?
    And your labour for that which satisfieth not?
    Hearken diligently unto Me, and eat ye that which is good,
    And let your soul delight itself in fatness.

    I will make an everlasting covenant with you,
    Even the sure mercies of David.
    Behold, I have given him for a witness to the people,
    A leader and commander to the people.
    Behold, thou shalt call a nation that thou knowest not,
    And nations that knew not thee shall run unto thee
    Because of the Lord thy God,
    And for the Holy One of Israel; for He hath glorified thee.

    Seek ye the Lord while He may be found,
    Call ye upon Him while He is near:
    Let the wicked forsake his way,
    And the unrighteous man his thoughts:

And let him return unto the Lord,
For He will have mercy upon him;
And to our God,
For He will abundantly pardon.

For My thoughts are not your thoughts,
Neither are your ways My ways, saith the Lord.
For as the heavens
Are higher than the earth,
So are My ways higher than your ways,
And My thoughts than your thoughts.

For as the rain cometh down and the snow from heaven,
And returneth not thither, but watereth the earth,
And maketh it bring forth and bud,
That it may give seed to the sower, and bread to the eater:
So shall My word be that goeth forth out of My mouth:
It shall not return unto Me void,
But it shall accomplish that which I please,
And it shall prosper in the thing whereto I sent it.

For ye shall go out with joy,
And be led forth with peace:
The mountains and the hills shall break forth before you into singing,
And all the trees of the field shall clap their hands.
Instead of the thorn shall come up the fir tree,
And instead of the brier shall come up the myrtle tree:
And it shall be to the Lord for a name,
For an everlasting sign that shall not be cut off.

[*From Isaiah* liv. 7–13, lv.

XII

OTHER ANONYMOUS PROPHECIES OF THE EXILE

1. THE FALL OF BABYLON

THE unknown prophet whose poems we have in Isaiah xl-lv was not the only one who in the latter half of the Exilic period had sufficient insight into the ways of Jehovah to discern the coming doom of Babylon. In the Book of Isaiah are gathered up also two or three poems by one or more other unknown prophets, poems striking in their imagery and dramatic force, but in spirit akin to the hate-poems of the nationalist prophet Nahum whose message we read on p. 85. These poems are to be found in Isaiah xiii, xiv. 4*b*–23, xxi. 1–10.

The Fall of Babylon

The burden of Babylon. The noise of a multitude in the mountains, like as of a great people; a tumultuous noise of the kingdoms of nations gathered together: the Lord of hosts mustereth the host of the battle. They come from a far country, from the end of heaven, even the Lord, and the weapons of His indignation, to destroy the whole land. Howl ye; for the day of the Lord is at hand; it shall come as a destruction from the Almighty. Therefore shall all hands be faint, and every man's heart shall melt: behold, the day of the Lord cometh, cruel both with wrath and fierce anger, to lay the land desolate: and He shall destroy the sinners thereof out of it. For the stars of heaven and the constellations thereof shall not give their light: the sun shall be darkened in his going forth, and the moon shall not cause her light to shine. And I will punish the world for their evil, and the wicked for their iniquity; and I will cause the arrogancy of the proud to cease, and will lay low the haughtiness of the terrible. I will make a man more precious than fine gold; even a man than the golden wedge of Ophir. Therefore I will shake the heavens, and the earth shall remove out of her place, in the wrath of the Lord of hosts, and in the day of His fierce anger. How hath the oppressor ceased, the golden city ceased! The Lord hath broken the staff of the wicked, and the sceptre of the rulers. He who smote the people in wrath with a continual stroke, he that ruled the nations in anger, is persecuted, and none hindereth. The whole earth is at rest, and is quiet: they break forth into singing. Yea, the fir trees rejoice at thee, and the cedars of Lebanon, saying, "Since thou art laid down, no feller is come up against us."

The King of Babylon in Sheol

Hell from beneath is moved for thee to meet thee at thy coming: it stirreth up the dead for thee, even all the chief ones of the earth; it hath raised up from their thrones all the kings of the nations. All they shall speak and say unto thee, "Art thou also become weak as we? Art thou become like unto us?" Thy pomp is brought down to the grave, and the noise of thy viols: the worm is spread under thee, and the worms cover thee. How art thou fallen from heaven, O Lucifer, son of the morning! How art thou cut down to the ground, which didst weaken the nations! For thou hast said in thine heart, "I will ascend into heaven, I will exalt my throne above the stars of God: I will sit also upon the mount of the congregation, in the sides of the north: I will ascend above the heights of the clouds; I will be like the most High." Yet thou shalt be brought down to hell, to the sides of the pit. They that see thee shall narrowly look upon thee, and consider thee, saying, "Is this the man that made the earth to tremble, that did shake kingdoms; that made the world as a wilderness, and destroyed the cities thereof; that opened not the house of his prisoners?"

[*From Isaiah* xiii and xiv

2. THE RETURN TO JERUSALEM

Isaiah xxxiv and xxxv also contain prophecies belonging to later times than the eighth century before Christ, to which Isaiah himself belonged. It is likely that parts of these two chapters were written in the years after the return from Exile, but chapter xxxv has such close affinities with the message of the great unknown prophet of Isaiah xl-lv that we give it here.

The Return to Jerusalem

The wilderness and the solitary place shall be glad for them; and the desert shall rejoice, and blossom as the rose. It shall blossom abundantly, and rejoice even with joy and singing: the glory of Lebanon shall be given unto it, the excellency of Carmel and Sharon, they shall see the glory of the Lord, and the excellency of our God. Strengthen ye the weak hands, and confirm the feeble knees. Say to them that are of a fearful heart, "Be strong, fear not: behold, your God will come with vengeance, even God with a recompence; he will

OTHER ANONYMOUS PROPHECIES OF THE EXILE 253

come and save you." Then the eyes of the blind shall be opened, and the ears of the deaf shall be unstopped. Then shall the lame man leap as an hart, and the tongue of the dumb sing: for in the wilderness shall waters break out, and streams in the desert. And the parched ground shall become a pool, and the thirsty land springs of water: in the habitation of dragons, where each lay, shall be grass with reeds and rushes. And an highway shall be there, and a way, and it shall be called "The way of holiness"; the unclean shall not pass over it; but it shall be for those: the wayfaring men, though fools, shall not err therein. No lion shall be there, nor any ravenous beast shall go up thereon, it shall not be found there; but the redeemed shall walk there: and the ransomed of the Lord shall return, and come to Zion with songs and everlasting joy upon their heads: they shall obtain joy and gladness, and sorrow and sighing shall flee away.

[*Isaiah* xxxv

3. A CURSE ON EDOM

In strong contrast to this beautiful message of hope is the passage in Isaiah xxxiv. 5-15, a hate-poem against Edom (or Idumea). It should be compared with the Edom passages in Psalm cxxxvii and in Obadiah (see pp. 151, 152).

A Curse on Edom

My sword shall be bathed in heaven: behold, it shall come down upon Idumea, and upon the people of My curse, to judgment. The sword of the Lord is filled with blood, it is made fat with fatness, and with the blood of lambs and goats, with the fat of the kidneys of rams: for the Lord hath a sacrifice in Bozrah, and a great slaughter in the land of Idumea. And the unicorns shall come down with them, and the bullocks with the bulls; and their land shall be soaked with blood, and their dust made fat with fatness. For it is the day of the Lord's vengeance, and the year of recompences for the controversy of Zion.

And the streams thereof shall be turned into pitch, and the dust thereof into brimstone, and the land thereof shall become burning pitch. It shall not be quenched night nor day; the smoke thereof shall go up for ever: from generation to generation it shall lie waste; none shall pass through it for ever and ever. But the cormorant and the bittern shall possess it; the owl also and the raven shall dwell in it: and He shall stretch out upon it the line of confusion, and the stones of emptiness.

They shall call the nobles thereof to the kingdom, but none shall be there, and all her princes shall be nothing. And thorns shall come up in her palaces, nettles and brambles in the fortresses thereof: and it shall be an habitation of dragons, and a court for owls. The wild beasts of the desert shall also meet with the wild beasts of the island, and the satyr shall cry to his fellow; the screech owl also shall rest there, and find for herself a place of rest. There shall the great owl make her nest, and lay, and hatch, and gather under her shadow: there shall the vultures also be gathered, every one with her mate.

[*Isaiah* xxxiv. 5-15

XIII

THE FIRST POST-EXILIC PROPHETS

1. INTRODUCTION

THE exile in Babylon lasted for about fifty years: that is to say, those who had gone as children into exile, after the fall of Jerusalem in 586 B.C., were elderly men and women when Babylon came into the possession of the Persians, led by Cyrus. For the next two hundred years Persia wielded the sovereign power in the affairs of the East.

THE EXILES IN BABYLON

Strange to say, the Bible gives us only one definite historical fact about the years of exile in Babylon—that, after a time, King Jehoiachin was released from prison and treated with kindness, respected alike by his captors and his former subjects (2 Kings xxv. 27). In spite of this scarcity of historical detail, the prophetic literature for the period is, as we have seen, so rich that from it we can build up a good conception of, at least, the inner life of the exiles. Compare, for instance, Jeremiah's letter, given on p. 77.

To this the inscriptions of the Babylonian kings add something. We know that Nebuchadrezzar was a great monarch, eager on constructive rather than destructive conquests; anxious to build up a happy, wealthy empire rather than to conquer merely for the sake of military glory. In this he far surpassed the Assyrians. He set himself, by building, to make Babylon a fit capital for his great empire. Workmen of all sorts were required: these workmen had to be fed. His deportation of the best elements in Judah contributed to the success of his building. There was scope for any craftsman, while the need for food supplies encouraged the development of agriculture. Thus the majority of the exiles were not prisoners: they settled in colonies near the city, where many of them tilled the land

and produced food, while others wrought divers kinds of craftsmanship. Gradually, as they mingled more freely with the Chaldeans, they developed trade with them; so began the growth of that wonderful commercial capacity of the Jews. Life in its material aspects was, during these years of exile, comparatively easy.

But the exiles were homesick men and women for many years, some of them until they returned again to Jerusalem. Their Temple and its worship were gone. No one thought of building a temple in Babylon; the new temple was to be in Jerusalem. A people, very particular about cleanliness and ceremonial, were cut off from all that in this respect they held most dear. But, as we noted on p. 90, one thing remained; their sacred writings, the words of the prophets, the old stories of their ancestors, the earliest laws and the new law-book found in King Josiah's reign. Time and place, however, were needed if their spirits were to be fed on these sacred writings. Thus the Sabbath began to be strictly observed, for then men might gather together to hear the word of God read and explained. So began that weekly worship in the synagogue familiar to Jesus; a custom to which our Jewish friends still adhere. We may remind ourselves that the Jewish Sabbath lasts from 6 p.m. on our Friday until 6 p.m. on our Saturday.

THE RETURN FROM EXILE

In 538 B.C. Cyrus, the Persian conqueror, defeated the Babylonians and took possession of Babylon. Thus for the next two hundred years the Jews lived within the Persian Empire. Cyrus showed himself a merciful and wise conqueror, trying to obtain the goodwill and gratitude of the subject peoples and succeeding in so doing. The great unknown prophet of the Exile saw in Cyrus the "Anointed of the Lord" (see p. 243). Here is a quotation from an ancient inscription made by Cyrus (Marduk is the god of Cyrus):—

I am Cyrus, king of the world, the great king, the mighty king, king of Babylon, ... king of the four quarters of the world, son of Cambyses,

THE FIRST POST-EXILIC PROPHETS

the great king, grandson of Cyrus, the great king, great-grandson of Teispes, the great king; an everlasting seed of royalty. . . . When I entered in peace into Babylon, with joy and rejoicing I took up my lordly dwelling in the royal palace. Marduk, the great lord, moved the understanding heart of the people of Babylon to me, while I daily sought his worship. My numerous troops dwelt peacefully in Babylon; no terroriser did I permit. The people of Babylon (I released) from an unsuitable yoke. Their dwellings—their decay I repaired; their ruins I cleared away.

. . . The cities (beyond) the Tigris, whose sites had been founded of old,—the gods who dwelt in them I returned to their places, and caused them to settle in their eternal shrines. All their people I assembled and returned them to their dwellings. . . . May all the gods whom I have returned to their cities pray before Marduk for the prolonging of my days, may they speak a kind word for me.

In other words Cyrus reversed the policy of the Assyrians and of Nebuchadrezzar and permitted those who had been transported to return to their countries and rebuild their temples. Among these were the Jews. This ancient inscription fully confirms the Biblical statement that Cyrus permitted the Jews to return to Jerusalem (see Ezra i).

How many of the Jewish exiles actually availed themselves of this permission to set out on a long, dangerous journey back to a ruined, desolate city, where neither homes nor Temple awaited them, we do not know. But it is clear that the counter-attractions of life in Babylon, under a friendly monarch, would keep the majority where they were. As far as can be known, at this time only a few representative persons went back to Jerusalem, among whom were Zerubbabel and Joshua, of whose work in rebuilding the Temple we shall read in the prophecy of Haggai.

In Jerusalem these returning exiles were met by exiles from Egypt, who had had a much less arduous return journey, and by the few weak elements of the nation which had remained in Judah all the years of the exile, many of them living in caves. At first these men set themselves to build homes on the site of the destroyed city; probably they intended to rebuild the Temple as soon as their own most urgent needs were met.

2. HAGGAI AND THE NEW TEMPLE

But spirits sank and hands were slack. For seventeen long years nothing was done. Of the events of these years we know little. Certainly at last a period of drought and famine set thoughtful men to consider their ways. Also we know that upheavals occurred in the dynasty of the Persians, resulting in the settlement of Darius as ruler of Babylon, and in his choice of Zerubbabel, of the house of David, as the Persian viceroy in Judah.

But in 520 B.C. the silence was broken by the message of the aged prophet Haggai, old enough to have known the first Temple of Jehovah, destroyed seventy years before. In simple, straightforward words the prophet pointed the moral of the drought and famine and called on the people to rebuild the Temple. Later, when they become discouraged in the task, thinking the Temple disappointingly small and bare, he appeared again with a message of cheer and hope. Haggai's efforts were successful: five years later the new Temple was completed.

We note how carefully this prophet dates his work: it reminds us of Ezekiel's methods in this respect.

The People called to rebuild the Temple

In the second year of Darius the king, in the sixth month, in the first day of the month, came the word of the Lord by Haggai the prophet unto Zerubbabel, governor of Judah, and to Joshua the high priest, saying, "Thus speaketh the Lord of hosts, saying, 'This people say, The time is not come, the time that the Lord's house should be built.' " Then came the word of the Lord by Haggai the prophet, saying, "Is it time for you, O ye, to dwell in your cieled houses, and this house lie waste? Now therefore thus saith the Lord of hosts; 'Consider your ways. Ye have sown much, and bring in little; ye eat, but ye have not enough; ye drink, but ye are not filled with drink; ye clothe you, but there is none warm; and he that earneth wages earneth wages to put it into a bag with holes. Consider your ways. Go up to the mountain, and bring wood, and build the house; and I will take pleasure in it, and I will be glorified', saith the Lord. 'Ye looked for much, and, lo, it came to little; and when ye brought it home, I did blow upon it. Why? Because of Mine house that is waste, and ye run every man unto his own house. Therefore the heaven over you is stayed from dew, and the earth is stayed from her fruit. And I called for a drought upon the land, and upon the mountains,

THE FIRST POST-EXILIC PROPHETS

and upon the corn, and upon the new wine, and upon the oil, and upon that which the ground bringeth forth, and upon men, and upon cattle, and upon all the labour of the hands.'"

[*Haggai* i. 1–11]

Rebuilding begun

Then Zerubbabel and Joshua, the high priest, with all the remnant of the people, obeyed the voice of the Lord their God, and the words of Haggai the prophet, as the Lord their God had sent him, and the people did fear before the Lord. Then spake Haggai the Lord's messenger in the Lord's message unto the people, saying, "I am with you," saith the Lord. And the Lord stirred up the spirit of Zerubbabel, governor of Judah, and the spirit of Joshua, the high priest, and the spirit of all the remnant of the people; and they came and did work in the house of the Lord of hosts, their God, in the four and twentieth day of the sixth month, in the second year of Darius the king.

[*Haggai* i. 12–15]

Words of Encouragement

In the seventh month, in the one and twentieth day of the month, came the word of the Lord by the prophet Haggai, saying, "Speak now to Zerubbabel, governor of Judah, and to Joshua, the high priest, and to the residue of the people, saying, 'Who is left among you that saw this house in her first glory? And how do ye see it now? Is it not in your eyes in comparison of it as nothing? Yet now be strong, O Zerubbabel,' saith the Lord; 'and be strong, O Joshua, and be strong, all ye people of the land,' saith the Lord, 'and work: for I am with you,' saith the Lord of hosts: 'according to the word that I covenanted with you when ye came out of Egypt, so My spirit remaineth among you: fear ye not.' For thus saith the Lord of hosts; 'Yet once, it is a little while, and I will shake the heavens, and the earth, and the sea, and the dry land; and I will shake all nations, and the desire of all nations shall come: and I will fill this house with glory,' saith the Lord of hosts. 'The silver is mine, and the gold is mine,' saith the Lord of hosts. 'The glory of this latter house shall be greater than of the former: and in this place will I give peace.'"

And again the word of the Lord came unto Haggai in the four and twentieth day of the month, saying, "Speak to Zerubbabel, governor of Judah, saying, 'I will shake the heavens and the earth; and I will overthrow the throne of kingdoms, and I will destroy the strength of the kingdoms of the heathen; and I will overthrow the chariots, and those that ride in them; and the horses and their riders shall come down, every one by the sword of his brother. In that day,' saith the Lord of hosts, 'will I take thee, O Zerubbabel, my servant, and will make thee as a signet: for I have chosen thee,' saith the Lord of hosts."

[*Haggai* ii. 1–9, 20–23]

3. THE VISIONS OF ZECHARIAH

THE DESIRE FOR A KING

The last quotation from Haggai shows clearly how great importance was attached by the people to the presence in their midst of Zerubbabel as the governor of Judah, duly appointed by the Persian monarch Darius. For Zerubbabel was a man of royal family, a BRANCH of the house of David, as the prophet Zechariah describes him. This man, they thought, might prove to be the ideal king that was to be: the people's hopes were set on a speedy restoration of the monarchy. In Haggai, Joshua the high priest and Zerubbabel the governor are put side by side: equal emphasis is laid on the civic and religious rulers, except for the special encouragement to the civic ruler in the above passage. Zechariah, however, expressed in his prophetic messages a greater sense of the importance of Zerubbabel and evidently hoped for a restoration of the monarchy. This hope was not realized. The Persian king may have taken offence, if not alarm, at the idea, and Zerubbabel drops out without a word. Judah continued a mere Persian province governed by a nominee of the Persian king.

Thus in the years following the rebuilding of the Temple we see the power of the high priest growing so that the restored community soon became more of a church than a state. But still in their hearts the people cherished through the centuries a hope for a king of the house of David, whose coming would ensure them both material and spiritual blessings: in short, they hoped for a Messiah.

ZECHARIAH AND HIS MESSAGE

Zechariah dated his work as precisely as did Haggai, but while all of Haggai's message belongs to different periods in the year 520 B.C., Zechariah's, although begun in the same year, is carried on for at least two years. His heart was deeply concerned with the moral and spiritual health of the new community, and it is likely that his messages did even more than

THE FIRST POST-EXILIC PROPHETS

Haggai's first inspiration to ensure the completion of the Temple in 516–515 B.C. These are contained in the first eight chapters of the book bearing Zechariah's name; the later chapters contain the messages of later writers. Compare the composite nature of the Book of Isaiah (see p. 269).

Zechariah may be compared with Ezekiel. Both men wrote in prose, both dated their work precisely, both saw visions and gave their messages in the form of visions. In the Book of Zechariah are eight visions which the prophet saw one night early in 519 B.C. We give some of these next, with a little additional matter incorporated with them.

First Vision: No Sign of World Upheavals to help Judah against Persia

Upon the four and twentieth day of the eleventh month, which is the month Sebat, in the second year of Darius, came the word of the Lord unto Zechariah, the son of Berechiah, the son of Iddo the prophet. I saw by night, and behold a man, and he stood among the myrtle trees that were in the bottom; and behind him were there red horses, speckled, and white. Then said I, "O my lord, what are these?" And the angel that talked with me said unto me, "I will shew thee what these be." And the man that stood among the myrtle trees answered and said, "These are they whom the Lord hath sent to walk to and fro through the earth." And they answered the angel of the Lord that stood among the myrtle trees, and said, "We have walked to and fro through the earth, and, behold, all the earth sitteth still, and is at rest."

[*Zechariah* i. 7–11]

Words of Comfort

Then the angel of the Lord answered and said, "O Lord of hosts, how long wilt Thou not have mercy on Jerusalem and on the cities of Judah, against which Thou hast had indignation these threescore and ten years?" And the Lord answered the angel that talked with me with good words and comfortable words. So the angel that communed with me said unto me, "Cry thou, saying, Thus saith the Lord of hosts; 'I am jealous for Jerusalem and for Zion with a great jealousy. And I am very sore displeased with the heathen that are at ease: for I was but a little displeased, and they helped forward the affliction.' Therefore thus saith the Lord: 'I am returned to Jerusalem with mercies: my house shall be built in it,' saith the Lord of hosts, 'and a line shall be stretched forth upon Jerusalem. My cities through prosperity shall yet be spread abroad; and the Lord shall yet comfort Zion, and shall yet choose Jerusalem.'"

[*Zechariah* i. 12–17]

Second Vision: Doom on Judah's Conquerors

Then lifted I up mine eyes, and saw, and behold four horns. And I said unto the angel that talked with me, "What be these?" And he answered me, "These are the horns which have scattered Judah, Israel, and Jerusalem." And the Lord shewed me four carpenters. Then said I, "What come these to do?" And He spake, saying, "These are the horns which have scattered Judah, so that no man did lift up his head; but these are come to fray them, to cast out the horns of the Gentiles, which lifted up their horn over the land of Judah to scatter it."

[*Zechariah* i. 18–21]

Third Vision: A City that has no Need of Walls

I lifted up mine eyes again, and looked, and behold a man with a measuring line in his hand. Then said I, "Whither goest thou?" And he said unto me, "To measure Jerusalem, to see what is the breadth thereof, and what is the length thereof." And, behold, the angel that talked with me went forth, and another angel went out to meet him, and said unto him, "Run, speak to this young man, saying, 'Jerusalem shall be inhabited as towns without walls for the multitude of men and cattle therein: for I,' saith the Lord, 'will be unto her a wall of fire round about, and will be the glory in the midst of her.'"

[*Zechariah* ii. 1–5

The Lord will be to Jerusalem a wall of fire like that which men make in the desert round their camp at night. In these days of disarmament conferences, when men are thinking of peace and war in new ways, this vision is surprisingly apposite. To Zechariah the true defence of a people is not in material things: walls may cost us more by cutting us off from good than they accomplish in protection. The true defence of a people is the Lord "in the midst of her".

Zechariah, as has been well said, is a man of "sanctified common sense", who faces facts, among others the most deadly fact of iniquity and sin in the midst of the community. His fourth vision shows Joshua the high priest in "filthy garments" of iniquity: then clothed by an angel with "change of raiment", and finally given the mysterious promise of the BRANCH. Whether the high priest in filthy garments is meant to represent the iniquity of the whole community, or whether Joshua himself has been in some personal trouble from which he is acquitted, is uncertain.

THE FIRST POST-EXILIC PROPHETS

In the fifth vision the candlestick is what we should call a lamp, fed with oil from the olive trees on each side. We may note how often Zechariah uses an angel as an intermediary between himself and Jehovah: he appears to be less intimate with the Lord than were the former prophets.

Fifth Vision: Light, Safety, and Peace maintained by Joshua and Zerubbabel

And the angel that talked with me came again, and waked me, as a man that is wakened out of his sleep, and said unto me, "What seest thou?" And I said, "I have looked, and behold a candlestick all of gold, with a bowl upon the top of it, and his seven lamps thereon, and seven pipes to the seven lamps, which are upon the top thereof: and two olive trees by it, one upon the right side of the bowl, and the other upon the left side thereof." So I answered and spake to the angel that talked with me, saying, "What are these, my lord?" Then the angel that talked with me answered and said unto me, "Knowest thou not what these be?" And I said, "No, my lord." Then he answered and spake unto me, saying, "They are the eyes of the Lord, which run to and fro through the whole earth." Then answered I, and said unto him, "What are these two olive trees upon the right side of the candlestick and upon the left side thereof?" And he answered me and said, "Knowest thou not what these be?" And I said, "No, my lord." Then said he, "These are the two anointed ones, that stand by the Lord of the whole earth."

[*Zechariah* iv. 1–6, 10, 11, 13, 14

The Lord's Spirit with Joshua and Zerubbabel

This is the word of the Lord unto Zerubbabel, saying, "Not by might, nor by power, but by My spirit," saith the Lord of hosts. Who art thou, O great mountain? Before Zerubbabel thou shalt become a plain: and he shall bring forth the headstone thereof with shoutings, crying, "Grace, grace." Moreover, the word of the Lord came unto me, saying, "The hands of Zerubbabel have laid the foundation of this house; his hands shall also finish it; and thou shalt know that the Lord of hosts hath sent me unto you. For who hath despised the day of small things? They shall rejoice, and shall see the plummet in the hand of Zerubbabel."

[*Zechariah* iv. 6–10

Again Zechariah's mind turns to the evil in Jerusalem. The sixth vision is of a "flying roll" which is a curse that devours all thieves and perjurers. The seventh vision passes from sinners to Sin itself, depicted as a woman in a barrel (ephah), kept in by a lid weighted with lead. The prophet sees clearly that the only hope of the people is absolute separation from sin. In the vision the ephah with its contents is despatched to the land of Shinar (i.e. Babylon) in the care of two women flying with the wings of a stork (see Zech. v). In the last vision Zechariah returns to view the whole world "before the Lord of all the earth". As the text which has come down is thought to be corrupt, the exact meaning of this vision is uncertain: so also is the exact meaning of the second passage about BRANCH which follows (Zech. vi).

The remainder of Zechariah's message is dated two years later. The rebuilding of the Temple made such good progress that the community lifted up their heads and began to think. For years they had kept as fast days such anniversaries as that of the Fall of Jerusalem. Should they continue to do so? The prophet points out the duties that matter far more than any fast, showing himself akin to the former prophets. His message closes with beautiful promises to the restored community.

Social Righteousness and Fasting

And the word of the Lord came unto Zechariah, saying, Thus speaketh the Lord of hosts, saying, "Execute true judgment, and shew mercy and compassion every man to his brother: and oppress not the widow, nor the fatherless, the stranger, nor the poor; and let none of you imagine evil against his brother in your heart."

"These are the things that ye shall do; Speak ye every man the truth to his neighbour; execute the judgment of truth and peace in your gates: and let none of you imagine evil in your hearts against his neighbour; and love no false oath: for all these are things that I hate," saith the Lord.

And the word of the Lord of hosts came unto me, saying, Thus saith the Lord of hosts; "The fast of the fourth month, and the fast of the fifth, and the fast of the seventh, and the fast of the tenth, shall be to the house of Judah joy and gladness, and cheerful feasts; therefore love the truth and peace."

[*Zechariah* vii. 8–10, viii. 16–19

Precious Promises

Again the word of the Lord of hosts came to me, saying, Thus saith the Lord of hosts; "I was jealous for Zion with great jealousy, and I was jealous for her with great fury." Thus saith the Lord; "I am returned unto Zion, and will dwell in the midst of Jerusalem: and Jerusalem shall be called a city of truth; and the mountain of the Lord of hosts the holy mountain." Thus saith the Lord of hosts; "There shall yet old men and old women dwell in the streets of Jerusalem, and every man with his staff in his hand for very age. And the streets of the city shall be full of boys and girls playing in the streets thereof."

Thus saith the Lord of hosts; "Behold, I will save My people from the east country, and from the west country; and I will bring them, and they shall dwell in the midst of Jerusalem: and they shall be My people, and I will be their God, in truth and in righteousness." Thus saith the Lord of hosts; "Let your hands be strong, ye that hear in these days these words by the mouth of the prophets, which were in the day that the foundation of the house of the Lord of hosts was laid, that the temple might be built. For before these days there was no hire for man, nor any hire for beast; neither was there any peace to him that went out or came in because of the affliction: for I set all men every one against his neighbour. But now I will not be unto the residue of this people as in the former days," saith the Lord of hosts. "For the seed shall be prosperous; the vine shall give her fruit, and the ground shall give her increase, and the heavens shall give their dew; and I will cause the remnant of this people to possess all these things. And it shall come to pass, that as ye were a curse among the heathen, O house of Judah, and house of Israel; so will I save you, and ye shall be a blessing: fear not, but let your hands be strong."

[*From Zechariah* viii. 1–13

XIV

A PERIOD OF DISILLUSION AND MISERY

1. MALACHI'S PICTURE OF HIS TIMES

ENCOURAGED by the prophetic work of both Haggai and Zechariah, the Jews had by 515 B.C. completed the new Temple in Jerusalem. But not yet was "the glory of the Lord" seen upon it. Men had returned to Zion with a great faith and a mighty hope in their hearts, and only trouble came upon them. They longed for political independence, the more daring spirits among them seeing in Zerubbabel a possible king of the house of David: but they remained subject to the Persians and had to pay them "tribute, custom and tolls" through very greedy tax-gatherers. The upkeep of the local governor and his servants was also a heavy burden for a poverty-stricken community.

Even their neighbours hated the Jews. The half-heathen Samaritans on the North, the Ammonites on the East, the Edomites on the South, all regarded them with intense dislike. Their territory was much less than in the old days, while its population was both small and poor. The civic life of the community was stained with injustice, lawlessness, deceit and treachery. Religious life was at its lowest ebb: people did not hesitate to cheat Jehovah Himself by bringing to sacrifice animals "which had died a violent death, and the lame, and the sick". The worship of the Temple was starved until it became almost impossible.

To this period, which covers roughly the half-century from about 500 B.C. to 450 B.C., belong the writings of an unknown prophet now called "the messenger" or "Malachi". His words reflect the sadness of his times, but they also express the hopes nursed by the men who remain loyal to Jehovah.

Disloyalty to Jehovah
  The burden of the word of the Lord to Israel by Malachi. "I have loved you," saith the Lord. "A son honoureth his father, and a servant

A PERIOD OF DISILLUSION AND MISERY

his master: if then I be a father, where is Mine honour? And if I be a master," saith the Lord of hosts, "where is My fear, O ye priests, that despise My name? And ye say, 'Wherein have we despised Thy name?' Ye offer polluted bread upon Mine altar; and ye say, 'Wherein have we polluted thee?' In that ye say, 'The table of the Lord is contemptible.' And if ye offer the blind for sacrifice, is it not evil? And if ye offer the lame and sick, is it not evil? Offer it now unto thy governor; will he be pleased with thee, or accept thy person?" saith the Lord of hosts. "I have no pleasure in you, neither will I accept an offering at your hand. For from the rising of the sun even unto the going down of the same My name shall be great among the Gentiles; and in every place incense shall be offered unto My name, and a pure offering: for My name shall be great among the heathen," saith the Lord of hosts. "But ye have profaned it, in that ye say, 'The table of the Lord is polluted; and the fruit thereof, even his meat is contemptible.' Ye said also, 'Behold, what a weariness is it!' and ye have snuffed at it; and ye brought that which was torn, and the lame, and the sick; thus ye brought an offering: should I accept this of your hand?" saith the Lord. "But cursed be the deceiver, which hath in his flock a male, and voweth, and sacrificeth unto the Lord a corrupt thing: for I am a great King," saith the Lord of hosts, "and My name is dreadful among the heathen."

"And now, O ye priests, this commandment is for you. The priest's lips should keep knowledge, and they should seek the law at his mouth: for he is the messenger of the Lord of hosts. But ye are departed out of the way; ye have caused many to stumble at the law; ye have corrupted the covenant of Levi. Therefore have I also made you contemptible and base before all the people, according as ye have not kept My ways, but have been partial in the law."

[*From Malachi* i and ii

Doubt of the Justice of Jehovah

Ye have wearied the Lord with your words. Yet ye say, "Wherein have we wearied Him?" When ye say, "Every one that doeth evil is good in the sight of the Lord, and He delighteth in them"; or, "Where is the God of judgment?"

"Your words have been stout against Me," saith the Lord. Yet ye say, "What have we spoken against Thee?" Ye have said, "It is vain to serve God: and what profit is it that we have kept His ordinance, and that we have walked mournfully before the Lord of hosts? And now we call the proud happy; yea, they that work wickedness are set up."

[*Malachi* ii. 17, iii. 13–15

The Reality and Goodwill of Jehovah

"Behold, I will send My messenger, and he shall prepare the way before Me: and the Lord, whom ye seek, shall suddenly come to His temple, even the messenger of the covenant, whom ye delight in:

behold, He shall come," saith the Lord of hosts. But who may abide the day of His coming? And who shall stand when He appeareth? For He is like a refiner's fire, and like fullers' soap: And He shall sit as a refiner and purifier of silver: and He shall purify the sons of Levi, and purge them as gold and silver, that they may offer unto the Lord an offering in righteousness. Then shall the offering of Judah and Jerusalem be pleasant unto the Lord, as in the days of old, and as in former years. "And I will come near to you to judgment: and I will be a swift witness against the sorcerers, and against the adulterers, and against false swearers, and against those that oppress the hireling in his wages, the widow, and the fatherless, and that turn aside the stranger from his right, and fear not Me," saith the Lord of hosts. "For I am the Lord, I change not; therefore ye sons of Jacob are not consumed."

"Even from the days of your fathers ye are gone away from Mine ordinances, and have not kept them. Return unto Me, and I will return unto you," saith the Lord of hosts. "But ye said, 'Wherein shall we return?' Will a man rob God? Yet ye have robbed Me. But ye say, 'Wherein have we robbed Thee?' In tithes and offerings. Ye are cursed with a curse: for ye have robbed Me, even this whole nation. Bring ye all the tithes into the storehouse, that there may be meat in Mine house, and prove me now herewith," saith the Lord of hosts, "if I will not open you the windows of heaven, and pour you out a blessing, that there shall not be room enough to receive it. And I will rebuke the devourer for your sakes, and he shall not destroy the fruits of your ground; neither shall your vine cast her fruit before the time in the field. And all nations shall call you blessed: for ye shall be a delightsome land," saith the Lord of hosts.

[*Malachi* iii. 1-12

The Faithful Remnant

Then they that feared the Lord spake often one to another: and the Lord hearkened, and heard it, and a book of remembrance was written before Him for them that feared the Lord, and that thought upon His name. "And they shall be Mine," saith the Lord of hosts, "in that day when I make up My jewels; and I will spare them, as a man spareth his own son that serveth him. Unto you that fear My name shall the Sun of righteousness arise with healing in His wings."

[*Malachi* iii. 16, 17, iv. 2

2. A PSALM OF HOPE

Psalm cxxvi appears to belong to this period of disappointment which followed hard after the time of enthusiastic hopes. In beautiful words it expresses the joy of the returning exiles,

A PERIOD OF DISILLUSION AND MISERY

and then with humble confidence beseeches Jehovah to grant His people a full deliverance.

> When the Lord turned again the captivity of Zion,
> We were like them that dream.
> Then was our mouth filled with laughter,
> And our tongue with singing:
> Then said they among the heathen,
> "The Lord hath done great things for them."
> The Lord hath done great things for us;
> Whereof we are glad.
>
> Turn again our captivity, O Lord,
> As the streams in the south.
> They that sow in tears shall reap in joy.
> He that goeth forth and weepeth, bearing precious seed,
> Shall doubtless come again with rejoicing, bringing his sheaves with him.

3. THE HOPE OF AN UNKNOWN PROPHET

THE BOOK OF ISAIAH

We have seen that the long Book of Isaiah contains not only the prophetic messages and some biographical account of the man Isaiah who lived in the eighth century before Christ, but the beautiful poems which contain the prophecies of a great unknown prophet, sometimes referred to as "Deutero-Isaiah" (i.e. "Second Isaiah"), as well as some short prophecies from minor men. We refer the reader again to pp. 36-44, to pp. 240-250, and finally to pp. 251-254. In other words the messages of anonymous prophets have been incorporated by a later editor in the book of the original Isaiah, and so have the support of his illustrious name. For a note on this characteristic of Jewish editorial work, see p. 18.

But just as chapter xl of Isaiah introduces a complete change from the previous chapters, a change alike in language, in outlook, and in the circumstances to which it refers, so with chapter lvi of Isaiah comes another complete change. It is generally agreed that all of Isaiah lvi-lxvi belongs to post-Exilic times, but a variety of opinions is expressed as to how far these chapters are to be attributed to more than one prophet. The main point is that they appear to belong to this same period of difficulty after the return from exile, when men's hearts needed the encouragement given by the prophetic poet often referred to as "Trito-Isaiah" (i.e. "Third Isaiah") as much as the exiles had needed the encouragement of his greater predecessor.

HUMILITY AND HOPE

The selected passages show us how aware this prophet was of the gloom and doubt and sinfulness of this period from about 500 B.C. to about 450 B.C. But they also express in beautiful words his hope for a restored and glorious Jerusalem, a new Zion, the City of God.

We note how keenly, after exile in Babylon, the Jews feel the contrast between themselves and the Gentiles or heathen. They hope too for a complete reversal of fate; as *they* had gone to Babylon, so may the inhabitants of Babylon and other countries come to Jerusalem. It is strange that this hope has been realized: every race turns to Jerusalem as the scene of the most poignant events of the life of Jesus Christ. Third Isaiah had some glimmer of the truth that this coming of all nations to Jerusalem would be spiritual rather than physical.

A Call to Humility of Spirit

Thus saith the Lord, "The heaven is My throne,
And the earth is My footstool:
Where is the house that ye build unto Me?
And where is the place of My rest?
For all these things hath Mine hand made.
To this man will I look, to him that is poor
And of a contrite spirit, and trembleth at My word."

Thus saith the high and lofty One that inhabiteth eternity,
Whose name is Holy;
"I dwell in the high and holy place,
With him also that is of a humble and contrite spirit,
To revive the spirit of the humble,
And to revive the heart of the contrite ones.

For I will not contend for ever,
Neither will I be always wroth:
For the spirit should fail before Me,
And the souls which I have made.

The wicked are like the troubled sea, when it cannot rest.
Whose waters cast up mire and dirt.
There is no peace", saith my God,
"To the wicked.
Cry aloud, spare not,
Lift up thy voice like a trumpet,
And shew My people their transgression,
And the house of Jacob their sins.

Yet they seek Me daily,
And delight to know My ways,
As a nation that did righteousness,
And forsook not the ordinance of their God.
'Wherefore have we fasted,' say they, 'and Thou seest not?
Wherefore have we afflicted our soul, and Thou takest no
    knowledge?'

Is such the fast that I have chosen?
A day for a man to afflict his soul?
Is it to bow down his head as a bulrush,
And to spread sackcloth and ashes under him?
Wilt thou call this a fast,
And an acceptable day to the Lord?

Is not this the fast that I have chosen?
To loose the bands of wickedness,
To undo the heavy burdens,
To let the oppressed go free,
That ye break every yoke?
Is it not to deal thy bread to the hungry,
And that thou bring the poor that are cast out, to thy house?
When thou seest the naked, that thou cover him;
And that thou hide not thyself from thine own flesh?"

Then shall thy light break forth as the morning,
And thine health shall spring forth speedily:
And thy righteousness shall go before thee:
The glory of the Lord shall be thy rearward.
Then shalt thou call, and the Lord shall answer;
Thou shalt cry, and He shall say, "Here I am."
    [*From Isaiah* lxvi. 1, 2, lvii. 15–21, lviii. 1–9

A New Hope

    Arise, shine, for thy light is come,
    And the glory of the Lord is risen upon thee.
    For, behold, darkness shall cover the earth,
    And gross darkness the people.
    But the Lord shall arise upon thee,
    And His glory shall be seen upon thee.
    And the Gentiles shall come to thy light,
    And kings to the brightness of thy rising.

    Lift up thine eyes round about, and see:
    All they gather themselves together, they come to thee:
    Thy sons shall come from far,
    And thy daughters shall be nursed at thy side.
    Then thou shalt see, and flow together,
    And thine heart shall fear, and be enlarged;
    Because the abundance of the sea shall be converted unto thee,
    The forces of the Gentiles shall come unto thee.

    The multitude of camels shall cover thee,
    The dromedaries of Midian and Ephah;
    All they from Sheba shall come: they shall bring gold and incense;
    And they shall shew forth the praises of the Lord.
    All the flocks of Kedar shall be gathered together unto thee,
    The rams of Nebaioth shall minister unto thee;
    They shall come up with acceptance on Mine altar,
    And I will glorify the house of My glory.

    And the sons of strangers shall build up thy walls,
    And their kings shall minister unto thee:
    For in My wrath I smote thee,
    But in My favour have I had mercy on thee.
    Therefore thy gates shall be open continually;
    They shall not be shut day nor night;
    That men may bring unto thee the forces of the Gentiles,
    And that their kings may be brought.

    For brass I will bring gold, for iron I will bring silver,
    And for wood brass, and for stones iron:
    I will also make thy officers peace,
    And thine exactors righteousness.
    Violence shall no more be heard in thy land,
    Wasting nor destruction within thy borders;
    But thou shalt call thy walls "Salvation",
    And thy gates "Praise".

A PERIOD OF DISILLUSION AND MISERY

The sun shall be no more thy light by day;
Neither for brightness shall the moon give light unto thee:
But the Lord shall be unto thee an everlasting light,
And thy God thy glory.
Thy sun shall no more go down;
Neither shall thy moon withdraw itself:
For the Lord shall be thine everlasting light,
And the days of thy mourning shall be ended.
[From Isaiah lx

The Prophet's Message

The spirit of the Lord is upon me;
The Lord hath anointed me to preach good tidings unto the meek;
He hath sent me to bind up the broken-hearted,
To proclaim liberty to the captives, the opening of prison to the bound;

To proclaim the acceptable year of the Lord,
And the day of vengeance of our God:
To comfort all that mourn,
To appoint unto them that mourn in Zion;

To give unto them beauty for ashes, the oil of joy for mourning,
The garment of praise for the spirit of heaviness:
That they might be called trees of righteousness, the planting of the Lord,
That He might be glorified.
[From Isaiah lxi. 1–3

4. A PRIESTLY CODE OF LAW

Other men besides poets and prophets contributed to the growth of the Old Testament in those years of gloom which followed hard on the rebuilding of the Temple in Jerusalem. No great events occurred of which to write narratives; no mighty men arose of whom to write biographies. But in the darkness the Spirit of God moved in men's hearts with the inspiration to bring their nation nearer to their God. Scholars tell us that most probably these writers were amongst the exiles who remained in Babylon and that there they accomplished this work, at a date some time round about 500 B.C.

THE OUTLOOK OF THE PRIESTLY WRITERS

The author or authors of this work belonged to the priesthood, and their task was to bring their own lofty ideas of God and of man's relation to God within the reach of the minds and hearts of the common people: like the earlier authors of the Deuteronomic Code, they set out to express the best they knew in a code of laws, a code of which the form was deeply influenced by the work of Ezekiel (p. 168) and by the Exilic Holiness Code (p. 172). These men cared much about the ritual of worship and of sacrifice.

But the work of this author, or, more probably, school of authors, was more than the composition of a code of laws, containing up-to-date regulations as well as many ancient ones. The priests embedded their law-code in an historical narrative, selecting just those parts of their national history which would best explain the origins of the sacred religious practices of the Jews.

For instance, we have seen how, during the Exile, much greater stress came to be laid on the observance of the Sabbath, as the exiles' opportunity for meeting together to worship and to receive instruction from the sacred writings. Thus we find in this "Priestly Code", as it is called, such an emphasis on Sabbath observance as led in the following centuries to that legalistic keeping of the Sabbath against which Jesus both spoke and acted with deliberate intent. But, in addition to these precepts, the priestly writers give a poetical account of the Creation (Gen. i. 1–ii. 4*a*), in which they expressly state that God rested from creating on the seventh day, so giving this ordinance of Sabbath observance, which they rightly wished all Jews to keep, the sanction of being in the ultimate order of the universe from its very beginning!

In the same way this writing gives a history of the origins of the rite of circumcision in the time of Abraham (Gen. xvii); of the Divine name Yahweh (or Jehovah) in the days of Moses (Exod. vi. 2, 3); of the priesthood and system of sacrifices at Mount Sinai (e.g. Exod. xxv–xxx; Lev. i–xvi); of the sacred

A PERIOD OF DISILLUSION AND MISERY

cities of the Levites and of the cities of refuge, on the approach to Canaan (Num. xxxv).

THE P DOCUMENT

In the Old Testament we do not have this P Document (that is, this Priestly Code with its narrative portions) set down apart by itself. It is embedded in the first six books of the Bible, having in later post-Exilic times been combined by one or more of the editors with such earlier material as the J, E, and combined JE Narratives, the Book of the Covenant, the Deuteronomic Code, and the Holiness Code (pp. 47, 57, 172, 178). Thus we do not dwell more on its peculiar features in this volume: we shall return to it in Volume II.

What interests us now is that, just as the Deuteronomic Code was formulated in a period of gloom and later published to the people in the reign of Josiah in 622 B.C., so in these years of gloom following the rebuilding of the Temple a work was quietly being composed destined to have a far greater influence on the future of the Jewish people than the Deuteronomic Code ever had.

We shall begin Volume II with some consideration of the events which led to the publication of this new and final law-code of Judaism, a code which set the origin of certain religious observances in a past of hoary antiquity. Here we have seen the great majority of the Hebrew nation scattered in distant lands and only a Remnant of them settled in or near Jerusalem. In Volume II we shall consider the literature which came from this Jewish Remnant.

INDEX

Abiathar, 20, 93
Abigail, 230
Abimelech, 197
Abner, 18, 233, 236
Abominations, 62, 72, 142
Absalom, 23–27
Ahab, 116–23
Ahaziah, 123, 131–3
Ahijah, 104
Altar, 30, 52, 62, 109, 120, 145, 168, 267
Amalekite, 184, 219
Amaziah, 32
Amel-Marduk, 147
Ammonite, 108, 184, 191, 211, 266
Amnon, 23
Amon, 57, 143
Amos, 30–31, 115
Angel, 121, 141, 187, 261–3
Annals, 90, 112
Anointing, 131, 210, 219, 273
Ark, 100, 206, 207, 237
Assyria, 36, 40, 42, 69, 84, 134–41
Authorship Anonymous, 19, 240, 251, 269

Baal, 51, 83, 115–7, 119, 133, 188
Babylon, 48, 69, 77–80, 146–9, 151, 155, 170, 240, 251, 255, 257, 273
Barak, 185
Baruch, 68, 73, 76
Bath-sheba, 21, 93
Bethel, 32, 109, 123
Blessing, 17, 65, 66
Blindness, 131
Bones, Dry, 165
Bow, Song of the, 16
Bribe, 32, 51, 61, 213, 215
Building, 96, 98–100, 237, 238, 255–9
Burnt Offering, 32, 35, 43, 46, 120, 168, 191, 238

Calf, 109
Call, 38, 71, 157, 205
Canaan, 48, 51, 181, 182, 202
Captivity, 77, 146, 147, 155, 245, 255
Carmel, Mount, 119
Chaldeans, 86. *See* Babylon
Chariots, 124, 130
Child, 22, 35, 44, 49, 71, 127, 152, 153, 160, 204, 205
Chronicles, 110, 112
Code of Law, 47, 48, 58, 172, 274

Comfort, Words of, 77, 164, 241, 249, 252, 259, 261, 265, 272
Commandments, Ten, 53
Compiler, 104, 110, 112, 116, 205
Confidence, 40, 87
Court History of David, 21–7, 95, 227
Covenant—
  Ark of the, 206
  Book of the, 47
  Messenger of the, 267
  New, 80
Curses, 65, 75, 253

D Document, 180, 209, 214
Damascus, 40, 131
Danites, 199
Darius, 258, 260
David, 15, 21–7, 93, 95, 219–39
Day of the Lord, 83
Deborah, 11–13, 184
Delilah, 193
Deliverance, 13, 42, 140
Deutero-Isaiah, 240–250, 269
Deuteronomist, 90–2, 95, 100–2, 104, 112, 116, 135, 145, 146, 184, 195, 202, 205, 219, 237
Deuteronomy, 56–68, 143
Disobedience, 174, 219
Dothan, 130
Dream, 96, 179, 190
Drought, 117, 258

E Document, 55, 179, 197, 209, 213
Edom, 105, 152, 253, 266
Egypt, 40, 48, 54, 81, 106, 108, 110, 141, 145, 150
Ehud, 184
Eli, 203–7
Elijah, 113, 115–24, 178
Elisha, 113, 124–34
Elohim, 179
Ephraim, 34, 35, 109, 200, 209
Excavations, 48, 110
Exile. *See* Captivity
Ezekiel, 155–171

Fable of Jotham, 15, 197
Faithfulness, 86–7, 268
Famine, 118, 153, 187, 258
Fasting, 22, 76, 264, 271
Feasts, 32, 43, 52, 53, 63, 64, 109, 264
Firstfruits, 53, 63

INDEX

Flight, 81, 106, 153, 224
Foreigner, 19, 51, 61, 136, 169, 192, 243, 272
Forgiveness, 36, 249, 250, 270
Friendship, 18, 224-7, 229

Gedaliah, 79, 80, 149
Gehazi, 127, 129
Gideon, 184, 187-90
Gilead—
  Balm of, 73
  Elders of, 191
  Jabesh-, 211
  Mount of, 189
Gleaning, 61, 173
Glory—
  after suffering, 246
  of the Lord, 38, 100, 157, 168, 259, 262, 272
God—
  Forgiveness of, 36, 249, 250
  Greatness of, 242
  Love of, 35
  Sorrow of, 35
  Vision of, 96, 156
  Wisdom of, 41
  Wrath of, 72
Gods, 52, 54, 62, 105, 109, 139, 199, 257
Goliath, 220
Grief, 27, 72, 73, 153, 161, 192, 203, 246
Groves, 62, 119, 136, 142, 145
Guilt, 22, 34, 43, 45, 72, 144, 160, 161, 168

Habakkuk, 86-8
Haggai, 258-60
Hammurabi, 48
Hannah, 203
Harvest, 52, 53, 61, 63, 64, 173
Hate, 43, 174, 251-3
Hebrew, 11, 12, 20, 46, 56, 177, 202, 209, 275
Helpfulness, 126-29
Herodotus, 82, 138, 141
Hezekiah, 40, 44, 45, 57, 67, 137-40
High Places, 52, 58, 62, 110, 115, 135, 142, 145, 210
Hiram, 96, 98, 103, 237
History, 20, 90-2, 112, 134, 176, 255-7
Holiness—
  Code, 172-5, 274
  Ezekiel and, 167-70
Holy One, 37, 41, 43, 270
Hope, 31, 84, 165, 175, 268-73
Horeb, 116, 179

Hosea, 33-6
Hoshea, 114, 135
Huldah, 144
Humility, 46, 170

Idols, 42, 51, 142, 143
Idumea. *See* Edom
Images, 52, 54, 62, 136, 199
Incense, 43, 105, 110, 136, 145, 267
Inconsistencies, 177-81, 184, 208, 219, 224
Individual—
  Religion, 80
  Responsibility, 160-1
Inscriptions, 48, 110-2, 137, 256
Isaiah, 36-44, 136-41
Israel, 30-6, 89, 107, 112-36, 179

J Document, 55, 178, 209, 275
Jael, 14, 186
Jealousy, 223, 225
JE Compilation, 180, 275
Jehoiachin, 69, 70, 77, 92, 146, 148, 255
Jehoiakim, 69, 70, 73, 75, 76, 148
Jehovah—
  Answer of, 87
  Confidence in, 40
  Cyrus called by, 243
  Disloyalty to, 266
  Greatness of, 242
  Pleading, 45
  Suffering Servant of, 244-7
Jehu, 131-3
Jephthah, 190-2
Jeremiah, 68-81
Jeroboam I, 105, 109, 110
Jeroboam II, 30-3, 114, 134
Jerusalem—
  Assyria and, 42, 136-41
  David and, 237
  Destruction of, 45, 68-79, 149, 153
  Restoration of, 248-50, 257-65
  Return to, 247-8, 252, 257
  The New, 166-71, 270-2
  Women of, 38
  Worship in, 58, 63, 64
Jesus, 18, 29, 42, 63, 90, 109, 239, 245
Jews, 36, 63, 147, 245, 256, 266, 270, 274
Jezebel, 116, 117, 121-2, 133
Joab, 21, 24-7, 236, 237
Jonathan, 17, 217, 218, 223-7, 235
Joshua, 257-60
Josiah, 67-71, 82-3, 143-5
Judah, 28, 37-45, 67-81, 83, 89-90, 107, 136-45, 235-7, 257

Judges—
  Book of, 13–6, 28, 176–7, 182–4, 195–6
  Stories of, 181–208
Judgment, 32, 43, 45, 60, 87, 173, 264. *See* Justice
Justice, 37, 46, 51, 61, 160, 245–6, 267. *See* Judgment

Karnak, 111
Kingdom—
  Division of, 93, 104–9
  Establishment of, 177–239
  Ideal, 43
  Northern. *See* Israel
  Southern. *See* Judah
Kings, Book of, 89–150
Knowledge—
  of God, 35, 36, 80, 155
  of Solomon, 97–8

Labour, Forced, 96, 99
Lamech's Cry, 12
Lament, 17, 27
Lamentations, Book of, 153
Law. *See* Code
Law Book. *See* Deuteronomy
Laws—
  Civil, 49, 50
  Early, 46–55
  Religious, 51–3, 62–4, 168–70
  Social, 51, 60, 61, 173, 174
Leaders, 163–4
Leaven, 63
Lebanon, 98, 99, 110
Leper, 128–30
Letter, 77, 140, 155
Levite, 167, 169, 200
Leviticus, Book of, 172, 175, 274–5
Literature, 1, 46, 90, 176, 255, 274
Local, 52, 58, 63
Lord of Hosts, 42, 72, 74, 75, 77, 258–68
Luxury, 32

Malachi, 266–8
Manasseh, King, 45, 57, 67, 142
Marduk, 256–7
Medes, 69, 135, 137
Megiddo, 14, 110, 133, 145
Mercy, 35, 46, 248–50
Mesha, 111, 125
Messenger, 140, 212, 231, 266–8
Micah—
  of Ephraim, 199–202
  Prophet, 44–6, 57, 74, 219
Micaiah, 76
Midianite, 181, 187–90

Moab, 105, 108, 125, 184, 228, 236
Moabite Stone, 111
Monuments, Ancient, 48, 110
Moses—
  Blessing of, 17, 66
  Law of, 19, 47–9, 58–9, 65
  Ten Words of, 53–5
Mother, 14, 54, 93, 118, 125, 127, 153, 194, 199, 204
Mountain, 45, 85, 167–8, 192, 241–2, 248, 265
Music, 32, 151, 211, 224–5

Naaman, 128
Naboth, 116, 122, 131
Nahum, 84–6
Narratives—
  Combined, 208–27
  E, 179
  Earliest, 20–29
  Elijah, 117–24
  Elisha, 124–34
  J, 178
  JE, 180
  of David, 21–7, 227–39
Nathan, 22, 93, 238
Nation, 47, 60, 96, 242, 243, 248, 249, 252
Nazirite, 193–4
Nebuchadrezzar, 69, 77–80, 146–50, 255, 257
Neighbour, 80, 173
Nineveh, 69, 70, 84–5, 141
North. *See* Israel
Numbers, Book of, 13, 17, 28, 275

Obadiah, 119, 152
Obey, 60, 81, 219
Offering, 32, 53, 62, 97, 110, 120, 168, 219, 267, 268
Oil, 46, 259, 263, 273
Old Testament, 19, 34, 80, 112, 177, 240, 273
Omri, 92, 111, 114, 116, 131
Oppression, 37, 39, 41, 43, 45, 61, 96, 111, 185, 247, 271
Othniel, 182–4

P Document, 275
Palestine, 48, 111, 192
Parable, 39, 159
Pashur, 75, 78
Passover, 63
Persia, 243, 256–61
Philistines, 27, 192–5, 206, 216, 220, 224, 228, 234, 235
Poetry. *See* Verse
Poor, 32, 38, 60, 84, 173, 264, 271

INDEX

Potter, 41, 74, 159
Praise, 13, 272, 273
Prayer, 101-2, 140, 147, 203, 213
Preacher, 29, 31, 42, 59, 70, 72-4
Priestly—
  Code, 273
  Writers, 274
Priests, 45, 100, 110, 116, 169-70, 199-202, 203, 228, 258-60, 267
Promises—
  of New Covenant, 80
  of Joy and Peace, 249
  Precious, 264
Prophetess, 37, 144, 185
Prophets—
  Exilic, 155-71, 240-54
  False, 41, 45
  of Baal, 119, 120
  Post-Exilic, 258-73
  Pre-Exilic, 29-46, 68-88, 105, 116, 124
  Schools of, 123-5, 211-2
Prose, 13, 29, 30, 162, 186
Psalm—
  of an Exile, 151
  of David, 19, 20
  of Hope, 268

Rabshakeh, 138-40
Rebellion, 25, 27, 35, 40, 69, 72, 107, 148
Reformation, 59, 89
  in Judah, 142-5
Rehoboam, 28, 56, 93, 106-12
Religion—
  Individual, 80
  of a Book, 90
  of Israel, 115
  of Jeremiah, 70
  True, 46, 57
Religious—
  Conditions, 83
  Laws, 51-2, 62-4
  Problem, 109
Remnant, 36-7, 40, 57-8, 67, 84, 89-90, 155, 245, 265, 268
Repentance, 31, 42, 70, 175, 239
Return, 35, 36, 168, 250
  from Exile, 256
  to Jerusalem, 247, 252
Reverence, 54, 174
Rhythm. *See* Verse
Righteousness, 43, 160, 173, 244
  Social, 60, 264
  Sun of, 268
  Trees of, 273

River, 129, 148, 151
  Vision of, 170-1
Roll, 75, 158

Sabbath, 43, 53-5, 174-5, 256, 274
Sacrifices, 30, 43, 52, 62-4, 100, 120, 267
Samaria, 44, 114, 117-8, 134-6
Samson, 15, 192-5
Samuel, 27, 182, 202-11, 213-16, 219, 224
  Books of, 18, 20, 28, 176-7, 180, 202-39
Sanctuary, 52, 58, 161, 169, 171, 174, 201
Sargon, 114, 135
Saul, 15, 17, 27-8, 208-12, 214-30, 232-5
Second Isaiah, 269
  Writings of, 240-50
Seer, 32, 209-10
Sennacherib, 42, 137-41
Sermon. *See* Preacher
Servant, 22, 26, 75, 98, 101, 107, 129, 139, 244-7
Sheba, 96, 103, 272
Shepherds, 41, 108, 163-5, 228, 241
Shishak I, 106, 110-11
Shunammite, 127
Signs, Ezekiel's, 159, 161
Sin, 21, 23, 35, 43, 104, 136, 161, 168, 239, 247, 263
Sinai, 13, 116, 124, 179
Sisera, 14-5, 185-6
Slavery, 49, 60
Solomon, 20, 29, 47, 94-106
Song—
  of Confidence, 87
  of Deborah, 13
  of Red Sea, 12
  of Sorrow, 153
  of the Bow, 17
  of the Well, 13
Sorrow. *See* Grief, Woe
South. *See* Judah
Spirit, 67, 166, 259, 263
Stocks, Jeremiah in, 75
Stories, 11, 90, 178-80
  of Judges, 181-95
  Two Primitive, 197-202
Stranger, 13, 33, 34, 43, 51, 61, 102, 169, 264, 272
Suffering—
  Jeremiah's, 75
  Servant, 244-7
Syria, 48, 113, 124, 128, 130, 131, 133

Tamar, 23-4
Tel-el-Amarna, 48
Temple—
  Annals of, 90
  Built, 96, 98-9, 238
  Dedicated, 100-3
  Destroyed, 149
  Ezekiel and the, 166-70, 173
  Importance of, 58, 91, 108-9
  Isaiah in the, 38
  Rebuilt, 257-266
  Repaired, 143
  Sermon, 72, 73
  Worship in, 38, 101, 140, 266-7
Ten Tribes, 105, 108, 115
Third Isaiah, 270-3
Tidings, 26, 27, 85, 159, 241
Trees, 16, 98, 171, 237, 250, 252, 261, 273
True Religion, 46
Trust in Egypt, 40-1, 138
Tyre, 96, 98, 100, 162, 163, 237

Unclean, 38, 170, 253
Uzziah (Azariah), 31, 37, 38, 40, 135

Valley, 44, 126, 165, 220, 241
Vanity, 38, 73
Vengeance, 12, 151-2, 252, 253, 273
Verse, 12-16, 29, 30, 82, 85, 162
Victory, 12, 13, 185, 189, 191, 207, 211
Vine, 36, 39, 87, 139
Vineyard, 32, 43, 44, 130, 139
  Naboth's, 116, 122, 131
  Parable of, 39
Vision, 38, 72, 87, 96, 156, 165-71, 205-6, 239, 261-4

Voice, 38, 41, 81, 116, 120-1, 139, 157, 241-2
Vow, 191-3, 203, 218, 267

Wall, 99, 127, 139, 262, 272
Watchman, 26, 132, 158, 164
Water, 108, 120, 128-9, 189, 248-9, 253
Weak, Strength for the, 243
Weary, 75, 86, 243, 267
Wickedness, 15, 35, 71, 85, 91, 117, 155, 160, 204-6, 271
Widow, 43, 51, 61, 117
Wife, 34, 37, 122, 161
Wilderness, 59, 121, 229, 252
Wine, 32, 35, 193, 249
Wings, 38, 156-7, 243
Witness, 54, 191, 215, 249
Woe, 38, 40-1, 45, 85, 158, 163, 164
Woodman in Trouble, 128
Word, 35, 59, 250
Worship, 32, 51-2, 57-8, 83
Writing, 29, 31, 40, 58, 75-8, 90-2, 146, 177-81, 256

Yahweh, 178
Yoke, 35, 106, 271

Zadok, 26, 93-4, 169
Zechariah—
  King, 134
  Prophet, 260-5
Zedekiah, 77-9, 148-9
Zephaniah, 82-4
Zerubbabel, 257-60, 263, 266
Zidonian, 105-6, 114, 117
Zion, 45, 73-4, 236, 241, 248, 253, 264-5, 269, 273

THE WORLD OF OLD

For Product Safety Concerns and Information please contact our EU representative GPSR@taylorandfrancis.com
Taylor & Francis Verlag GmbH, Kaufingerstraße 24, 80331 München, Germany

www.ingramcontent.com/pod-product-compliance
Lightning Source LLC
Chambersburg PA
CBHW061435300426
44114CB00014B/1700